MAKING MODEL
Railway Buildings

At first glance this model could be set anywhere, at any time: a typical English half-timbered cottage, a standard Mackenzie and Holland signal box and a generic platelayer's hut; all of which could be found almost anywhere, more or less, and at any time in the first half of the 20th century. But look again. Those chalk cliff-faces suggest the south coast, the South Downs or perhaps Wiltshire. Ah, but that cottage is rather mean in size and sparse of timbers, quite unlike anything found in the well-wooded, rich chalkland pastures of Kent or Sussex, so it's probably Wiltshire. But where are the station nameboards – and isn't that an ack-ack station camouflaged on the hill behind, complete with gun, tractor and tents? If so, it must be war time. Of course – it's Salisbury Plain in World War Two! Obvious when you know what you're looking at – and all without a train or a specific railway structure to help you. It's amazing how much of a back-story you can tell, if only you set about making the right type of iconic model railway buildings.

MAKING MODEL
Railway Buildings

Andy McMillan

THE CROWOOD PRESS

First published in 2013 by
The Crowood Press Ltd
Ramsbury, Marlborough
Wiltshire SN8 2HR

www.crowood.com

British Library Cataloguing-in-Publication Data
A catalogue record for this book is available from the British
Library.

ISBN 978 1 84797 340 5

Dedication
This work is dedicated to Laney and Anne, for it was their
encouragement, patience and sagacity over several decades
which so helped me chase my dream of turning an
oft-disparaged hobby into an art form.

USEFUL BOOKS ON VERNACULAR ARCHITECTURE

Billett, Michael *Thatched Buildings of Dorset* (Robert
Hale Ltd., 1984, ISBN 0 7090 1962 9)

Brown, R. J. *The English Country Cottage* (Robert Hale,
1979, ISBN 0 7091 7381 4)

Brunskill R. W. *Vernacular Architecture: an Illustrated
Handbook* (Faber & Faber, 2000, ISBN 0 571 19503
2)

Evans, Tony and Lycett Green, Candida *English
Cottages* (Weidenfeld & Nicholson, 1982)

Reid, Richard *The Shell Book of Cottages* (Michael
Joseph Ltd., 1977, ISBN 0 7181 1630 5)

Young, David *More Cobblestones, Cottages and Castles*
(Obelisk Publications, 1992)

Typeset by Jean Cussons Typesetting, Diss, Norfolk
Printed and bound in Singapore by Craft Print International

CONTENTS

INTRODUCTION

It is a fact not commonly observed but, at its best, a real model railway is a genuine art form with the highest of pedigrees. Most railway stations, if modelled in 4mm scale, would need a space perhaps seventy feet long to get it all in, whereas many of us are lucky if we have as much as twenty feet in which to squeeze a representation. Therefore, for all but the very simplest prototypes, precise replication of reality in miniature is often simply impossible. This is just as well, for a simple reproduction would be mere craftsmanship. Art, by definition, requires 'the personal input of the artist' into the representation of something. Nowadays that means feelings, moods, events: in fact all the emotional repertoire that we once traditionally considered applied only to music. Sadly, people today apply it to piles of bricks, unmade beds and dead half-animals in formaldehyde. One ridiculous 'installation' was nothing but a room light which winked on and off now and again. I had a room light like that once when I was living in a student flat but I never called it 'art'…

Traditional pictorial art, however, has always been the representation of something, someone or somewhere definable: be that imaginary characterization or portraiture, fanciful imagery or a representation of a real event, place or landscape. So, following that logic, a model of a railway indeed becomes a true art form the moment you move beyond simple slavish representation and begin deciding what to put in and what to leave out.

The major difference between a working model and a painting is that we need to work in five dimensions because to length, breadth and height (x, y & z), we are adding the extra dimensions of movement and time (v & w). By movement, I mean by 'instants' of action, the passing or shunting of trains in particular; and by time I mean by the representation of 'period' or era. This latter can be effected in several ways which, unlike those of a two-dimensional painting,

are not necessarily 'fixed'. For example we can, with a model, change both some of the content (i.e. the trains, which can come and go at our command), and our perspective (or viewpoint) by moving around the model. This allows us to place a horse and cart, which can only be seen from one angle, on the same layout as a car which can only be seen from another, thus changing the time context as the viewer moves. Such a layout seen from one angle might represent 1930 while from another 1950: the potential lying therein will be obvious.

By adopting the age-old traditions of artistic composition, we, the modellers, are making cogent choices about our trains and the landscapes we run them through and so can rightly claim to be artists with all that that implies, even if we are not always particularly good ones! As with all genuine art forms, excellence is something which only comes with study, understanding, and some practise in execution! We do need to understand the 'tools of art' for we cannot rely on the trains alone to create impressions of space and location: to do that we need scenery and, since we do not normally have the space to copy real landscapes, we need to create our size-limited versions by picking suitable icons and modelling those as individual structures which we then arrange in a suitable fashion. And that's called art!

Aside from the fact that all the model railways depicted in this book are the sole work of the author, which is not always the case, it is perhaps rather different from others on the subject of model railway buildings because it also deals with the landscapes within which those buildings are set. After all, there's little point in refining some subtlety in your scenery when just a few feet away there are bare baseboards, structural timbers, perhaps even open storage sidings which need hiding, and all backed by wallpaper instead of a proper backscene.

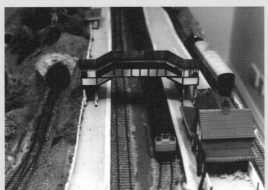

Photos 1–4. TOP LEFT: *If you begin to design your scenery only after you have laid and tested your track then you cannot expect realism when you've finished (TOP RIGHT). (MIDDLE LEFT) Fortunately, as this 1980 re-design of boy's trainset plan 5.5 shows, even the smallest variation in depth is a help! Indeed, careful grouping of a few simple structures can improve things further, as can a hint of village (BELOW).*

**Photo 5. *If you want realism then there is just no substitute for looking at reality and modelling it.
This applies as much to a homogenous whole of landscape and structures as it does to this passing
mid-1950s tank wagon train. It is through creating such surroundings that the train really appears to be
going somewhere, not just circling aimlessly.***

Engines, coaches and wagons are simple – you just take them off the track and when you do they retain their value since you can either sell them or just as easily put them back on again. But scenery's not like that. You will not want to put a hundred hours or more into building a fabulous Devonian cottage only to decide later that you need to 'move' your layout to Wiltshire to accommodate a new favourite train. Therefore this book will certainly go into considerable detail about the nitty-gritty of how you can and should cut card and other materials (even noting how you should *not* do so in such a way as to endanger yourself), but there are only so many ways you can photograph various sharp edges cutting things. So this book not only deals with the construction of the model buildings themselves but also challenges you to think about what buildings to make models

of, what level of detail to apply to them, and where and how to place them. It will even suggest what colour to paint them and what scale to build them in – notwithstanding the chosen scale of your trains!

But this is not a book about landscape per se. There are so many of those (a whole world full, of course), and so many different ways of creating them that it would take an entire book by itself to even begin to do that subject justice. Nevertheless, before we start cutting card in Chapter 2, Chapter 1 will consider just what we are attempting to achieve with our model railway, because this allows us to understand what buildings we should choose to put in our landscape, what level of finish to attempt and where to put them.

And please note that use of the word 'in' as in 'in our landscape', for this is the first change in perception you need when moving from a toy train set (where you would traditionally glue something 'on' to your baseboard), up to a 'proper' model of a railway: you need to begin thinking less about gluing things onto a flat 'board' and more of creating a model of a landscape which apparently just happens to have trains running through it. Perhaps, as it were, just a 'little bit of Old England' or Wales or wherever: as long as it is recognizable in both period and location and suits your preferences. Here you will find buildings which sit 'in' a landscape as an integral part of it, not just as another individual bit thrown 'on' to the baseboard to fill a bit more space – and behind that simple concept is a whole new world of perception: one where we are going to make a model of a believable location, not just a three-dimensional representation of our own imagination. Our imagination is a 'good thing' of course; it is a vital asset to our first 'trainset' because when our new pride and joy trundles around an oval of track devoid of any other features it is our imagination which completes the picture. However, when it comes to filling in that imaginary landscape with actual models, then there is far more variety out there in the real world than one single imagination could ever envisage – and since no matter how much we attempt to suspend reality we *know* that to be the case, so it is that our

model will never look realistic until we base what we model on reality.

So: having in Chapter 1 established first principles, including properly thought-through planning, we can then move confidently on to Chapter 2, reaching for the knife and the cardboard with at least a fair idea of what it is we will be attempting to recreate and why. In Chapter 3 we will look at choosing and using commercial, 'ready to plant' buildings'. In other chapters we move on to adapting commercial models so they suit location or purpose, then through making more drastic alterations to turn them into something else, before progressing to building from scratch when that remains the only means of getting exactly what we want. Finally, in the last chapter, we look at ways of lighting your models and landscape so that, like the real thing, your trains can run both day and night.

But the last word of this introduction must be to record my thanks to the many photographers, from the famous and lauded to the 'unrecorded' and unsung, without whose inspiration in the pages of myriad railway books I would not have begun the complex task of turning images of fleeting moments of history into miniature working realities. Thank you, chaps, one and all.

Photo 6. The whole model – trains, landscape and period – is best decided upon in advance. Having done so, if you then chose to include a model bank* barn you will, naturally, already have designed a suitable bank to build it on! (*Yorkshire for slope.)

CHAPTER ONE

BUILDINGS: AN OVERVIEW

WHY ARE BUILDINGS NECESSARY TO A MODEL?

There is a question which needs to be thought about before you even consider picking up a knife or a paintbrush: 'Why bother'? Why model any buildings at all? Certainly most people want to have a station on their model, somewhere to stop a train and do some shunting now and again, and most stations have station buildings, perhaps a goods shed and a few huts, but why bother with a townscape or village as well? In fact, as was practically universal on model railways before the Second World War (and remains so to this day on many 0-gauge layouts), why model anything outside the railway fence at all? Good question! Actually, there's a good answer. A good landscape enhances your trains. (Photo 7)

Yes, we've all heard of the station five miles from the village and thus called 'Xyz Road', and there's nothing wrong with modelling such a place, but if you do, what do you load in your trucks? How would you know? What fun is there in shunting a handful of meaningless wagons into a goods yard without any purpose in doing so beyond that of filling a siding? Where's the 'play value' in that? Perhaps you've read a book which tells you what the traffic was, but are you going to have to explain that to every visitor or is there some way of inferring a particular trade or traffic by modelling something? If your trains just amble through your model with no visible link to the landscape they are passing through, what is the railway for? What is your model for? Where's the connection between a train stopping at your station and the people and businesses or farms it is meant

Photo 7. In time-honoured fashion a local train arrives at a small-town junction station with passengers for onward main-line travel to a city. Substitute a steam train and a forest of semaphores, and this scene would have been recognizable to its Victorian inhabitants.

to serve? Every railway was originally built with a purpose; why not bring that purpose out where people can see it?

Even if you are modelling an actual station and are thus limited by what was factually there, you might consider which period would best suit the model from the point of view of traffic (you can always build or buy trains more appropriate to that period later). Then ask, 'which is the best side to model it from'? 'It will only fit one way', is perhaps one answer but you might find that alongside the tracks on one side was a feature which detracts from the model's story, and on the other, one which enhances it. Consider swapping them over if it illustrates the story of that station all the better for the viewer. It's your model and you're building it: if there's a great feature 400 yards beyond your space-imposed scenic break, move it! Get it in there; use it to enhance your guest's understanding of the line. Could you pinch a feature from another station down the line and 'move' it into yours, perhaps? That feature closed before your period? Fine. Either change your period or model that feature derelict: it may still explain 'why', whether defunct or not. Besides, there can be a very particular sublimity in dereliction, especially if that dereliction is partial rather than total.[1]

Consider this: could your guests tell you what part of the country your model represents from your landscape alone, without seeing any trains? Perhaps the landscape itself is sufficiently dramatic (like Tupdale's Yorkshire), but that's very rarely the case. The simple fact is that if you decide to represent a particular county, line or locality on your model, then often the best way of illustrating that location is to use architectural features to give your railway a sense of place and time; a reason, if you like, for just 'being'. Local vernacular structures evolved with experience; local people using local materials learned to use them in the most effective way they could to deal with the material's properties and the local conditions. Individual builders' preferences also

tended to further characterize buildings in one or two villages or perhaps one particular valley (Photos 8 & 9). These peculiarities gave their buildings a particularly local as well as a general regional character. Of course, materials differ as localities change, as do building practices, but that is what led to the almost infinite variety of 'the vernacular'. That is why it is so called; for no architect designed these buildings, no planner made them conform; it was just local builders learning and following their local traditions, adapting them over time as different styles came and went. But if you want to take advantage of that individuality (Photos 10 & 11) you will need to represent it and if you can't buy it, you have to make it: which is where we come in with this book …

GENERIC VERSUS VERNACULAR

Once you have decided to have a village, or part of one, then immediately you face another question: that of 'generic modelling' versus using a *particular* local architectural vernacular. Some modellers maintain that they want a generic type of landscape because then they can 'run anything'. That is perfectly plausible at face value but my answer is always, 'If the landscape can be anything why have one at all? And if you do, why does it matter where it is if you are going to ignore it anyway'?

My point is that if a Great Western engine is going to look wrong passing a Scottish croft, then an LMS Duchess is going to look equally wrong passing an oast house! Suppose there are no trains to see at all? Even then, a landscape with a Devonian cob-walled cottage next to ship-lapped East Anglian one will always look 'wrong' because it is wrong. At least if the landscape is appropriate for one particular area then you create interest before a train even appears – and when one does, at least some will sit comfortably within it, even if others still look out of place. After all, an expressed desire to model some indefinite place called 'Generic Britain' (or more likely 'Generic England', which is what the speaker usually

---

[1] Think how much we all love wandering around a largely-ruined castle but note that it has to have substantial remnants of towers, walls and walkways we can use to stimulate our imaginations and some high-points to get great views from. The total dereliction of a heap of collapsed stones is just boring – there's nothing remotely romantic in rubble!

Photo 8. This seventeenth-century mill in Derbyshire is a typically solid structure in stone.

BELOW: Photo 9. Another one 200 miles away in Dorset is of much the same age, and although the size and form are similar, the details are entirely different.

Photo 10.　Warehouse in the main street in Dunster, just over the Devon border in Somerset.

Photo 11.　This warehouse is beside an estate near Budleigh Salterton, in South Devon – the same purpose of storage on the same isthmus and enclosing similar areas, yet entirely different in appearance and construction. Each would look wrong in the other's situation.

has in mind), commonly means you are listening to someone who can't be bothered to move beyond the train set stage – but if that was you then you wouldn't have bought this book so I think I am on safe ground!

Of course, it's your railway and you can put what you like wherever you like it, but if you've bought this book I am going to presume you have a particular wish to 'do it properly' and that you want to learn how to build what you would like to see, rather than having to rely entirely on mass-produced items by Superquick, Hornby or Bachmann. If so, where do we start? The possibly surprising answer is with 'scale'.

SCALES WORKED TO IN THIS BOOK

As a professional model maker, most of the work I do is to commission so it will come as no surprise to learn that nearly all of these illustrations are to 00 or N gauge. This assertion is, of course, poppycock – how can you build a house to a gauge? Nevertheless, most model buildings are still sold as '00/H0' or 'N' gauge, although more recently the words 'suitable for' have appeared on boxes even though the actual scale, i.e. 4mm, 3.5mm or 2mm to the foot, is often missing. Odd that; the terms have been familiar to modellers for over 50 years so why not use them? On the plus side, Oxford and other model car manufacturers are now including the numerals '76' for '1/76th scale' as part of the item description, so let's hope that customer intelligence is finally being recognized.

Of course, building your own structures sooner or later involves measurement of some kind, so knowing what 'scale' you are working in becomes much more than just a convenient title, it becomes a practical 'factor' by which to divide prototype dimensions. Let's take a simple example. You have a photograph of a building you want to model (Photo 12). In the corner is a 'person of known height' whom you placed there deliberately. (If not, there is always the 'counting bricks' option: a standard brick is 2½in high, mortar is ½in, so 3in per row times the

Table of common UK gauges/scales/ratios

Gauge	Scale in metric	Ratio
I	10mm to the foot	1:30th or 1:32nd
0	7mm to the foot	1:43rd
S	³⁄₁₆in to the foot	1:64th
00	4mm to the foot	1:76th
HO	3.5mm to the foot	1:87th
TT	3mm to the foot	1:100th
N	2mm to the foot	1:148th
Z	1.39mm to the foot	1:220th

number of rows …) You also paced out the frontage, of course: 14 paces and your pace is 33 in (84cm) long. (And if you forgot to do that, a standard brick is 9in long …) So you have two known dimensions and can now use your favourite graphics programme to change the perspective of the building until the bottom edge (if horizontal!), first floor, eaves and roof line are all parallel – or as nearly as the sagging age of the thing will allow – thereby removing the perspective. Then adjust the length to something which seems more or less correct, as in Photo 13, and print it off. Now, because you know the scale you are working to, you can easily use a calculator to obtain the dimensions you need for your model.

Theory

A word of explanation for the young. As you know, we railway modellers with pretensions to accuracy work in a scale known as '4mm to the foot', (or 2mm or 7mm, or even 3.5mm ditto). As such it is also known as a 'bastard scale' because it has two parents who are not 'linearly married' in that we have Metric at one end of the equation and Imperial at the other. It is not a happy marriage but the test of time shows it's a good way of keeping the numbers simple for mental arithmetic. For example if a book tells you a real bridge is 100ft long then your model needs to be 400mm long. Just multiply the one number by four (or two or seven, etc.), to get the other. Easy! Much easier than trying to divide 100ft by 76 without reaching for a calculator – and how do you measure 1.31579ft anyway? (Perhaps us 'old 'uns' ain't quite as daft as you thought …) So if you post-

Photo 12. *A photo of a prototype building I wanted to model, the major dimensions being accounted for by pacing out the length and by knowing the height of my then wife, Jenny.*

Photo 13. *The same photograph after being 'corrected' by a graphics programme. It's not perfect, but it saves a long drive to Buckinghamshire with an assistant, a 30m tape, a notebook, a pencil and a tower of mobile scaffolding ...*

date being taught Imperial: now and again, just for practice, try working in '2/4/7mm to the foot' scale because all you who have been brought up using purely Metric measurements might one day find you want to model an engine using copies of the original Imperial drawings. These will be in feet and inches, of course, so the earlier you learn to understand them the better! I will just mention 'S gauge' here because it *is* a totally Imperial scale, albeit one for the truly devoted scratchbuilder.

Practice

Let's begin our example with height. It doesn't matter whether you work entirely in Imperial, entirely in Metric or use one at each end because scale is a 'ratio' so it's just a number to divide or multiply by, whichever denomination you choose to record the result. But I have to write something and, as I'm ancient, I'll use Imperial for the 'real thing' and Metric for the model, which was to be 4mm to the foot. Find your calculator.

The lady in the photo was 5ft 7in. That's 67in – a convenient whole number for calculator input. Her height measured on the photograph is (say) 9.8mm. Her 'real size' to 'photo image' ratio is therefore 67 divided by 9.8, or 6.9367 to four decimal places, which we can call the 'ratio of real height to photographic measurement'. Now we are, for current purposes, working to '00' or 4mm to the foot scale. Therefore a model of the lady would need to be a scale 5ft 7in (67÷[12÷4]) or properly 67÷3, which equals 22.3 recurring; that being her 'real-to-model height' in millimetres, of course. By combining the two ratios, i.e. both the photographic-to-real and the real-to-model scale ratios, we can come up with what we will call a 'Vertical Constant' or 'Vk' for that photograph. To do this we divide her 'intended model height' – 22.3mm – by her 'photographic height' – 6.9367mm – and get (22.3÷6.9367=3.2196), again to four decimal places. In fact, allowing for angular distortion and a certain generalization, a 'Vk' ratio of 3.22 will be perfectly adequate!

Remember this number is a *ratio* called Vk but the number it allows us to calculate will be recorded in millimetres because that's what we used when we measured her height on the photo. We can now put '3.22' into our calculator's memory as a 'constant' and we are ready to turn our photograph into a 'working drawing'. Sketch out the building roughly on paper (Fig. 14) and then, using your Vk constant, simply read off any height on the face of the building, in millimetres, directly from the photo; multiply it by Vk and write the answer on your sketch against the dimension you measured. (I have numbered some suggestions.) You will soon have the heights of the doors, windows top and bottom, joist heights for the jetty and an eaves height. (Hint: if you photocopy the sketch before you add the dimensions and you can use it for 'Hk' too.)

Remember your roof apex is not in the same 'plane' as the front of the building and any attempt to simply read off its height from this photo will include an unacceptable distortion, so don't try it! You might however, notice that the photo suggests the roof slopes at an angle of pretty much 45°. With this information, and with another 'de-distorted' view of the gable end (Photo 15) you can use the 'measured height' of the eaves to calculate the overall height of the arch at the top and thus that of your roof apex. Note that the window opening and squared steps on the gable are a great help in squaring up this end view on your computer since they are, by definition, both square and straight! Then, by projecting a line through the top of the side at 45°, you can use simple geometry to work out the building's width.

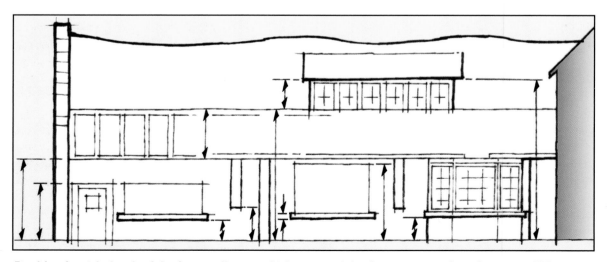

Fig. 14.   A quick sketch of the front wall upon which to record the dimensions resulting from your 'Vk' factor (see text).

Where possible I prefer to use actual measurement or 'paces' but, where these are not available, you can either use geometry to establish your width or visual evidence which, if available as it is here, is generally safer. To describe the latter: on the original image I can see that the blind niche is two bricks wide, as is each gable step, which gives us a brick width of 23ft 9in at the eaves. Thus with an eaves height of approximately 11ft 6in, and half an overall width of about 25ft, (allowing for the jetty), calculation suggests the roof apex is some 24 feet above ground, or 96mm.

Length is arrived at by a similar calculation to height but it needs its own constant since, unless you were extraordinarily lucky, the scale of the photograph will not be the same in both planes. Thus 14 paces multiplied by 33in would be 462in, which sum divided by 12 to give feet provides 38ft 6in, the actual length of the building. Since our scale is 4mm to the foot, our model will need to be 4 x 38½ which is 154mm long. Because the building in the photo measures (let's say) 71mm, we can now arrive at a Horizontal Constant of 154÷71=2.17, which we can call 'Hk' or, if we have photos of two or more sides, 'HkSF' for South Face, etc. If we note that figure on our sketch, we can now use it to calculate approximate dimensions for the width of the doors, windows and where along the side they are located. I say 'approximate' since although adequate for reading a 'nearly side-on' photograph, the stronger the perspective, the more factors there are which cannot readily be calculated precisely; perspective, parallax, lens deterioration across the focal plane, etcetera – but of course if you were *really* determined to be precisely accurate you would have measured the building properly in the first place![2] As it is, you have there an excellent and simple way of turning a photograph into a pretty good approximation which will be instantly recognizable to anyone who knows the subject.

Photo 15   Again taken from the same photo, this 'perspective-corrected end view' would be impossible to pace out, of course, but this is where 'brick counting' comes to our rescue.

BALANCE

Of course, you may equally ask, 'Why do we need to model to scale if an approximation is apparently good enough? After all, our engines run on electricity, not steam or diesel; the flanges are over-sized, the gauge is probably incorrect and the passengers are plastic'! These are fair points but in fact it is a simple matter of balance: your trains are 4mm to the foot, their passengers will be the same so the doors on the station buildings they need to pass through should be the same scale too. Forget that and start inventing new dimensions for buildings which sit right beside

[2] A closer approximation of horizontal distance on a photo with a plane of considerable perspective is possible by describing an arc, centred at eye-height on the vertical plane at the nearest corner of the building, and of a length to cut through the Vanishing Point at the horizon. Vertical lines can then be projected from the required features up or down to the arc and the length required measured *along* the line of the arc itself. Sadly, without accurate details of the lens which captured the image, the method remains only a rather better approximation than reading measurements directly from the photo. In such photographs too, the VP can be used to project any feature's vertical position to the nearest corner of the building from where all your vertical measurements can be accurately taken.

your trains and that sought-after realism will be lost the moment you glue them down! When kept away from the fixed scale of your trains however, the scale of your buildings can certainly vary and not just overall but throughout the depth of that model too. Such is called 'perspective modelling' and it is commonly seen in dioramas. It can look superb too, as long as you are careful to ensure that the perspective 'works' from all the likely viewing angles.

It should also be remembered that early railway station buildings were designed to be impressive and substantial: the 'new-fangled' railway had to look as if it were intended to be here for ever. Thus even a simple wayside station was often a substantial structure built of stone with strong architectural features, fancy windows and heavy detailing given to such as barge boards, canopies and doors (Photo 16). These features were not only large to look impressive but large to cope with ladies with skirts hugely widened by crinolines (Photo 17) and gentlemen made taller by top hats of Dickensian dimensions! (Photo 18) An assumption that a door in a station building can be reproduced by copying the dimensions of the average house door would usually be quite wrong, therefore, although more than one commercially available model has made that simple mistake! So the first thing to do is to look at reality, find something you like and begin modelling it. You will find that far more satisfying than copying somebody else's model and perpetuating their mistakes.

CHOICE OF SCALE

Of course, by the time you come to make buildings to go on your own model railway your choice of

Photo 16. **The Bristol and Exeter Railway-designed station building at 'Sandford and Banwell' station, once on the Cheddar Valley line in Somerset. The massiveness of the stonework, the fanciness of the barge-boards and the generally huge dimensions compared with local cottages were all quite deliberate and designed to impress locals with the permanence of this then-new form of transport. Sadly, the railway proved to be less permanent than was once hoped.**

MRS. DURBY CHARGES A LOCOMOTIVE

Photo 17.   An image by an unaccredited artist from an illustrated railway novel published in 1865. One chapter – entirely irrelevant to the plot, incidentally – describes a works such as Crewe or Swindon in considerable detail and has been often quoted as a prime example of an early railway record. (From the author's collection)

Photo 18.   We are on more familiar ground here with an illustration from a lesser Dickens novel of the same period showing what look like early District Line clerestory carriages behind some hugely hatted characters. (From the author's collection)

scale will already have been made through your personal preferences and purchases of trains. That fact might lead you to wonder which of the techniques featured in the following chapters will be of use to you. Well, all of them I trust! The point is that the techniques remain much the same whatever scale you are working to: it is where and how you apply them that makes the difference.

Let's side-step for a moment and think about the 'rivet counter' or 'armchair modeller': you know, the sort who knows everything, criticizes everything and

delights in pointing out every single mistake he can and yet, by definition, has never completed a model railway in his life. Despite his insistent, vocal and vituperative presence on far too many e-groups he can, fortunately, be completely ignored with safety until he can show you a completed model all of his own work. I suggest that will never happen because he is far too busy expounding his theories to listen to the voice of practical experience and is therefore quite incapable of acually making anything. He has yet to learn to stand back and see the 'overall picture' and thus the relationship of its component parts, each one *in balance* with the other.

Sadly, while his mere existence has, over the years, put powerful pressures upon the increasing quest for *dimensional* accuracy he's had a negative one on the quest for better 'realism'. Now with mass-produced train models greater accuracy is, generally speaking, to be encouraged because if a plastic moulding is produced to the right dimensions then we all benefit from a better model. But once you begin talking about hand-made models you

Photo 19.　*This may be a fantasy model but it was built to roughly 10mm:ft scale on 16.5mm chassis with the figures over an inch high – so that's a big building in the background. Even so, the smallest details are those hinges on the first-floor loading doors – but with rope-knotted bridges and stock like that, who's looking at door hinges?*

Photo 20.　*Modelling an open sash window means making two frames but the effect is usually worth it if the model is prominent enough. However, adding the ropes and pulleys to make it look as if it might work is probably not worth the extra effort, although some armchair pundits might deride that as omitting a vital component ... If so they would be missing the point as an open window not only adds a touch of humanity, but it is also a deliberate invitation to the viewer to look more closely.*

move from the world of mass reproduction into that of at least the craft world, if not the art one. Here the difference between technical accuracy and visual realism might best be explained by reference to the difference between a 'technical drawing', whereby every detail of a subject is faithfully reproduced, and that of the 'artistic sketch' where it is not. The one is a basis for making a practical item in a workshop or as a means of illustrating its dimensional or technical aspects in an image; the latter is a means of capturing the 'feel' of something, or its 'visual essence', with the minimum of strokes. You will note that already we are leaving behind the precise language of the technical and beginning to use the vague, almost ethereal language of art. For the former, think Hamilton-Ellis and *Locomotives I have Known* and for the latter think Turner and *Wind, Rain and Speed*.

But remember, if it is an 'art' it can be learnt. In model railway terms what it really comes down to is the difference between those who spend a lifetime capturing every rivet or brick of everything on their railway and those who decide that 'capturing the essence' of some particular item or structure is, all things considered, probably the better approach. The suggestion therefore is that with a bit more thought, but with considerably less effort, a model can be made which alone is less than perfect but which *in situ* improves the overall impression created by the railway as a whole. Putting that another way; with a little imagination, obfuscation and a modicum of skill, one might achieve 90 per cent of the effect of a 'Pendon' for perhaps just 10 per cent of the effort.

Generally speaking this is a better way to proceed, largely because you give yourself the chance to complete a model in just a few years rather than spending a whole lifetime on just one. You can tell the almost complete lack of artistry of the pedantic type of modeller because they never have a proper backscene and prefer to let you see wallpaper (or worse, a 'bit of human operator') behind their model rather than an artistic and appropriate background setting. They have no 'vision', no overall 'impression' of their subject – which in their own home is fine but when they exhibit their work publicly they too often convey to us a scene without form or structure, merely working on layer upon layer of detail in the misguided belief that 'more' is by definition 'better'. Now if that's what you want to do with your own time that's fine, each to their own after all, but I know which I prefer looking at ...

One notable society has the tag line, 'Getting it *all* right' – a phrase which is open to several interpretations. If they mean that everything you model should be based on a prototype, not your imagination, then I am with them 100 per cent but many people seem to presume it means that every detail should be faithfully modelled to the last rivet, in which case I could not disagree more! You should find fairly quickly that the level of detail you put into any model depends upon how many structures you have to create and their relative positions in the grand scheme of things, rather than the particular scale you are working to. Thus a 4mm scale cottage in the middle ground of a model – or even a 7mm or 10mm scale one in the background of a large one (Photo 19) – does not need any great detail of tiling or feature, whereas a lone building in the immediate foreground of a layout might need door handles, individual tiles and possibly even the representation of separate sash window frames if it is to look accurate (Photo 20).

POSITION IN THE LANDSCAPE

As examples of what I mean, look at the following photos of structures on Tupdale, a 4mm or 1:76th scale model. In the foreground of this model (Photo 21), right in front of any visitor, is a pub which positively invites closer inspection. In fact we demand it from the viewer by placing a small, unexpected detail which catches the eye; a pile of bottle crates waiting to be placed into what we now realise must be a bottle store behind it (Photo 22). Any visitor aged 50 or over will instantly recognize those once-familiar wooden boxes filled with brown-glassed bottles of stout, light or brown ale; each with a label on the front. They had a bright metal cap, for which one needed either a bottle opener or very stout teeth! The building itself has a commensurate level of detail although readers of the aforementioned age will spot the 'Airfix Norman Church kit' origins of many of its components ... We'll ignore the signal box and barn for now because I want to turn your attention to that large goods shed in what is, from here, the middle distance (Photo 23). But of course as the operator sitting at the panel sees it, while it does not exactly become a foreground model, it certainly looms a lot larger so we do need to be very careful about how we tackle it (Photo 24).

If we get in really close (Photo 25), we can see that there is a fair amount of detail present; for example, each stone is precisely defined with a cut line, the windows are etched (specially made for this model,

in fact), and the down pipes have mountings onto the wall carefully detailed – everything you'd expect of a foreground model in fact – but note also the very muted colours in which the whole shed is painted: the colours are different, yes, but the tones are very similar. Then look at the texture: the walls are almost entirely flat. Stone which in reality is quite fat and rounded on the prototype has almost no depth here other than the odd more deeply-carved mortar course, the odd stone with the surface missing and a protruding string course around the base. Yet this is not noticeable because up this close the eye is

Photo 21.   *A huge landscape looks tiny if you can see it all at once and take in everything at a single sweep. Therefore it is vital to add eye-catching detail such as this pub which, with its rectangular black notices and square white windows, is immediately at odds with its undulating, flowing, natural surroundings. Further entice the eye with dark corners, repeated angular shapes and hidden detail begging the questions, 'What's in that porch?', and 'What's that beside it'?*

RIGHT: *Photo 22.   Small, fine details in the right place attract interest way beyond their size but need to be chosen carefully. Too much detail is self-defeating and makes a rural idyll too 'busy', though unfortunately not everyone understands this.*

BELOW: *Photo 23.   The goods shed in the middle distance is by far the largest building on the model yet it does not stand out and considerable thought went into ensuring it did not do so. (See text)*

Photo 24. *From the operator's viewpoint however, it becomes a lot more important and blocks the view of the backscene, thus giving the railway more impact than its surroundings. The viewer from the outside sees the railway in its landscape but the operator is more intimately conscious of the railway – which is how it should be.*

attracted to the details such as the windows, down pipe and the handrail protecting the steps; so it does not notice the texture of the walls.

But the texture of a distant, substantial building is not provided by its wall's surfaces, it is provided by its overall shape, the shadow the roof casts, the darker depths of the odd open door and the depth of the window reveals. If you now go back to the overall view which the visitor sees you will realise that none of this fine detail is visible from that distance and yet the building looks 'right' because the colours blend together and, because there is very little shadow detail showing, the structure sits back into the landscape in a way totally acceptable to the

eye. And this is the whole point of this introduction; if you get the level of detail and colour right for the position of each model within its setting, then the overall effect can be fabulous.

If everything across the board from front to back is detailed down to the nth degree then there is no separation: no recession from foreground into middle ground, none from that to the background and so 'through' that to the horizon. The 'mist of distance' is lost as a result and thus any illusion of reality is lost with it. And don't take my word for it: Ruskin, Turner's very own Victorian Bosworth, loudly insisted that, 'without obfuscation there can never be clarity', and of course Turner, our greatest

Photo 25.   The detail may be very fine and precise but the colours are muted and the shadows subdued: by such means a large building can look great from both close-up and from a distance.

ever British artist, could handle both fine detail and 'obfuscation' equally well, having been first an architectural painter of note before he moved on to the landscapes 'of soapsuds and froth' for which he later became so famous.

And it's not only Turner; Claude, Constable and Stubbs (of horses fame) all notably recede their detail as they move further from the foreground of their pictures into the landscape. Indeed, about the only famous landscape painter not to do so is Lowry who is known, of course, for his rather 'flat' paintings of matchstick men and matchstick cats and dogs ...

Therefore depending upon your type and size of model railway and the particular structure you are currently making for it, I trust you can see how any or all of the following methods might prove useful to you whatever scale you are working to, and that some techniques will work for all scales but others hardly work for any. I'll end this section with another quote from Ruskin who, to my mind, remains the most understandable of all art critics:

> No good work whatever can be perfect, and the demand for perfection is always a sign of a misunderstanding of the ends of art.

What better authority could you want? I rest my case.

Photo 26. A selection of typical research books, each dedicated to one particular subject. Copies are easily sourced on the internet.

CHOOSING THE RIGHT PROTOTYPES

For railway structures, choosing the right building to model is easy these days. Books are available on practically every line which was ever built in Britain and often you could do no better than buy several and pick the line you like best (Photo 26). But most of these books stop at the railway fence (understandably), and while they may feature some local hotel or a row of railway houses which overlooked the station, you will have to look elsewhere for interesting 'non-railway' buildings to create that local ambience previously suggested.

All kinds of internet resources are of course available. If you use the internet you will not need me to list them here while websites change so quickly that what is current as I write this may well have gone by the time you read it! Fortunately there also remain the traditional methods.

SITE VISITS

You can, for instance, make the once-obligatory 'site visit' – and I mean in a personal, not a virtual sense, although that too can be revealing. Interestingly, a personal visit often reveals a lot of useful information, even if the location is now unrecognizable

from the photographs which created your interest in it in the first place. Railway details themselves are often remarkably long lived, as this 1860s masonry culvert bridge shows (Photo 27). The original, rather soft, 'rusticated' sandstone has been considerably patched using engineering blue bricks and while the main body of the arch, largely protected from frosts, retains its original stonework that too has a new arch face, repairs probably effected by the Southern Railway during the 1920s or 30s. British Railways would have just replaced the whole thing!

Many station locations have changed out of all recognition since the days when the railway was king but the landscape surrounding a place, and the ambience that gives the locality, are all valuable insights for the visiting modeller, even if his beloved station is now a housing estate. If so, there usually remain some useful details to be found not too far away, such as this fencing on the old Somerset and Dorset line near Templecombe (Photo 28). The use of old rail for braced fence posts was a good choice: they obviously last! From the other side we see that the post is flat-bottomed rail, with holes in its flange for the wire tensioning bolts, but that the bracing rail is bullhead to allow clearance around it for the wires (Photo 29). Clever! Despite this, one had only to walk along a few yards to the next occupation

Photo 27.   Old Somerset and Dorset (S&D) culvert over a stream but with many and varied repairs over its 150 years. The low parapet is probably a British Railways addition.

ABOVE: Photo 28.   Although the S&D closed in 1966, in 2011 this fencing made from worn-out rail remains a very modellable feature.

RIGHT: Photo 29.   Such finds are also a great and accessible record of early rail sections, albeit not necessarily from the same line.

TOP: **Photo 30.** *The Southern Railway was a great user of reinforced concrete for fence posts, bracing and even some level-crossing gateposts. Many still survive.*

MIDDLE: **Photo 31.** *On close inspection this field gate proved to have some substantial flecks of cream paint on it. The local farmer confirmed he had 'rescued' it after the railway closed from an occupation crossing used to access his land. There are the remains of several others precisely like it within a mile so it's probably an S&D original rather than a SR or BR replacement.*

crossing to find a concrete version, for the use of which material the Southern Railway was particularly famous (Photo 30). For the lateral thinker therefore, a nose around the vicinity with a camera will almost always turn up a few really interesting and attractive prototypes which you will probably want to add to your layout: details which rarely appear in books, such as this original railway occupation crossing gate (Photo 31), which still had cream paint on it under

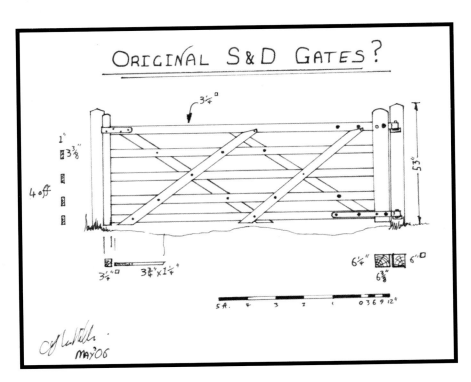

ORIGINAL S&D GATES?

Fig. 32. *As the only surviving complete occupation crossing gate in the area it was measured carefully and drawn up, as shown here, to record it for posterity. Then I sent that to the HMRS Journal editor, who kindly published it so anyone can refer to it.*

the horizontal timbers. It was well-worth measuring and drawing up for future reference. You should also try to find and photograph some local stone and brickwork as accurate colour references, invaluable if otherwise you have to rely on old black-and-white photographs.

Finally, with regard to non-railway buildings, there exist a few particularly valuable reference books on vernacular architecture in general and cottages in particular (Photo 33). These are listed on page 5.

RESEARCHING THE PROTOTYPE – CONGRESBURY, SOMERSET

Having looked first at the surroundings of our railway, let's now take Congresbury on the Yatton-Wells line as an example of researching the specifically railway aspects of a station and its environs. The prime source of information for this entire line is the book by Derek Phillips, *Steaming Through the Cheddar Valley* (OPC 2001) (Photo 34). This not only shows some eleven photographs of the station but, because it covers every station on the line, it also providentially provides excellent photos of the trains and their stock too. With this base to build upon, a site visit a year or two later (see Photos 35–47) revealed the station buildings long demolished but the station master's house intact. The platform faces still existed here and there but mould and algae had discoloured the stone to the point where they were no longer effective historical records. On the plus side, although both bridges had been removed (one by which the railway crossed a nearby Levels drain, another by which the road crossed the railway), the formation both East and West of the station site remained accessible and largely untouched, although much overgrown, so that the approaches were recordable much as they must have been in the 1950s. The surrounding landscape was also photographed for the backscene.[3]

Photo 33.   A selection of excellent books on vernacular architecture.

Photo 34.   A typical reference 'bible' for anyone modelling a particular line of railway.

---

[3] The photos, which individually can be found on page 31, have been stitched together on pages 32–33 to show what a backscene for this model might look like.

Photos taken on a 'site visit' to the remains of Congresbury Station, Somerset Levels.

Photo 35

Photo 36

Photo 37

Photo 38

Photo 39

Photo 40

Photo 35. The last remaining railway building standing at Congresbury – the stationmaster's house.

Photo 36. Sadly 'end of the roll' carelessness in film processing spoilt this image, but it still provides a valuable record for the modeller.

Photo 37. Note that the garden is at the level of the surrounding land, but that the station approach road on the other side of the hedge is at a raised level and climbing higher.

Photo 38. A 'Levels drain' some twenty feet wide, once bridged by the railway.

Photo 39. The drain is protected by a raised embankment on either side. Pedestrians crossed the line using gated 'occupation crossings', this being one of five close to the station.

Photo 40. This view from the trackbed of the railway clearly shows the remains of the second crossing gate, pure GWR and still largely intact.

Photo 41

Photo 42

Photo 43

Photo 44

Photo 45

Photo 46

Photo 41.   Today, with the road embankment up to the bridge over the railway removed, the widened main road to the right has been raised to reduce flooding using the spoil from that embankment. Despite this, the view of the distant hills, trees and housing must remain much the same as it was throughout the life of the railway.

Photo 42.   Panning the camera left we can begin to collect photos to stitch together for a backscene ...

Photo 43.   ... while also noting the huge size of this particular field.

Photo 44.   Being regularly grazed the grass remains short, but the line of the disused railway has become overgrown, quite substantially in places.

Photo 45.   Close by the railway's fence is a remaining gatepost, seen distantly in the previous view.

Photo 46.   It and this waggon-way over the drainage ditch are both features worth modelling in what is otherwise a flat and largely featureless field.

Photo 47.   Looking back from here towards the road and drain, the stationmaster's house marks the start of the station site. The line of the railway is roughly where the gap in the trees is, the rather poisonous ballast and noxious weedkillers used in the 1950s still restricting the undergrowth even decades later.

Site visit to Congresbury, south-eastern end.

Photo 48

Photo 49

Photo 50

Photo 51

Photo 48. *Just beyond the east end of the station site a green lane, now just a bridleway, sits alongside a small drain. These are crossed by both the main line to Wells (in the background) and the branch to Blagdon (not visible) in distinct crossings separated by perhaps a hundred metres. I believe the gate on the right is an old Bristol & Exeter original since it is different to the few remaining GWR examples and matches early Victorian etchings of that railway's main line. It has been removed for further use nearby, probably by a farmer as we saw previously on the S&D.*

Photo 49. *Moving closer, the small drainage culvert disappears from sight for quite fifty metres but reappears the other side of the Wrington Vale line. These typical but very varied railway structures are rarely recorded, yet even the shallowest embankment needs one every few hundred metres.*

Photo 50. *At the crossing itself this fence post is a wonderful survivor of the cast-iron bridge rail initially used on the originally broad-gauge Cheddar Valley line. Turned into a fence post, it has lasted over a hundred years!*

Photo 51. *From a little north of the line; after a hundred metres or so of tree-lined lane with several narrow, almost medieval-width fields to the east; the vista opens up again and another patch of potential backscene reveals itself. That very tall church spire, which was hardly noticeable at all from the west, now obviously needs to feature on it prominently. Thus a short walk has provided several useful details that will make for a much more accurate and convincing model.*

BELOW & RIGHT: Backscene image stitched together from the photos on page 31.

It was a shame about the lost station buildings but fortunately, local enquiry around Congresbury duly confirmed the report in Mr Phillip's book that the next station of Sandford and Banwell, a few miles up the line and precisely similar in construction, not only remained standing but had been sympathetically restored. Moreover, it was accessible during normal office hours. The photographs in the accompanying panel (Photos 52–60), show the results of 'going the extra mile' – or three in this case!

Today, in 2012, a new housing estate occupies the site of Congresbury station and has obliterated those few final remains entirely. However, much of the charm of the vicinity remains in the approaches from either side so a visit even today would not be entirely wasted and would certainly give you the 'feel' of the Somerset Levels. However, the detail and overall perception gained from that trip again proved the value of site visits, even forty years after the sound of the last whistle had blown away on the wind.

FURTHER SOURCES OF INFORMATION

Returning to Mr Phillip's book, a polite written enquiry enclosing an S.A.E. to the author, care of the publishers, produced contact details for the late Joe Moss, whose photographs feature so prominently. As was suspected, there were quite a few more he had taken of the station during several visits, those taken in 1949 being of particular value. These prints had not made it to the book but I was able to buy copies of them from dealer Roger Carpenter who now markets Joe's collection. Some showed extra details which are not available in any other way since it appears nobody else photographed them while they existed. This proves that unless you think to ask about other photos from part-published collections, and are prepared to pay for what turns up, you may unnecessarily remain ignorant of some features of your chosen prototype. I had hoped to include a few of them in another panel as an example of what is available but, not wishing to pay a second time for what was effectively an advertisement, I decided not to. However one has to say that for the time, skill and materials it takes to print old film negatives, not to mention the space and very particular conditions needed for their prolonged storage, the fees for printing off copies are entirely justified and, whilst enabling otherwise unobtainable period detail to be retained for future generations, they still cost a lot less to acquire than yet another new engine! One has to hope however that these collectors too have made suitable dispositions for saving the unique images they are looking after so that they remain available when, in due course, the collector too 'passes on'.

Whilst on the subject; although it can be a remunerative choice to dispose of your own, or a loved one's, painstakingly assembled collection of photos by selling them to a private dealer, this is may be less than ideal. Certainly it is better than losing them, which is what seems to have happened to much of the National Railway Museum's photographic collection, most of which, I understand, moulders in

Surviving buildings at Sandford and Banwell station –
photographed on the same day as the trip to Congresbury

Photo 52

Photo 53

Photo 54

Photo 55

Photo 56

Photo 57

Photo 58

Photo 59

Photo 60

Photo 52. Although styled like an estate cottage, the proportions of the B&E station buildings are, to say the least, substantial.

Photo 53. The very fine stonework of the quoins around the openings and on the corners are quite definitive features which just have to be modelled ...

Photo 54. ... while the individual stones have all been very carefully sawn into rectangles with very closely fitting joints – beautiful workmanship!

Photo 55. The cast-iron drainage fittings and finely detailed, pierced barge-boards are both quite distinctive and require some thought as to how best to reproduce them ...

Photo 56. ... while the blank window detail in the gable end and blank 'plinth' below it all shout 'quality' loud and clear. The promoters of this line wanted you to bank on their company's solid credentials, an attitude completely at odds with that of the railways today, which is why these things are so worthwhile modelling properly.

Photo 57. Note, too, how far the doors are set back behind the walls, emphasizing the latters' thickness and solidity – all clever marketing by design!

Photo 58. The windows are not set anywhere near so far back but use very fine timbers, carefully shaped to match the opening and thus to let in the maximum light: more of the very fine quality work so notable on some of the early railways' structures.

Photo 59. The booking hall, complete with ticket window, remained in 2006 an internal delight complete with period décor – ceiling tiles apart!

Photo 60. Beside the main station building is a small porter's lodge which was once the signalman or 'bobby's' cabin. Being for staff its more lowly status is reflected in the relative plainness of the barge-boards – but they are still fine pieces of work.

Photo 61. This delightful photo of Aberdovey station's water tower and cattle dock also shows three attractive villas on the cliff in the background, including one with fancy castellations: a fun challenge by way of a little 'perspective modelling', should they take your fancy. It is typical of photos in the HMRS collection. (Historical Model Railway Society)

storage, unviewed, awaiting the funds to pay for sorting and catalogueing, the work of which is often considerable when accompanying notebooks are slung out as 'useless junk' by the unknowing. Your photos however, may usefully be made much more accesible by offering them to an appropriate railway line society (if a local collection), or to the Historical Model Railway Society if the collection is more of a national record, because such societies normally use volunteers for catalogueing work and thus progress, albeit often slow, is normally a continous process. In other words, the photographs will, in time, usefully become available to future generations. In the same vein, when you are searching for images, although searching for locations in the various commercial collections is one route, joining one or more of these societies so as to gain access to their various photographic collections is another. (Details below.)

Photo 62.
The cheap but reasonably effective coal office from the 'Scenix' range.

BELOW: *Photo 63.*
A resin-moulded station building from Hornby's 'Skaledale' range, adapted to suit a West Country location.

In addition to these four resources ('line books', line societies, site visits and photo dealers), you might, whilst on your field trip, look out in local shops or post-offices for village books with names like *Victorian Borset* or *Borsetshire in Old Photographs* or some such, which can provide an invaluable and often unique collection of local period images. While these tend to be mainly village and farm photographs the station is often included, even if sometimes obscured by a charabanc full of smiling locals! Nothing for Congresbury was available at the time of my visit but who knows what's available these days?

Reverting to purely railway structures, apart from the huge selection of new and second-hand specialist books available to buy, there are also the traditional resources: libraries, museums and, generally of far more use, a multitude of 'Line Societies' which specialize in collecting and distributing information and photos of not only the trains of their favourite railway, but normally their recorded architecture too. For lines which are not covered by these mainly 'pre-Grouping' and 'Big 4' societies, the Historical Model Railway Society is the 'senior society' having recently celebrated its 50th birthday. It covers all the British railways and its collection of railway books is probably the largest to be found outside the British Library while its collection of photographs is approaching a hundred thousand items (Photo 61).

SOURCING YOUR MODEL BUILDINGS

It will not have escaped your attention that there are now regular releases of complete, cast resin, painted, 'ready-to-plant' model buildings of both railway and residential types, not to mention a considerable variety of industrial structures. So the first option is to just buy a few appropriate examples – and probably a few inappropriate ones – and bed them into your scenery (Photo 62). If they are chosen carefully and neatly bedded in, it seems reasonable to include them and I have certainly used them now and again – but it is a rare model that can rely entirely upon such structures. Of course, anyone happy with those

all over his railway would be so unlikely to buy this book that I am going to assume *all* you readers are prepared to put in at least a *little* more effort …

The second option is to look carefully to see if any of the pre-made resin buildings might, with a little work, be adapted to your purposes – as with this Hornby building which has had its 'stepped gables', so reminiscent of the North East, replaced by the tapered stone copings so familiar in the West Country (Photo 63). You will find an example of a more complex adaptation detailed in a later chapter, but to remain with the theme of sourcing for now, if you can't buy it ready made the next option is to see if there is a suitable kit available. Kits are now myriad and vary from simple card – we will tackle one as our first project – through plastic, such as this popular platelayer's hut (Photo 64), and resin, some of considerable age, to etched brass examples of varying value for money depending upon their ease of construction and usefulness.

Beyond these are the 'kits of bits' which are either laser-cut wooden structures, many of obviously American parentage, or packages by Wills and others which provide appropriate amounts of sheet plastic materials, some detail frets of greater or lesser usefulness, depending upon your skill levels, and a set of written instructions. By the time you get to these you are practically scratch-building anyway and although they can be useful as a means of learning new techniques and working with different materials, unless they suit your proposed model admirably you are probably better off scratch-building. To do so will probably be quicker and it will certainly be cheaper!

Do beware of mixing too many different types of materials though, without thinking it through first. It takes a good eye to mix cast resin, plastic, plaster and cardboard structures and get them all to fit together harmoniously and believably. It can be done, I've done it, (Photo 65), but it may not be the best approach for a relative beginner without an eye for what will sit happily next to what.

Of course the answer to all these options is actually an easy one: if you are happy with an easy solution in a particular place then use it. If it does

Photo 64.   A simple but beautifully effective plastic kit by CooperCraft of a Great Western platelayer's hut.

Photo 65.   Cast resin, cast plaster and cardboard kit buildings here sit happily cheek by jowl on a town street but beware: mixing different construction materials is not always effective.

TOP LEFT: **Photo 66.**   *Another version of the same CooperCraft kit but this time used in multiple to make a different, bigger structure with a new tiled roof in paper on a card former. Something similar would be an ideal beginner's project.*

TOP RIGHT: **Photo 67.**   *This hut, however, is completely hand made except for a bit of Wills' stonework for the sides and chimney. It is based closely on an example found on the Settle and Carlisle line.*

LEFT: **Photo 68.**   *Sometimes an observant eye and some imagination is really all that you need for a very simple building. This one is made from cardboard and an offcut of embossed brick sheet.*

BELOW: **Photo 69.**   *A 'double closet' (his and hers, presumably) found in South Perrott, Dorset and modelled in cardboard.*

not satisfy you however, merely move up to the next level. In all probability, once you have scratch-built a few buildings you will have the experience to know which is the best route to take to get the effect you want to achieve. Above all remember one thing: if you can, finish the entire model. Showing anybody a half-built scene will only elicit the comment, 'It'll be nice when it's finished', and you'll not gain very much from that, will you? Besides, spending more than a few years on any one project is probably pointless; what is the point if, as has happened, you spend an entire lifetime on 'The Grand Project' but never actually finish it? What have you achieved? Nothing! Far better to take on a smaller, simpler project, get it finished, learn from it, and then start another project armed with a lot more experience and the benefit

Photo 70.   Open structures require careful thought about how to provide strength. The large-section main girders are fine modelled in plastic but sometimes metal construction is the best way, as with the thin ironwork used for the roof support structure which has been soldered up using angled brass sections.

of knowing that not only you can do it, but that this time you can do it better!

CHOOSING THE RIGHT MATERIALS

When you do decide to jump in and begin scratch building, choosing the right materials to work with will certainly become important. Knowing what to use for any particular job will certainly come more easily with practice but, apart from some obvious choices, a few words now might save you some wasted effort.

The first thing to consider is the size of the model. A small platelayer's hut is easy; you can make it from scratch in card or plastic, adapt a card, plastic or resin kit or make it using individual paper brick 'chads' or 'slate' tiles and they can all work (Photo 66). It's a small, relatively quick project and as very few were

precisely the same, as long as you pick a type suitable for your chosen line of railway then just have a go and see what you make of it (Photo 67). Since most only have one door and one window, they make excellent starter projects. On the non-railway front, the 'privy' or outside loo is another small building with much the same qualities, although this time you can forget the chimney (Photo 68)! Of this particular (and genuine!) double structure (Photo 69) we need say nothing, except that 'Dualism' is supposed to be relaxing, isn't it?

Next for consideration comes the general type of the building. If it is closed and has walls on all sides then, again, almost any material remains appropriate because it can be well braced inside if necessary, but open structures such as engine sheds, barns and shelters require a little more thought. Consider the main surfaces of the building. For brick, embossed plastic sheet might be a nice exterior but a strong, cardboard structure behind it will be vital if it is not to warp. It certainly is perfectly possible to laminate a thick structure in plasticard but, if you do not leave adequate vents, the fumes from the last joint cannot escape and the whole structure will eventually become soft and warp. On the other hand, a similar lack of air in a cardboard construction will prevent PVA glue from going off quickly too, so before you start you need to think through not only what finish you want on the outside of your model but how you are going to support it, too. The thicker types of embossed plastic sheeting are, if to scale for your project, fine for most sorts of walls including corrugated ones while their flat back surfaces certainly make construction simple. Where you need to show a thin corrugated edge however, or where you can see both sides — as with open fronted barns or roofing — thin, clear 'corrugated glazing' sheet

painted as opaque material is usually much better. You can support it on brass sections, soldered into a substantial support structure, as shown by my gas-works purifier (Photo 70).

Windows in thin plasticard sheet are wonderfully easy to cut out and can be made delightfully complex, but larger examples tend to warp rapidly and besides, without a hearty coat of black paint they let light through them if illuminated from the inside. A decent quality business card, on the other hand, is much less prone to either warp or let light through and easily accepts quick-drying PVA wood glue. This is helpful if you are using cotton thread as glazing bars. These three photos — outside, inside and illuminated from behind — show the use of cotton thread for window bars (Photos 71, 72 & 73). Note that in this case I used 10 thou. plasticard window frames so as to allow filed, neatly-rounded tops — always

MIDDLE LEFT: **Photo 71.**   *Thin but good quality card is often a useful material for rectangular windows but can be difficult to shape neatly around tight curves.*
MIDDLE CENTRE: **Photo 72.**   *Plasticard was therefore chosen here because it is easy to file it into neat semicircles which fit the wall openings.*
MIDDLE RIGHT: **Photo 73.**   *If you paint thin plasticard black before finishing and fitting it, this overcomes its translucency — vital if you want to illuminate the interior.*
BOTTOM LEFT: **Photo 74.**   *For fancy windows, etched brass is the only real option. Bill Bedford made these especially for me, although they are now available from his standard range.*
BOTTOM RIGHT: **Photo 75.**   *Brass is, of course, entirely opaque!*

Photo 76.   Where the interior of a building can be seen, as where the track enters this goods shed, thick cardboard makes an excellent representation of a timber framework.

difficult in cardboard. For large, complex lights such as those found in factories or my Settle and Carlisle Midland goods shed, etched brass is the perfect answer. (Photos 74 & 75).

Attempting to make a large, ship-lapped or weather-boarded structure from plasticard is fraught with potential problems of warping, whereas cardboard layered with wood glue is both strong and represents wood very well. Thick cardboard makes an excellent 'timber framed' support structure where it will be seen, as in this timber-framed goods shed (Photo 76). Etched brass is great in kit form where the designer is experienced, but it is difficult to solder properly joints which are too close to each other. In larger structures brass, being an excellent heat sink, can also quickly get the better of the iron. Brass is not really a great base for paint, either, especially if a model is

going to be handled regularly. If that is your problem, then two-part epoxy paints provide the ideal 'pre-undercoat' prior to normal painting. On the plus side, the strength of metal comes into its own for very fine details. Metal is also perfect for signal arms and their bearings, which can be firmly soldered to a plate. They will work well if aligned properly, while plastic ones are feeble and last no time at all in regular use so, as with all things, pick your material to suit the job in hand, or even be prepared to mix timber (post) metal (working bits), and plastic (butchered kit details) if that works best (Photo 77).

Stone walls come in such variety that your choice of material is really decided by the visual effect you wish to achieve. I make great use of the Wills embossed plastic stone sheets, especially for repetitive struc-tures like bridges and viaducts, while Squires' less

Photo 77.   Sometimes your best option is to mix your materials: here a tall wooden post (tapered, sanded rocket stick), is given a long metal ladder (etched brass stiles with tcw rungs and landing handrails allied to tinplate support brackets and hoop), while a plastic signal kit provided the lamps, arms and other details.

BELOW: Photo 78.   Wills' stone sheet is used for the viaduct stonework above, Squires' for the retaining walls below.

Photo 79. *This wall's face was made by carving out small, V-shaped slices from quality cardboard. The 'Kings and Queens' on top are individual bits cut from the scrap waste of window and door openings.*

detailed and more regular vacuum-formed sheets have their uses too, especially in N-gauge (Photo 78). For flatter finishes, such as those seen on most limestone cottages, cardboard is my personally-favoured material (Photo 79), although others swear by plasticard for the same thing. Try both and see which you prefer! Where the rougher stonework found beyond the limestone belt is your subject, a smear of car-body filler or some other spreadable material, carved, might be your best answer. (Photo 80) One chap I know swears by Pyruma fire cement for his stonework but it crumbles rapidly if not cured properly. 'Cooking' fire cement buildings in an oven is not easy, and the smell does not go down well with the 'household authorities' either, but I did once give it a try long, long ago with tolerable results (Photo 81). Plaster has its enthusiastic adherents too but it crumbles too easily to last very long, although Dental

Plaster is certainly useful for casting repetitive details as once thoroughly dry it is practically indestructible! Sadly it is difficult and expensive to obtain.

For really open stonework such as dry stone walls, where the gaps are as important to the finish as the stone itself, try using chopped up bits of roofing slate glued together with wood glue. I made two 8-inch long 'originals' for Tupdale's 4mm scale dry stone walls and had them commercially moulded in resin, otherwise the fifty feet or so of walling needed would not have been possible (Photo 82)! Used both ways up, the four possible arrangements of 8in lengths of stone obviated any sense of repetition. Where both sides would be visible I used two, back to back, but where not the vertical capping stones – also cast from two originals – hid the lack of width. The sides could be stacked vertically too, making a higher wall when the need arose (Photo 83). Mind you, it took

125 castings, each one carefully trimmed, curved or sawn and re-joined as necessary, to finish that one model, so it is neither a quick nor a particularly cheap solution! But then of course, hand-building fifty-odd real feet of 4mm scale dry stone wall was not really an option either ...

Finally, the choice of tools and fixatives needed when working with different materials is worth some consideration too. Knives require a certain level of precaution and common sense, of course,

and a proper 'self-healing' cutting mat is highly recommended; it is certainly the best answer for any prolonged work. But sharp edges of one kind or another are a prerequisite for any kind of model-making be it card, plastic, metal or wood you are fettling, so there really is very little to choose between the different materials on that score.

Working in plasticard or metal, however, does lead to working with some unpleasant smells. Butanone and Methylethylketone, the standard chemicals for

Photo 80. Again, Wills' plastic sheeting is used for the viaduct stonework but mouldings of my own, based on chipped-slate pieces, form the dry stone walling above right. Hand-carved car-body filler created the 'rubble' embankment retaining wall below – therefore three different methods giving three different finishes.

gluing plasticard together, are noxious, liable to spill-age and violently explosive too, which makes them less than ideal if there are children or open fires about, or for those who smoke. Solder for brass or metal construction also usually requires noxious fluxes which can be quite dangerous if acidic – and they need to be strongly acidic for steel and iron work, as in fencing made from real steel rail. These chemicals are especially unpleasant when vaporized by heating in a joint, so get yourself a mask and cer-tainly *do not* breathe in the vapours!

And do be aware that certain of the chemicals used in modern, leadless solders are *far* more car-cinogenic than the resin flux that used to be in old

TOP: *Photo 81.   An old photo from the 1970s shows a village I once made from Pyruma fire cement. It was relatively quick but neither very accurate nor very long-lived. These days there are better materials available, such as fillers and polyester or composite resins.*

BELOW: *Photo 82.   Some five or six of the fifty-odd feet of 'drystone walling' on Tupdale. Hand-building such quantities is entirely unrealistic but casting multiple replicas from a few new originals is a sensible, practical answer.*

Photo 83.   Here the same castings are ranged three deep to support a raised roadway – not that you'd realize it.

fashioned tin/lead solders because they are designed to be used in fume-extraction cabinets. Nobody considered us poor model-makers without such facilities when the EU outlawed lead for commercial soldering, thus making it very expensive and all but impossible for the amateur to obtain today: pretty cavalier of them, you will agree. Lead, although poisonous if you got it on your hands and then swallowed some through eating or chewing your fingers, was perfectly safe if one used it for the job and then washed one's hands immediately afterwards. Just because a few people got lazy we now all have to risk cancer because that's deemed 'safer' than possible lead poisoning. And that's progress? I just wish decisions on these things were made by people who knew something about the subject.

In fact the biggest problem with soldering has traditionally been burnt fingers from having a hot iron lying around the workbench on a stand – still a problem today, whichever solder you use! This problem can be avoided by using a low voltage, 'instant heat' resistance iron which is only on when you depress the trigger – but then I've had a lot of practice at judging different temperatures by counting the seconds! Be warned: resistance irons can get so hot they melt the bit, so beginners – read the instructions!

So; at the end of the day (and that's not just an idiotic idiom, that's also a common modelling time), while all these methods and materials are perfectly safe for the mature adult who uses them without any untoward distractions, a modicum of common sense and a few simple precautions, there remains a lot to be said for the completely harmless if annoying mess caused by the drop of PVA glue spilt on the carpet, which is the worst thing likely to happen to the happy builder in cardboard! And after all, card was good enough for John Ahern, George and Doris Iliffe-Stokes, Peter Denny and Roye England when he began Pendon; and look at the stunning work they managed with it!

CHAPTER TWO

SUPERQUICK BUILD: THE VILLAGE SCHOOL

Learning basic hand-tool skills by building a Superquick cardboard kit, with 'improvements'.

INTRODUCTION

The 'Superquick' kit has long been considered the standard entry point when it comes finding a practical start for beginners wanting to learn how to make good models. The kits are simple card structures, the bits are largely pre-punched out and only a few tags need nicking with a knife to remove them. Therefore any sensible child can assemble one with patience, the minimum of tools and a bit of art glue. Indeed, any adult could probably assemble one too without any help from this book, given they had child-like patience, so they remain an excellent and cheap way of learning the basic skills needed to model buildings. Indeed cardboard remains the material of choice for probably the best – and certainly the most famous – structure modellers in the country; namely Pendon. It is proposed, therefore, to simply build one of these kits to show you the best way of doing so and to point out pertinent features as we go so you learn as much as possi-

ble from the experience. At just a few pounds each anybody can afford a Superquick kit so it is experience of great value which can be learned at very little cost. You do not even have to pick the same kit as me because most of the methods used will work with any similar card kit. Not only that but while the odd feature will be different, depending upon which kit you take on, the *process* of assembly will be very similar, as will the tools, materials and the kind of thought processes which go into considering ways of 'improving' it. From there it is but a short step to designing your own 'kit' of parts which you then create ready to assemble later; a process we call 'scratch building' …

INVESTIGATING THE KIT

So let's begin by looking at 'Superquick Series B No.31, the Village School' (Photo 84) .

As you can see (Photo 85), this simple but attractive brick structure comes 'flat-packed' in a plastic cover with a card title page, the latter a handy source of good quality thin card as we shall see later. The

SERIES B No. 31

VILLAGE SCHOOL

OR MODEL VILLAGES & OO & HO GAUGE RAILWAYS

Photo 84. Superquick's Village School kit is a 'Series B', which is really a price band for a particular number of sheets of printed cardboard.

Photo 85. Like most cardboard kits, it comes as a 'flat-pack' in a plastic bag with printed parts and a glazing sheet.

LIST OF TOOLS

- Steel straight-edge
- Ruler with a selection of metric and Imperial Scales
- Sharp general-purpose knife with retractable, snap-off blades
- 'Self-healing' cutting mat
- Standard HB pencil and rubber
- Warding file and/or some kind of abrasive sheet
- Tweezers or pliers for holding small items
- PVA-based wood or art glue
- Sellotape or impact adhesive, as preferred
- A selection of acrylic paints and brushes

The following are also useful:
- Water-based builder's glue
- Large black felt-tip pen
- Various rectangular wooden sections for bracing
- Junior hacksaw and blades
- A selection of household pegs, bulldog clips and/or hair clips
- Some spirit-based enamel paints and thinners
- Cheap talcum powder

Photo 86.   All you really need to make a cardboard building kit!

of instructions printed on a thinner card, which also contains a few more bits, more instructions on another sheet and some clear plastic glazing material with windows printed on it (Photo 87). The first thing to do is to ensure you have all the bits, glazing included – so check the packaging to ensure you are not about to throw it away! Then settle down to read the instructions *first*: do that with the kit itself in front of you so you can familiarize yourself with the bits, their names, and where they go in relation to each other. These days, with the almost universal availability and ease of use of digital cameras, it is probably worthwhile taking a photo or two of the various sections, (Photos 88 & 89) and try to get close enough to be able to read the names on each part – once you start separating them from the sheet it is all too easy to forget which bit goes where!

A photo is useful because, unlike a plastic kit where you can leave the parts on the sprue beside their part number until you need them, with a card kit, as you cut out the walls, odd bits of bracing, flooring and parts for later use become detached from their surroundings. If they are printed all over then their labels, often printed beside them, can be lost too, so the idea of being able to refer to the whole sheet in a photo is not as daft as it sounds, even for an experienced builder. A simple precaution like writing the name of each bit on the back as it is removed from its neighbour will usually be of value sooner or later,

building itself is made up of three simple rectangles: schoolroom, office and an entrance lobby topped with one flat and two gable roofs – perfect! It has a chimney (ideal 'thin card' working practice), and a number of other features which will not only show us how to create a three dimensional model from flat card but also how to help improve its authenticity, strength and realism as you build it.

Having removed the packaging, we can see that the kit consists of a single folded sheet of reasonably thick printed card with most of the major parts almost entirely pre-cut out for you. There is a set

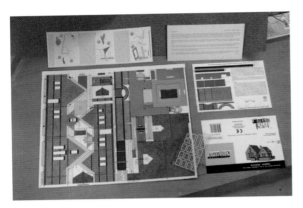

Photo 90. You will need to remove certain parts from the middle of others to be able to assemble them, but do not risk losing these among the 'scrap material'. Provide yourself with a tray and use it assiduously!

Photo 87. Once inside you will find a large, folded sheet of printed card, some lesser items on a smaller, thinner sheet, some paper instructions and the glazing sheet.

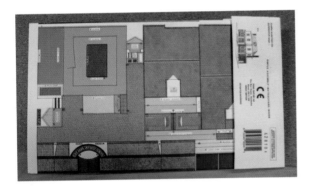

Photo 88. This is the second side containing roofs, floors, doors and the odd dormer or two. The playground walls are really there just to fill up the sheet.

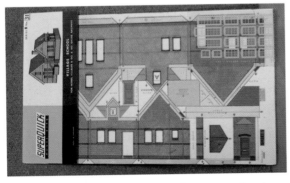

Photo 89. The first side, shown here, contains the main walls and a few other bits and pieces.

as will finding a high-sided tray to put these odd bits in so you don't loose them (Photo 90). So, now we are ready to find ourselves an uninterrupted hour or two and make a start.

SPOTTING 'MISSING BITS'

I know we all like to get stuck in straight away but before you begin, just stand back a bit and look carefully at the kit itself. Is it really all there? The point is, whereas in the early days of these kits back in the 1950s they really were 'complete', it soon became obvious to the designers that if they could miss off a few minor bits here and there they could improve the variety and sizes of models they could fit onto the same printed sheet, sheets which were limited to two standard sizes and prices – range 'A' and range 'B'! And so it is with this kit. Look closely and you will find only two 'barge boards', yet there are four gables, two for each of the two main rooms of the building. Therefore, if you want to finish the model 'properly' you will need to duplicate each board for the second gable ends.

Duplicating a shape in outline is simply achieved by placing the original over a piece of plain white card of similar thickness, scoring lightly around the edge with a blade, and then cutting it out carefully (Photos 91 & 92). It might therefore be handy to get in a good supply of different card thicknesses from an art shop before you go too far with any model making, although to be true to the ethos of the

Photo 91.   *The kit only provides one barge-board for each room, not one for each gable. Any 'proper' building will need one at each end so, to save measuring and marking out, merely score around the one provided to create another.*

Photo 92.   *With the original safely back in the component tray, carefully cut right through your card to make the new part. Use a number of light strokes and a sharp blade.*

cardboard kit you can often 'find' suitable materials by collecting 'useful-looking' varieties of cardboard packaging. Avoid corrugated cardboards, which have few uses, but cereal boxes and other plainly-printed cardboard with two non-glossy surfaces are always useful while the backing sheet of calendars is another good source; and free too! Sometimes huge calendars already several months old are flogged off very cheaply, and are not only an easy way of getting some good card but, with an 'English Cottage' or 'British Village' type, you might find some inspirational prototypes into the bargain. Of course, not everybody needs a perfect scale model of Anne Hathaway's cottage …

For the unwary however, there's one potentially frustrating problem which you might care to consider. All these card kits are very carefully and generally pretty well thought through but if they only provide barge boards at one end, this probably means there was not enough space on the card to provide a full set. Furthermore, the roof may be cut long enough to only cover the building if fitted with one barge board at one end – as is the case in this kit (Photo 93). So if you decide to 'improve' the kit by adding matching barge boards at the other ends, you will need either to extend the roofs to cover them, or to trim down the sides to fit the existing roof. Now I never was,

even as a lad, happy with printed card roofs and their complete lack of relief and neither should you be, because get the roof wrong and you spoil the whole thing. Anyone looking down at your model is going to see the roof first so if that disappoints, they are not going to waste time looking at the rest of the building. It was Alec Guinness in *The Ladykillers* of 1955

Photo 93.   *The kit only provides one barge-board for one end of each room: if you fit one at each end the roof will be too short, as shown here on the left-hand side. There is a 'workaround', however.*

who said that 'windows are the eyes of a building' – and so they are, but the roof is the 'hairdo'; the thing you notice first and a printed roof looks as wrong as a wig! A roof is bigger than any window and because of the angle it reflects light better so, if there's no relief in it, no physical representation of the separate sloping planes of each row of slates or tiles, and no hint of that physical separation into individual units which we all know is the reality, then the brain will reject it as being incorrect and any further attempts at realism on the rest of the model will be wasted. Fortunately, creating interesting roofs is a simple if not exactly rapid task, and we'll look at them in a later chapter, but for this project let's start at the bottom and work up by looking first at the walls and what goes into building them.

FREEING THE BITS FROM THE SHEET

At last we can now proceed to nick the tiny sections of card (called 'tags') which keep the bits together in the packing, thus enabling us to remove the walls from the sheet (Photo 94). Do note however, that some lines are deliberately part-cut as 'pre-scored' lines and are to be folded, so do not cut through these too (Photo 95)! If you look closely beside the blade in the next photo you will see that these lines are marked with red arrows (Photo 96) – look out for them and take care *not* to cut through them, although in places you may need to extend the part-cut through the odd tag if these remain as solid card. If you do accidentally cut right through a line

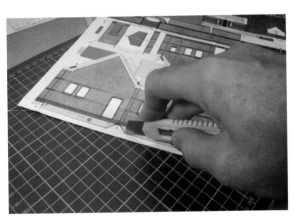

TOP LEFT: *Photo 94.   Cardboard kit parts are largely pre-cut but are retained in the sheet or 'fret' by tags which need cutting through.*

TOP RIGHT: *Photo 95.   However, some joints are deliberately not pre-cut but part-cut and are supposed to be folded over as tabs: do not cut right through these without thinking as they are intended to be part of the bit you are cutting out!*

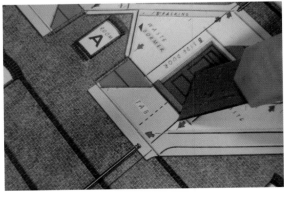

BOTTOM RIGHT: *Photo 96.   Look out for little red arrow indicators first, before cutting through any particular line. Once you see how it all goes together you may decide to remove some of these tabs and replace them with more substantial bracing – but you can decide that later so it is suggested you keep them for now.*

Photo 97.   When cutting out bits you will use later, don't forget to write on the back what they are because later you are bound to have forgotten which bit was which!

Photo 99.   You will need to be careful, attempting curved cuts with a straight blade!

which should remain 'part-cut', use a narrow strip of masking tape on the back to re-make the joint temporarily, removing the tape and gluing the joint properly later in the assembly process.

As you progress you will have to remove a number of other odd sections which will not be needed until later: identify them with a pencil so that later you know what they are! (Photo 97)

With the walls removed from the sheet, you can now remove the window waste from the walls by cutting through the small retaining tags in the

Photo 100.   Carving through the printed surface is all too easy to do. You will not be alone in that!

Photo 98.   Window and door blanks are often very nearly cut right through, but do get into the corners with a sharp blade or you will get rips and tears which will be white, the colour of the card beneath.

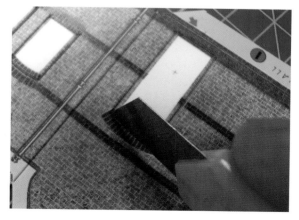

Photo 101.   Sometimes just pushing the blade tip into the corner is sufficient, without drawing it along the card.

corners (Photo 98). Do be careful with the knife; slicing a lump out of the bit you are removing is one thing, carving a chunk out of your brickwork (Photo 99) would however spoil the job (Photo 100). Try therefore, to line the blade up with the previously-cut edge as precisely as you can (Photo 101).

The window blanks should lift out easily if you have cut all the tags properly, so try it prodding it gently before pushing any blank out with force (Photo 102). It may help to work your way with the knife along all the tags from one side first (Photo 103), and then turn the card ninety degrees and do the next lot, and so on until all four quarter angles have been cut, removing any loose blanks as you go (Photo 104). Do watch out for odd bits where the card had not been completely cut through before the blank was removed because the slight tear will leave small 'furry' area of torn card (Photo 105). Remove these with a sharp blade as soon as you spot them! Also try looking from behind at the plain side of the card

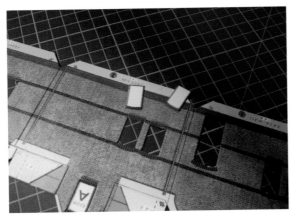

Photo 102. Try just lifting the blank with the tip of the blade. If it is free it will lift easily; if not, check and cut again.

Photo 103. Once it is loose, just move on to the next window. You can tap the whole wall on the table when you've done and they will all fall out – assuming you've done it properly, of course!

Photo 104. You will probably find it worth popping the 'waste' bits into a heap at the side: useful part-cut extra bracing!

Photo 105. If you do rip a blank out you may get these 'feathers' left in the corner. Cut them away carefully as soon as you spot them.

Photo 106.   *If you check the openings from behind, you can often see a mis-cut edge. Trim it now, before you add the windows, as it is always difficult to correct such things later.*

Photo 107.   *That same corner from the 'right' side shows a card edge that will be noticeable on the finished model, as will the poorly printed brick on the opposite side.*

Photo 108.   *If you have successfully cut out both rooms, they should look like this!*

Photo 109.   *Try gently teasing the corners to shape: you'll soon spot any bits you should have removed first!*

where any anomalous misshapes are often easier to spot without the distraction of printed colours (Photo 106). Remove these bits too (Photo 107). You should now end up with two complete sets of walls which look like this, if you are doing this particular kit (Photo 108). No doubt you will be keen to attempt a 'trial fold' to see what each piece should look like – at which point you may, like I did, spot an errant barge board which should have been removed earlier (Photo 109). Turning the piece over I found this unfinished cut (Photo 110) (probably my fault, not Superquick's), but it was easily remedied with the knife (Photo 111).

Still it did not want to 'let go' however, and turning it face up I found this missed tag. (Photo 112). This was soon sorted (Photo 113)! But even with the barge-board removed, still the corner would not fold and, rather than force it, I looked again closely and found the reason was that the scored line did not reach the edge of the card. (Photo 114). A quick 'nick' with the blade and success (Photo 115)! Far better to look for reasons as to why something won't go than to use brute force and rip your card; repairing torn printed surfaces neatly is rarely successful ...

You might care to notice that the smallest dormer's sides on 'room B', and the roof-mounting tags

Photo 110.   Here's a missed corner that wants cutting away to release one of those bothersome barge-boards.

Photo 113.   Success at last!

Photo 111.   There is no reason why you cannot work from the reverse side as long as you are careful.

Photo 114.   This corner did not want to bend when 'teased'. Look carefully and you can see that the scored line does not reach the edge of the card. Just nick it with the knife.

Photo 112.   Even so, the part still refused to 'let go'. Here's why: a missed 'tag'.

Photo 115.   Right! Ready for the next stage.

TOP LEFT: **Photo 116.** *It was at this stage that I became aware that the fold lines beside the dormer were for the vertical sides, while those along the top of the wall were for horizontal bracing. These were supposed to be two parts!*

TOP RIGHT: **Photo 117.** *They were duly cut to shape.*

RIGHT: **Photo 118.** *After a test fold, these parts were also ready for the next stage.*

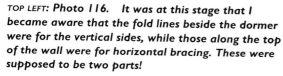

beside them, were *not* partly cut through, (Photo 116) as they had been on 'room A'. I decided at this stage to make matching cuts myself (Photo 117), largely in the hope that this was the right move as the instructions mention nothing about it. It would have been right, in fact (Photo 118), had I not later superseded the requirement by replacing it with my own 'improved bracing' (or '... had I not later replaced it with my own 'improved bracing').

MORE MISSING BARGE BOARDS

With duplicates of barge boards for the two main gable ends completed as described, it was felt that a smaller one would be a good idea for the small gable along one side of the main school room (called 'room A' in the kit). Two bracing strips were added from scrap therefore, ready to accept it. In reality, bargeboards for minor gables are often smaller versions of those fitted to the main gables and a reduction of about a third in the general proportions should suit

nicely, allied to matching the length of the new board to the gable.

To do this, first copy the angles of the gable onto some spare card (Photo 119) and then extend the lines a bit. This last is because barge boards are always slightly wider than the gable end (unless they are trapped between two adjoining walls, of course, but that's not the case here). This is because the roof overlaps the walls on most properties so the bargeboards need to do the same since their one reason for existing, beyond pure decoration, is to protect the ends of the roof timbers (battens) from the weather (Photo 120). You might therefore perhaps take the width of your new barge board's overhang from that of the previous ones. These extend 1/16th of an inch beyond the gable each side, so ours should do the same if they are to match. (If the dimension had been a particular number of millimetres I'd have

Photo 119. *To help create depth in the otherwise totally flat sides, the barge-boards are to be raised away from the wall face using thin card strips.*

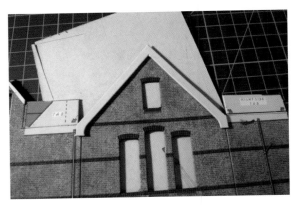

Photo 120. *Once dry, add the barge-boards. Note how they are wider than the wall.*

noted the dimension in Metric but it wasn't and, as most rulers have both scales, why not use the one most appropriate for the job? After all, we work in bastard scales of two, four or seven millimetres to the foot so working in both Metric and Imperial is something any railway modeller will just have to get used to!)

To decide upon the total width at the end a simple calculation is required. The width of the dormer's gable measures one and 1/16th of an inch (Photo 121), so our barge board will need to be one and 3/16ths of an inch to suit. To find the centre to measure that from, draw lightly around the window gap with a pencil point and 'guesstimate' the middle

of the bottom (Photo 122). (You can check, and if necessary correct, this 'centre-line' by measuring the distance from the slopes of the two gables at 90 degrees; it matters not what the figure is, nor what measurement type you use to record it, as long as they match. A draughtsman would use the arc from a pair of compasses to find the centre but that's 'proper' geometry and for our purposes, a quick once-over with a ruler is an easy way to keep things looking balanced.)

Now measure the width of the flare on the card, each dimension from the centre-line being half of nineteen 'sixteenths'; which would be nine and a half 'sixteenths', more correctly known as nineteen

Photo 121. *This tiny gable was not provided with a barge-board. Something else to correct! First measure the width.*

Photo 122. *Cut round the edge on to fresh cardboard, as previously, then mark in the window and estimate the centre.*

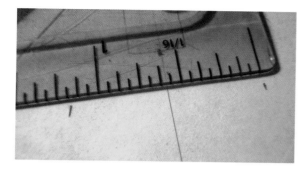

Photo 123.   You can then mark the width of the gable correctly either side of centre.

'thirtyseconds' (19/32nds), of course. The great joy of working in fractions is that one simply plays around with the relationship of one whole number with another, which is a very easy way of halving a dimension without having to resort to a calculator! Mark it on the card (Photo 123).

Having found our basic 'overall width' dimension, we now need the 'vertical drop' from the gable point to the squared-off bottom of the barge board. The large one measures a quarter of an inch (Photo 124), so make the small one some 3/16ths, 75 per cent being an acceptable compromise in this scale. Precision is less important in this kind of model-making than in making locos, largely because buildings don't move; they don't have to 'work'. Then again, the 'chippie' who built it would have picked a timber he had to hand and done a similar estimate so that the job 'looked right' when he'd finished; nobody

was likely to climb up a ladder just to measure it, were they? So do what he did and 'guesstimate' it; a method traditionally known as 'rule of thumb'.

To get the width of the main part of the smaller board, deduct roughly a third from the width of the large one and shape the new barge board to match the shape of the 'prototype' (Photo 125). You will note that there is also a tiny wooden gable on 'room B' – probably the bell tower for summoning the little bligh- er, the delightful children to school (Photo 126). This, not being in stone, probably represents an 'afterthought' to the main design. This being so, a simple, plain, parallel 'V-shaped' barge board will

Photo 125.   A suitable shape was then marked up and cut out, as here.

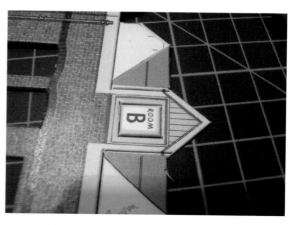

Photo 126.   A small wooden dormer, and this has no barge-board either. It has one printed on, so why not make a new one from card to 'do it properly'?

Photo 124.   Suitable dimensions were estimated by using the original boards provided for the ends.

Photo 127. *Again, by using the original dormer as your template, the new boards must match the angles!*

Photo 130. *Where not, cut your own from 'scrap' or offcuts.*

Photo 128. *From only two barge-boards supplied in the kit, a total of six are now ready for painting.*

probably be more in keeping than another fancy one, so make one (Photo 127). You should now have a full set of barge boards ready for your model (Photo 128). Now, as per the kit's instructions, you can fit and glue in place the packing pieces where they are provided (Photo 129) and cut new ones from waste card (from the edges of the kit, perhaps?), where

BOTTOM LEFT: *Photo 129. Where packing is supplied, it makes sense to use it to hold the barge-boards away from the walls.*

BOTTOM RIGHT: *Photo 131. Once the glue has dried, ensure these do not overlap the gable and if they do, trim them back.*

they are not (Photo 130). Should there be any hint of card overlapping the gable ends afterwards, do trim it off or you will ruin the fit of the roof (Photo 131).

PAINTING THE RAW CARD EDGES

Reading the instructions you will note that they advise colouring the raw edges of the card to improve the look of the building. This is generally worthwhile, although the dull, brown tone of the base card in this kit actually matches the greyness of the walls

Photo 134. *The easiest answer, however, is to leave the kit as it is and just colour in the edges. Felt-tip pens are hopeless on dark cardboard but acrylics are easy to mix and match reasonably well.*

Photo 132. *If you look at these kits from an acute angle you will notice that the brickwork is only represented on the face; no colour can be printed around edges, of course.*

Photo 135. *Paint the edges from the inside where you can, to help prevent spoiling the printed surfaces.*

Photo 133. *The same problem applies to the folded corners, too. (You could cut them at 45 degrees and re-make the joint but the walls would then be shorter by twice their depth. Nevertheless this is certainly a good ploy if the construction allows it.)*

tolerably well and I would normally leave well alone (Photo 132); but I'll show you how to do it anyway as a matter of principle. Once all the window and door openings are clear, you can fold up the sides into their correct shapes and thus expose the edges of the corners too (Photo 133). Note that you will need two colours for this kit; a warm grey to match the plain wall colour and a red to match the string courses. First create a little mixture of acrylic paint to match the main grey colour – mainly white with a bit of burnt umber and the merest touch of black – (Photo 134) and paint the edges of the door and window openings. The trick here being to paint them

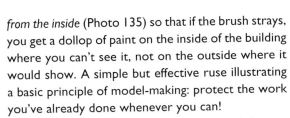

from the inside (Photo 135) so that if the brush strays, you get a dollop of paint on the inside of the building where you can't see it, not on the outside where it would show. A simple but effective ruse illustrating a basic principle of model-making: protect the work you've already done whenever you can!

When it comes to painting the corners it is impossible to work from the inside, so you just have to paint the exposed edges as well as you can (Photo 136) but you are almost guaranteed to get some paint on the printed card face (Photo 137). Fortunately, by using acrylics, if you use a finger to wipe the excess away instantly, before the edges have time to begin drying (Photo 138), then the surface is cleaned of paint before it has time to 'grab' and start to soak in (Photo 139). Note that I have only wiped away half the edge so you can see the difference. You, of course, will wipe the whole length clean! The same method will sometimes work with enamels too,

TOP LEFT: *Photo 136.   Where you can't, as on the corners, you will have to work from the outside.*

TOP RIGHT: *Photo 137.   Here, merely paint the colour on thickly ...*

BOTTOM LEFT: *Photo 138.   ... and wipe the excess off the surface almost immediately.*

BOTTOM RIGHT: *Photo 139.   It will not mark the printing if you are quick enough, as shown here on the right!*

should you wish to use those, but then you'll need to use a bit of rag wrapped around your finger.

Inspiration might suggest that one way round the problem would be to fold the joint back completely (Photo 140), thus giving you a flat edge to paint but unfortunately this degrades what little cardboard remains at the corner to the point where it loses

Photo 140.   If you do not fancy that process, then fold the corner flat – but that will weaken the joint, so be careful.

courses', although what it's there for only the kit manufacturers know – it's an odd feature to print! Plinths are generally proud and are found normally only where there is a significant change of ground level, while any foundations which might possibly have used a different brick are generally hidden underground. When brickwork is painted a light colour, the lower few feet are often painted black or dark brown to help hide dirt from rain-spattered flower beds or passing vehicles – but these are not painted walls so it is most odd. Still, since it's there you might as well make the best of it by matching the colour – easily achieved by adding a touch of black to your grey (Photo 141). Next you could mix up a red colour to match the string course to finish the job but hold on a moment, what about those sills? And what about that door missing its brick arch? (What door? I did say it was worth checking the kit over first …)

most of its strength. Make it wet by soaking it in paint and you may end up with a collection of separate bits if you are not very, very careful with your handling! When you've gained a little more confidence, you might consider deliberately cutting the walls back at 45 degrees and making a butt joint anyway, which could also solve the roof length problem, but I'd still paint the edges before gluing.

With this particular kit you will also need a darker grey to match the darker colour of the 'plinth

LACK OF SILL DEPTH

One notable omission from most cardboard building kits is the lack of any projection of the window sills away from the wall (Photo 142). Almost every building of this period had such features, probably right up until the 1960s in fact, and even today most

Photo 141.   Use a separate paint for any bands of other colours.

Photo 142.   The illusion is quite effective but where are the window sills?

SIMPLE PROTOTYPE FEATURES

I took these photos locally one afternoon when walking the dog. No doubt an amble around your own locality would produce a similar variety …

In sequence, these are a) a traditional Victorian timber sill; b) a Victorian sill made from roof tiles; c) examples of both (note also the fine old timber lintel); d) a wood sill with brick 'quoins' and arch over.

e) A stone sill, similar to the brick quoins and arch but with stone 'keystone' decoration – and note the use of alternate horizontal and vertical bricks to produce the arch; f) evidence of the window tax? A wide, short window filled in; later, a timber-silled, deeper replacement fitted off-centre under the original timber lintel; g) a modern UPVC sill for comparison; h) a 'hand-made' sill of standard bricks laid horizontally.

traditional buildings still feature sills which are proud of the wall's face. (*See* panel above for examples of real cottage sills.)

They are usually proud because sills only work properly if they protrude to a certain degree: they exist to prevent rain water running under the window, through the joint between it and the wall below, and so making the wall damp inside. If they were flush, and there were the slightest crack in the mortar, water would simply fill the gap and creep inwards by capillary action. The reason this doesn't happen is because proper sills have a secret feature; there is a slot or 'rebate' all along the bottom and, since water cannot run uphill, it collects along the

i) A similar sill, probably from 'reconstituted stone' path edgings; j) another of bricks laid on edge; k) bevel-edged bricks, laid flat; l) specially shaped, moulded decorative bricks.

m) Victorian wood lintel above a modern replacement window; n) a modern steel lintel hidden behind a reconstituted stone façade; o) a traditional stone arch that looks flat but is in fact made of lozenge-shaped stones which work as an arch; p) a modern high-density concrete lintel – note the extreme thinness compared to wooden beams.

q) Replacement window and sill under an original wood lintel; r) lead flashing and a repaired crack are evidence of a brick arch rendered over; s) a seventeenth-century example of no lintel at all except for a bit of lead flashing; t) the exception which proves the rule; 'dressed stone' window surround with mullion and transom but neither 'proud' drip stone above nor 'proud' sill below. Note the stone block 'relieving arch' above to relieve any strain on the decorative stonework and prevent it shearing. An example from our own local Victorian village school, as it happens …

outer edge in increasing mass until it drips off under its own weight. (Laying standard bricks or the like at a slight angle produces much the same effect by creating a low-point outside the wall's face.)

Therefore, almost any building we are likely to want to model should have window sills which are proud of the walls or it will look wrong. The point is that our subconscious will be aware that window-sills stick out from walls, even if we didn't know why until now. Therefore, if our model building is to look right its sills must be modelled proud of the walls. Fortunately, adding this feature is simplicity itself and, having learnt here how to do it, you can always go back and add them to previously-constructed

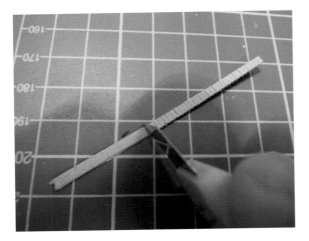

Photo 143.   Cut some from card scrap and just nick the surface with the blade to score it into individual bricks.

buildings if you need to – and now you have noticed them, if they are missing you will probably want to, of course. So here's how it's done …

In the case of this school I suggest the use of brick sills because they are easy to reproduce. Bricks will also match the brick 'string courses' and window arches featured in the kit, although with bricks there are as many options as there are examples around the country. These include standard bricks laid at a slight angle, either horizontally or on edge; specially-shaped bricks which include an angled slope on the top corner; and ones pre-moulded with particularly fancy shapes. The choice is yours. Why not go and look at how it was done in your local area?

For other buildings wood, stone or concrete sills might be more appropriate, and plain card will do

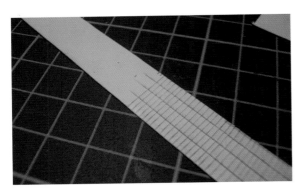

Photo 144.   Even better, cut from a broader piece and score lots at the same time!

Photo 146.   Do note, however, that the printed surface does not always reach the edge of the backing card, so first check both sides of your intended material.

Photo 145.   Most kits will have sufficient 'land' around the edge to provide a suitable section.

Photo 147.   One use of this mismatch is to provide a sill with a sloping upper edge by creasing the overlap and filling with glue before attaching.

Photo 148. *Trial colour of a sill strip. Perhaps a bit too much black ...*

nicely for them, but in this case we can also use it to give an 'impression' of bricks. To do this, merely score the strip across every millimetre or so (Photo 143). The job becomes even easier if you part-cut several strips and then score across them all at the same time, thus creating several bricks at each stroke! (Photo 144) If you want to get *really* clever you can use the edging of the kit (Photo 145), where the printed card overlaps the backing card (Photo 146), to create 'angled bricks' where the upper face of the sill is angled nicely at its edge, simply by filling the gap with glue and creasing the edge slightly before attaching to the wall (Photo 147). This is probably rather too clever for a simple card kit, but it does illustrate another technique you might want to use on a 'special' building one day.

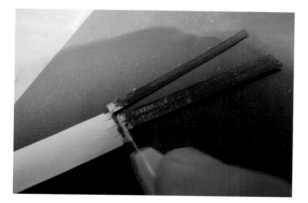

Photo 149. *If using the 'multiple strip' technique, merely paint the edges of the outer strips first, then cut them away.*

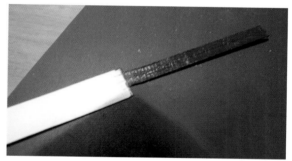

Photo 150. *You can now paint the edges of the inner strips. Easy!*

Photo 151. *Mix up a colour to match the existing 'string courses' and paint your cills.*

Now you can paint your strips to match the existing brick detailing of red string courses. I used raw sienna with a touch of black (Photo 148). When painting multiple strips paint the face and outer edges first, then cut away the outer two strips (Photo 149), so leaving yourself a handle to hold while you paint the outer edges of the inner pair (Photo 150). Leave to dry (Photo 151), while you paint the raw edges of the red string courses where they run around the corners and cross the sides of the taller windows (Photo 152), then come back and complete any remaining raw edges on your sills. Next, paint the upper edges of all the openings, and the lower edges of the window openings, using the same mix.

Photo 153. Look at the wall openings carefully: here's one without a brick arch over it.

BELOW UPPER: Photo 154. You can create one by shaping the edge before painting the brickwork in.

BELOW LOWER: Photo 155. The toilet window has an arch at the top but it is cut flat at the bottom, not curved. You can correct that by carving a matching curve in the lower edge and touching up the raw edge later.

Photo 152. You can also paint the edges of these courses where they cut across the window to some advantage.

THE MISSING DOOR ARCH

Correcting the missing brick arch over the back door (Photo 153), is of course optional but it would be normal for a real builder to adopt a particular method and use it throughout the build. Since all the other doors and windows in this kit have brick arches then another one here is the logical expectation. Begin by carving the upper edge of the door opening to an arc of similar shape to its neighbour (Photo 154) and, while you are at it, you might care to carve the upper edge of the toilet window into an arc too; the tool-maker has punched it as a straight edge despite the upper edge of the brickwork showing as an arc on the print (Photo 155). These are now ready to be touched in with the rest.

The missing arch is simply added by painting the shape of the arch above the door in red and leaving it to dry. We will slice a series of nicks in it later to represent the mortar. When you have done that you can either paint your new sills or, if done already, 'touch them up', finishing any unpainted surfaces.

When dry, cut your sills to length (Photo 156). Do the same for all your windows one at a time, noting that some sills overlap the wall either side and some don't: mine do. Before glueing the new sills in place, it probably helps to lay them out roughly in order so you don't get confused as to which one is to go where (Photo 157), and don't forget to touch in the ends where you cut them to length, either (Photo 158). Your walls should now look like those in photo 159. Already the shadows make the wall look better! We can move on now and fit the windows.

Photo 156.   While these 'extras' are drying, trim each individual sill to length and put to one side.

Photo 158.   ... and paint red the white card ends thus exposed too, of course.

Photo 157.   Lay all your sills out on the walls first before gluing on, just to make sure you have the right ones in the right places ...

Photo 159.   The surface of your walls is now looking better, with sills and barge-boards offering some attractive 'relief' to the otherwise flat printed cardboard.

Photo 160.   *Now you can add the glazing, but note it has a dull side and a glossy side.*

Photo 161.   *This is the 'proper' side, with dull printing. Non-white painted windows are not a recent idea, but they have not been common since Victorian times.*

FITTING THE WINDOWS

The first thing to notice about the glazing sheet is that it is printed on only one side. This will be matt, but if you happen to fit the glazing back to front it will be glossy, which looks entirely wrong! Check by holding each piece of glazing so that it reflects the light before fixing it on. The wrong side is shown in photo 160 and the right side in photo photo 161.

The instructions suggest using Sellotape to fix the windows in place. This is an ideal method for the beginner since he will then avoid getting glue all over the glazing, but it will not last longer than a few years as the Sellotape eventually looses its grip and then the windows fall out – which will happen even more quickly if the building ever gets damp! So if you want to preserve for posterity what is perhaps your first attempt at building a kit, or if you want to actually fit your kit onto a model railway, then use glue – but use it carefully and sparingly!

For this type of glazing I would normally use 'Evostick', first spreading a layer over the card behind the windows and letting it dry. Next add a few fine spots to each corner of the glazing face and one or more down each window edge and mullion, depending upon size (Photo 162), and then, reverting to the technique recommended in the instructions,

Photo 162.   *Having cut out the individual lights, add an appropriate glue sparingly but sufficiently.*

Photo 163.   *It is probably best to lay the glazing on the bench and lower the side over it if you want to get the printed windows 'centred' properly first time. Moving them into place afterwards by sliding is a great way to get glue on the printing!*

Photo 164.   *Leave for a few moments to get tacky before moving on to the next window.*

Photo 165.   *Turned over, you can see how little glue is required to make a good joint, but the various contact 'footprints' are showing an ample 'grab' area.*

place the wall over the window and ensure that the glazing's surround at each side is equal at each side (Photo 163). Only then press the wall down firmly onto the glazing to secure it (Photo 164). It will grip almost instantaneously and remain attached for donkey's years, given sufficient glue to grip properly in the first place (Photo 165). Any excess glue which does get onto the glazing should be left for a minute or two to go 'rubbery' (practice on packaging!), because it can then usually be teased away from the glazing without any damage at all by using a sharpened matchstick. Provided it was smudged

when nearly dry, a state which happens naturally if you take your time to carefully line up each piece behind its opening, you should be fine. As you will note from the photos, I tried a new method using 'Stix All', a white builder's glue. While this is less easy to use than Evostick, being white it does show the technique well in the photos and is one possible alternative. It would not normally be my glue of preference for this particular job however, so in this instance you may be advised for once do as I say, rather than as I did!

Photo 166.   *It was at this stage that I noticed the little wooden dormer did not have a proud sill either.*

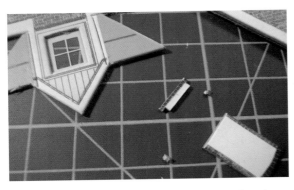

Photo 167. *The glazing was thus fitted higher than centrally to allow for adding a new cardboard sill below.*

Photo 168. *Trimmed to fit between the sides, it is ready for painting.*

ANOTHER SILL!

Even a most careful perusal of the kit before you start will not always uncover simple but desirable improvements – in this case the fitting of a sill to the small, timber-framed gable (Photo 166). As some

paint was going to be mixed to paint the new barge boards anyway, a new cardboard sill would take but a few moments and it would add a little more 'relief' to what is basically a flat wall!

Take a spare bit of window waste and trim some corners off it so it will fit into the opening at the

MIDDLE LEFT: **Photo 169.** *First, the slope required was ascertained by looking from the side and the edges cut at angles to suit.*

BOTTOM LEFT: **Photo 170.** *Barge-board supports were added at the same time. Note the original printed 'shadow' along the top and left-hand edges of the window casing. Clever!*

MIDDLE RIGHT: **Photo 171.** *With the new woodwork all cut to size, it can be painted to match the printed card. If in doubt, paint that too!*

rear and overlap it at the front (Photo 167). If the space around the glazing for this window is a bit tight after a trial fit (Photo 168), one can simply elongate the window opening sufficiently to accept the new sill without loosing any space for the glazing. Glue it in place, remembering to tilt it to a slight angle so that a 'drip edge' is formed at the bottom (Photo 169). To achieve a good fit against the glazing it is worth cutting the rear edges at a slight angle, cutting inwards, while the front edge also benefits from being cut at an angle outwards to produce slopes which will be vertical when the sill is installed. I then fitted spacers for supporting the new barge-board (Photo 170) and painted them and the boards while I was at it (Photo 171). 'Primrose Yellow' straight from the tube seemed ideal!

Photo 173. *It is an easy job to make a new one from scrap.*

DOOR RELIEF

No, it's not a charity; I simply observed that, probably for lack of space, this door and its frame are one flat piece (Photo 172). It then occured to me that as a panelled door its panels should be recessed but like all the doors in this kit they are flat. It is also coloured blue, whereas the rest of the building's woodwork is primrose yellow. Contrasting colours for doors is hardly something a money-conscious school board would waste money on so I decided to replace it with a proper panelled example which could be painted yellow. Here's how it's done …

Photo 172. *The large school door is printed with a flush door frame, but that just looks silly!*

First find a piece of card of reasonable quality and thickness, probably somewhere between a business card, although these are often a bit too thin these days, and a cereal packet, which is what I favour, although this card came from a box of dry dog food. Choose whatever is to hand of an appropriate thickness but do pick something with a matt or partially matt surface so it accepts glue and paint easily. A highly glazed surface will accept neither wood glues nor pencil marks so avoid them because for this type of job they are quite useless!

Begin by holding an over-sized rectangle of roughly the right shape behind the opening and draw round it, using the sides of the opening as your 'ruler' (Photo 173). If the gap formed when you cut the line out would be a fair representation of the width of a door frame then fine; if not, draw a second line with a ruler where you think it should be; ensuring that your line is parallel with its mate on the opposite side. Door sides are always parallel, even if their tops and bottoms have to slope to fit a gap. Doorways, however, are not always parallel sided, especially in older buildings, so watch out for that.

Also use the ruler to draw a straight line across the top where the door frame is straight, even though the arch above it is curved. This is the normal way of framing a door; only a few fancy or deliberately 'picturesque' cottages feature curved frame heads

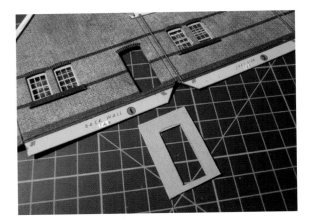

Photo 174. *Keep the edges of the frame straight: it is the bricks that are arched, not the door!*

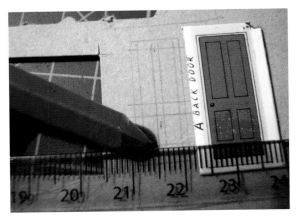

Photo 175. *In fact, why not make a proper new panelled door – another quick and effective detail.*

You can now cut out the panels but do leave a good margin around the door's outer edge. There always seems to be one piece which delights in remaining stubbornly attached (Photo 176) but the pest is easily thwarted by turning it over and noting which corner is retaining it; in this case it is the one nearest the middle of the door (Photo 177). Re-cut that corner and the piece will drop out.

Now select a plain piece of card as the panelling, remembering that the top openings could instead

Photo 176. *Use your window-opening trimming skills to good effect when removing the panels.*

and curved door tops to match, these being architectural 'gimmicks'.

Cut out the frame (Photo 174), remembering that while window frames have four sides, door frames only look to have three since the bottom side, and there often is one, is generally set flush with the floor. The kit's printed door panel proportions and arrangement however, are as excellent as its colour is fanciful, so it makes a good 'model' to copy onto fresh card for your new door, something which is easy to achieve with a ruler (Photo 175).

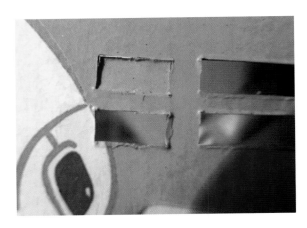

Photo 177. *Here's a rectangle with only three sides cut right through. Try again!*

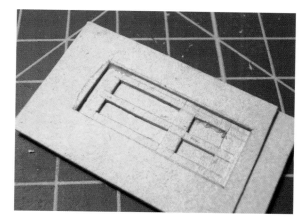

Photo 178.   *Glue the frame to the door and that to the infill, then leave to go tacky.*

Photo 179.   *Before the glue goes off, however, remove any excess with a suitable tool.*

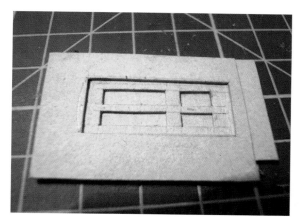

Photo 180.   *One much more realistic door and frame ready for painting.*

Photo 181.   *Give darker-coloured cards a thin coat and leave that to dry before adding a second.*

be left open for later glazing if desired. The three pieces can now be assembled with generous smears of PVA wood glue (Photo 178). The excess which escapes when the parts are squeezed together is in fact a good sign that you've used enough glue to ensure a sound joint. It is easily smoothed away with the unburnt end of a used matchstick (Photo 179). This should leave you with a much more convincing door in full (even exaggerated), relief, which is both more authentic and a lot stronger (Photo 180). When the glue is dry, paint it to match the barge boards (Photo 181).

While you wait for the glue to dry you might care to consider producing similar examples for the other doors. With this particular kit you should note that the main front door of the school entrance (between the two rooms, bottom right in photo 182), has a number of minor maladies which can be cured while you are at it. The basic kit leaves the door as part of the wall (!) which is both unprototypical and all the more noticeable because the other two doors are separate and glued *behind* their openings. This problem is partly disguised by only scoring the door down one side to use as a hinge, thus suggesting it is

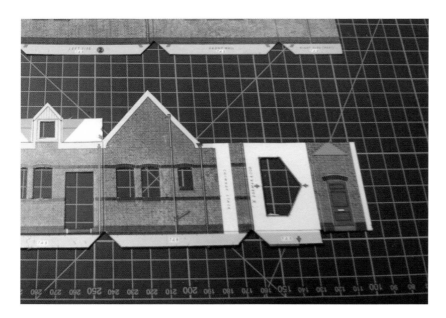

Photo 182.   The front door in the passage is even worse since it is printed flush with the wall without even a recessed opening ...

Photo 183.   ...so here's another new door, painted and fitted.

left open, but my guess is that a small board school of the 1920s (note the date on one wall), would have locked the children in so they couldn't escape the moment the teacher was distracted!

This problem could be corrected by cutting the door out completely, making a new door frame from card (as previously), and then gluing the door back in place behind it but sadly the door-frame is oddly cut on the left-hand side so that the brickwork suddenly turns yellow. A most unfortunate problem. But this door is also odd because it has a single pair of wide panels rather than two narrower pairs; a not impossible combination assuming a replacement door, but it was still felt better to replace the whole thing with one which matched the others. The errant coloured edge was therefore merely trimmed back to plain bricks and the replacement door and frame made a little bit wider to fit the new opening (Photo 183). We, of course, deem not to notice the missing red string course on that wall ...

If you recall the door missing its brick arch mentioned earlier, you will remember how we carved that to its new curved shape and painted the grey brickwork red to match, more or less, the window arch next to it (Photo 184). We now want to replicate that brick arch (Photo 185), by first making a

light curved cut across the top and then adding short, radial stokes below to allow the card beneath to show through to represent the mortar (Photo 186). My arch is rather lop-sided, one end being deeper than the other, but even so it is best left as it is: the printed one next to it is no better in this respect

TOP LEFT: **Photo 184.**   *You will remember that we cut out a missing brick arch and painted it red.*

BOTTOM LEFT: **Photo 185.**   *Next to it is a window with printed mortar lines, so it might be nice to attempt to replicate that.*

TOP RIGHT: **Photo 186.**   *Score the dry red paint with a sharp knife to approximately match the spacings, not forgetting to score an arch across the top of the brickwork, too.*

BOTTOM RIGHT: **Photo 187.**   *Fill the score lines with a little thin paint, et voilà! You will have to look very closely to see the difference!*

and from even slightly further away the discrepancy all but disappears – thus at normal viewing distance I can assure you that no-one will notice! (Photo 187) (If you cut into white card you may want to mix up a light 'wash' of mortar colour to deaden the brightness a little. If so, just add enough fluid to colour the cuts then immediately wipe away any excess.)

CONTINUING WITH THE GENERAL ASSEMBLY

With all the details on the walls sorted out (apart from gutters and down-pipes, which will be dealt with in another chapter), we can finally begin assembling them around their bases. At this point I depart drastically from the kit instructions but remember the makers must attempt to provide all the young modeller needs to complete a building, whereas we 'older kids' can easily obtain stronger, thicker card for things like bases, and have the wherewithal and experience – or we soon will have – to cut much thicker card safely.

With a little opportunism we have access to other resources, too: for example, back in the early 1990s an industrial heating company asked an acquaintance of mine to throw out some old exhibition advertising materials and he very thoughtfully threw them my way (Photo 188). I'm still using them. Those bereft

of such sources can buy large sheets of similar card from art shops where it is termed '3mm mounting board'. I also go out every November 6th and, with the excuse of walking the dog, collect every unclaimed rocket stick I can find. As a free source of generally neat, squared timber of different sizes, the method procures materials for modelling projects, provides bending and stretching exercises, tidies up the neighbourhood and gets the dog walked at the

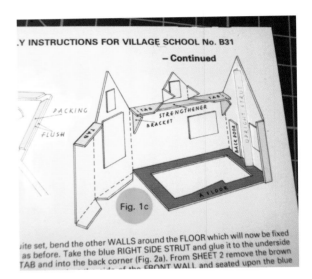

ABOVE: **Photo 189.** *The thin and flimsy printed card sheet the instructions suggest using for bracing is considerably less effective at this job and is best replaced.*

BELOW: **Photo 190.** *You can always use the original as your template, of course!*

Photo 188. *Old, unwanted advertising material makes excellent 'flooring' and bracing.*

Photo 191.   *With new doors and frames to cope with, the best method is to arrange the building so you can mark these intrusions and cut away the excess flooring before fitting.*

same time – perfect recycling with a zero carbon footprint earning oodles of green 'cred'!

Therefore, where the instructions suggest fitting their rather thin cardboard base (Photo 189), it was replaced with a solid piece of 3mm thick card which will create a far stronger and more durable structure. You can still usefully detach the original

base section from the kit and use it as a 'master' for your own by dint of scoring round it with a knife or drawing round it with a sharp pencil (Photo 190). If you have replaced your doors with new ones several layers deep you will then need to allow for that by marking either side of the new door (Photo 191) and cutting away a section of floor.

With three millimetres of edge with which to make a firm butt joint, you can dispense with the yellow 'tabs' which the kit provides. This will help reduce or even eliminate that nasty black line you so often see around the base of model buildings and which loudly shouts 'toy' at you. To be fair to Superquick, they intend you to use that gap to glue their 'printed playground' into and then in turn glue the boundary walls around that. I never find such bits convincing, however, nor is it very likely that the 'plot' you allocate for your school will match the outline of that the kit provides – if it did, the children would have a very small playground!

With the fit of your new floor carefully checked, you can now add glue to three of the edges (Photo 192), and then assemble the floor to those walls, leaving the fourth side open for access. Put this assembly one side and use some weighty objects to hold everything firmly while the glue dries (Photo 193).

Photo 192.   *When you are ready, apply a thin but continuous bead of glue along two or three edges ...*

Photo 193.   *... and glue three of the walls in place. Support the joints until the glue has hardened.*

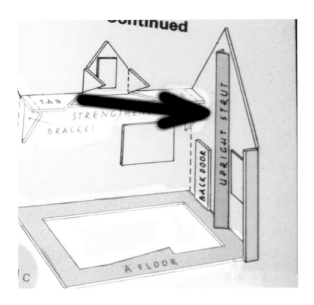

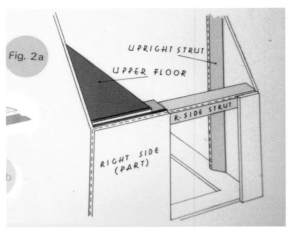

TOP LEFT: **Photo 194. The instructions suggest fitting a cardboard brace to keep the gable upright and strong.**

TOP RIGHT: **Photo 196. To save card, there is a gap in the inner wall where the kit instructions suggest fitting a folded card 'strut' or brace. However it is far better, and easier, to fit a whole new ceiling.**

To increase rigidity the instructions suggest folding up a cardboard brace and then gluing it to the wall (Photo 194), but here you may find a length of that spent rocket stick quicker and easier. Certainly it provides all the strength you are ever likely to need, and then some … (Photo 195)

Superquick then recommend folding down all sorts of tabs and glueing in place several card braces which they duly provide (Photo 196), but don't go there! Ceilings help the rigidity of any building, if made in one piece, and also give you a good surface to glue your roof supports to, therefore a ceiling is

a sound idea. So instead of messing about with all those odd bits, just cut out a single new piece!

Here the original floor might do the job well enough and would certainly be an improvement on the lots of odd pieces the kit provides while the missing centre would suit particularly well as rooms of this period often used their dormer window as a 'clerestory' light and so no ceiling was fitted. (This

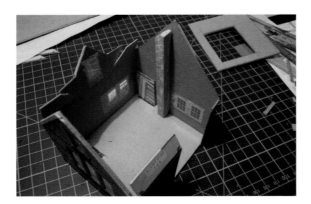

Photo 195. *I thought it easier, quicker and a lot stronger to fit a brace made from rocket stick.*

Photo 197. *Trim away any excess glazing to ensure a card-to-card joint to all the walls.*

Photo 198. Support folded corners with braces made from matchsticks and your building will last a lot longer.

Photo 199. Trim the new floors and ceilings around other bracing and glue in place. Add a 'ridge brace' to support both the roof and the opposite gable.

made such rooms icy cold in winter but in the 1960s I was still being taught in Victorian classrooms which lacked a ceiling!)

To allow light in while still providing some much-needed strength, I used 3mm card to make a ceiling with the middle cut out, a shape otherwise known as a 'collar'. To fit such a deep piece meant trimming the odd bit of glazing down to make room for a card-to-card joint 3mm deep (Photo 197), but do not glue your collar in place yet, merely ensure it fits properly for it will, of course, need trimming to fit around your 'brace'. At this stage I usually find it helps to reinforce the corners of any card building by glueing in spent matches and with these delicate folded corners some reinforcement is certainly advisable (Photo 198). For longer joints by the way, you might find 'cooks' matches useful. If you do not have any matches then strips of mounting board would do almost as well. Now fit the collar. I also used 3mm cardboard to cut and fit a 'ridge' to support the roof (Photo 199).

I had intended repeating these procedures for 'Room B' but noted that the floor provided in the kit was made up of more than one piece – never a good idea as it (or 'can then') get out of 'square' as the glue dries. This would not matter with a model of an ancient cottage which has 'settled' over the years but 20th century schoolrooms found to be out of

true would call for immediate demolition! Therefore, since no template exists, (I now offer) a method of shaping and fitting your own floor *without* a template .

MARKING OUT A FLOOR

First use a set-square to ensure you have a right-angled corner to an over-sized piece of thick card (Photo 200). Now fit that known, square corner into one corner of your walls, and hold it tightly in place. Then fold a third wall over the base and mark where it comes with a pencil (Photo 201). Now unfold that wall, then do the same in the other direction with

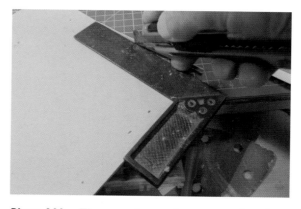

Photo 200. The second room has no complete floor so you will need to provide one. Start with a right-angled corner on a sheet of stout card.

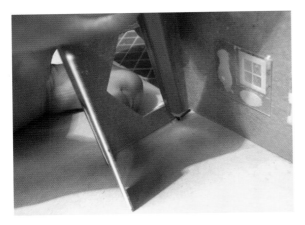

Photo 201. Place a right-angled corner between the two longest walls and mark off their lengths ...

Photo 203. Use a square to ensure the two opposite sides of the floor are parallel.

the fourth wall (Photo 202). Remove the base from the walls and 'project' your marks with a pencil, using the square, to make a rectangle (Photo 203). For a simple four-sided shape this would suffice but here we have the entrance hall as part of the construction so we must provide for that too. Although that is easily done with two more marks and use of the square, note that one of the walls extends into the floor space so as to give a good joint with its neighbour. Therefore cut a slot into the floor where that wall requires it (Photo 204).

There are two doors to make for this room – if you have not already done them – and if a door is a bit wider than normal, as is this door to room B,

you ought to ensure the 'stiles' of the door are broad enough to take the extra strain (Photo 205). If you simply angle the pencil a bit more than normal when marking out, this is a doddle (Photo 206), and if the height is the same as before, just mark up the 'rails' as you did with the standard door (Photo 207).

For outside doors I like to add a decent step (Photo 208), which I 'set back' into the basic floor shape where possible (Photo 209). This allows you to carve away some card as 'wear', and to fit the door *above* the step, rather than behind it; a useful ploy should you ever want to fix a door in an 'open' position.

We can cover another minor point here in that the door, and in particular the card frame surrounding it, will need to be kept clear of any glazing or

Photo 202. These marks will show you where to cut the edge of your floor for the next wall.

Photo 204. With this kit the front entrance wall is longer than necessary, but this makes for a better joint. Allow for it by slotting your new floor to suit.

TOP LEFT: **Photo 205.** With a little thought you can remove two corners of wall to allow room for a proper width doorstep.

MIDDLE LEFT: **Photo 206.** Laying your pencil over at an angle allows you to create a wider door frame when required.

BOTTOM LEFT: **Photo 207.** You can use your printed door as a template for cutting out a new panelled one.

TOP RIGHT: **Photo 208.** Consider raising the door above a suitable doorstep. Choose some thick card and cut one to fit.

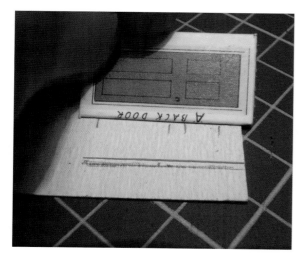

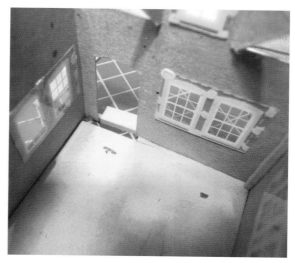

Photo 209. By carving away a bit of the flooring the step can be rebated, which looks more natural.

Photo 210. *Check that the glazing does not intrude into your gluing area. It is best to mark the edge on to the wall inside.*

Photo 211. *Then test fit your new door frame. If it obtrudes, decide to carve away either the door-frame or the glazing, or some of each as seems best, and mark appropriately.*

Photo 212. *Trim away what you don't want but leave enough to ensure a good gluing surface.*

Photo 213. *Glue the frame around the door and add plain sheet to represent the panels behind it, as previously, but do check your alignments carefully before the glue dries ...*

other obstacles nearby. To check this, make a mark in line with the edge of the obstacle (in this case the adjacent glazing sheet), but higher up the wall where it can be easily seen (Photo 210); then offer the intended frame up and mark that too (Photo 211), before cutting out (Photo 212). Unlike me, be sure you set the door in the middle of the jambs (Photo 213), although if you spot it quickly enough it is usually a correctable fault. Trace the outline of the floor onto another piece of card for possible use as a ceiling, then again, glue three of the sides to it.

Once all is dry the two rooms can be 'test fitted' together, at which point it was noted that they didn't quite fit because the gap allowed for the entrance hall in the wall of 'room A' was not quite long enough (Photo 214). To get round this problem, instead of fitting the usual spent match corner brace, fit a much larger brace of rocket stick in this corner (Photo 215). Once dry, you can carve away as much cardboard as you need to get a good fit without the joint falling apart. To ensure the two rooms stick together firmly and permanently, add a pair of 3mm thick braces across the opening to give ample surface for glueing (Fig. 216).

Again with the future in mind, you might decide to add a rectangular opening in the base for a possible lighting tube. (See 'cutting safely' panel.)

Photo 214.   With both rooms assembled, you can try a practice fit together. Sadly, these do not quite fit by a millimetre or so.

Photo 215.   Carving back the interior wall until it fits the gap can remove card you need to join it to the back wall. Get round this by glueing in place a stout brace from more rocket stick.

CUTTING SAFELY

Once a model has been assembled like this, cutting a hole into thick card already part of a model is a **really** dangerous trap for the unwary, which is why I mention it. I once planted the entire length of an exposed Stanley blade in my leg doing this very job; I needed four stitches and a new pair of jeans, so take my advice and be *very* careful if you have to do something similar! Of course, it could have been much worse ...

'A modelling chappie called Blacker,
Once wielded a knife like a hacker,
It wasn't the tool,
But misuse made the fool,
Carve a great bloody chunk from his lacquer.'

The *only* safe method is to place the model well back onto the work top (*not* near the edge where the knife can slip off the bench into an unwary leg – or worse!), fit a new blade and above all do NOT attempt to cut through in a few firm strokes. Take your time and just cut through a few fractions of a millimetre at a time, taking 10 or even 20 cuts to get even nearly through. Carve well into the other three sides of your rectangle *before*

Fig. 216.   Be very careful cutting through thick card unless it is resting directly on the bench.

attempting to cut right through the first; the gaps you make by doing so will allow the card in the middle to move slightly, thus making it easier for the blade to penetrate. (Photo 218). Take your time and finish the job slowly, even returning to it another time if you start to get frustrated or annoyed with yourself for forgetting to do it earlier. Even if you give up for the night and continue another day, it will still be far quicker than having to leave the job entirely alone for a few weeks while a nasty gash heals ... If you are careful, this should be the result (Photo 219).

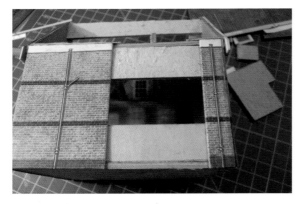

Photo 217. *Support the joint to the main school-room with additional card bracing. This ensures that once joined no man may put them asunder ...*

Photo 220. *Once the two rooms are completely ready to assemble into one building, coat the two surfaces amply with wood glue.*

Photo 218. *Cutting lighting holes into thick card bases requires the slow, careful use of repetitive light strokes.*

Photo 221. *Press the two parts firmly together, and after ensuring the perfect fit, apply light pressure (with books or clothes pegs, for instance), until the joint has taken. Leave to dry thoroughly before further handling.*

Photo 219. *With patience, a neat hole can be achieved without any personal damage.*

Photo 222. *With the wall assemblies completed and attached to each other, you can begin to see the results of all your hard work!*

TOP: **Photo 223.** *If using the kit's guttering, you will find it on the sheet of thin, printed 'extra bits'. Score any arrowed joints.*

MIDDLE: **Fig. 224.** *When scoring joints, check how effective they will be by looking at the back. If you cannot see the dent in the surface, score harder; if you have cut through, you will know you should have been gentler!*

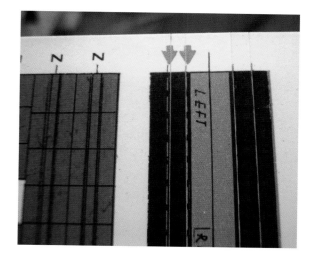

After carving such a deep hole, trimming the thin edge of 'room B' to fit in the gap in the wall of 'room A' should be easy. Then, with a final check for alignment and squareness, the braces were given a good coating of PVA glue (Photo 220) and the two rooms joined together at last (Photo 221). The building with its walls finished should look like this (Photo 222).

CONCERNING CARDBOARD GUTTERING

For the sake of completeness only, I point out that the kit does provide what it calls 'gutters' on the 'accessories card'. The theory is that you should first score along the red-arrowed lines (Photo 223), so they can be folded up. (Your scoring from the under-side should look like the horizontal lines in Fig. 224, as compared to the vertical cut line.) The black sections are then folded in half and glued together while the 'tabs' are glued to the underside of the roof as per Photo 225.

As a means of providing a very particular feature this method really is a non-starter! It is flat where it should be rounded, it is incredibly flimsy, and the finished guttering is unlikely to outlast initial construction, never mind any length of use on a model railway, especially as they are liable to be bent every time you handle the model. A pointless inclusion, really, and even as a youngster I never could see the point of creating something so delicate that a child who has spent some 12–15 hours building a model should see it damaged and spoilt so quickly through poor design. Right – rant over!

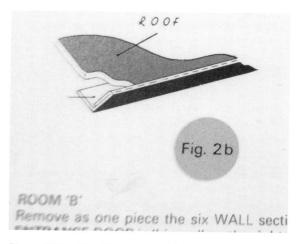

Photo 225. *The kit suggests folding one piece over itself to create depth to reinforce an angle but this is a poor method.*

LEFT: **Photo 226.** I once used thin card to represent guttering and, as you can see, it soon fell off with handling, as did the bent plastic rod I used for the downpipes. The rest of it however, has lasted, pristine and intact, for over 30 years – a testament to cardboard construction.

BOTTOM: **Photo 227.** As for the roof, that will need to be secured properly too. Thick card cut at an appropriate angle will provide ample gluing surfaces.

On a model of this quality gutters are a feature probably not worth bothering with, especially as there really is no good way of creating realistic, long-lived and firmly attached guttering from cardboard. Cardboard is a sheet material and works very poorly when creased, shaped and formed without adequate bracing. Plastic, however is ideal. You can buy moulded plastic guttering (Ratio have some in their structural detailing packs), but it is simple enough to make and later in the book I'll show you how. Now then, let's get on with this roof, shall we?

PREPARING THE ROOF SUPPORTS

If the roof of any model is to retain its shape for many years and remain firmly attached to its building, then it is going to need proper support. The same applies to the gable ends and any dormers which protrude. The more firmly you fix them in place, the more likely they are to remain where you put them. I have cardboard buildings I made over 30 years ago and they are still in excellent condition – apart, that is, from their flimsy cardboard guttering and some bent plastic rod which I used as downpipes! (Photo 226) I use metal downpipes now.

We have already fitted a rocket-stick to brace one gable of our school and a substantial 3mm card 'ridge timber' glued firmly between them will be more than sufficient to hold them both firmly (see Photo 199). Another worthwhile addition is to dramatically increase the area of the eaves joint by cutting a shoulder of 3mm card at something like the roof angle and gluing it along the eaves (Photo 227). Anything which helps the roof stay where you glue it is a help and a 4mm wide butt joint is a lot stronger than attempting to glue a roof to a 90 degree corner of thin card, which is all the basic kit provides.

Photo 228. *Again, when cutting thick card at obtuse angles, ensure you cut away from the supporting hand.*

Photo 229. *Cutting towards the supporting hand is a great way of losing chunks of it. Don't do it! Blood ruins the surface of card kits …*

Just remember when you cut at an angle like this that you must cut away from the supporting hand (Photo 228), not towards it (Photo 229); that way lies considerable digital danger of a most painful kind! Besides, blood ruins the colours printed on your model …

Again, with plenty of good card to hand you may care to ignore the instructions and make two of your own hearty braces for the dormer sides. These would be glued to both the inside faces and to our

supporting collar, but while doing so we can also add further support to the opposite roof by extending the braces right across to that side (Photo 230). All we need is a pair of narrow rectangles which we position 'dry', hard against the dormer face, so we can mark off where we want to cut them, this being in line with the roof's opposite slope, the initial mark being made by eye. Transcribing the angle for that edge is easy: merely hold the mark behind a gable end and draw the slope on with a pencil (Photo 231). Both braces can now be glued in place (Photo 232).

Photo 230. *'Clever' bracing can sometimes support several things at the same time.*

Photo 231. *Finding such angles is easy: just hold an off-cut in place and mark off with a pencil. This is the easy way to transfer these angles to your bracing'.*

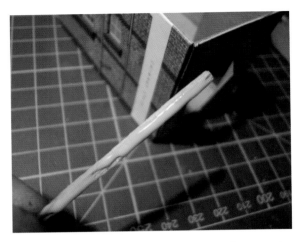

Photo 232. *Ensure you glue bracing in place amply*
well: you will not want it rattling around inside if it
comes loose.

Photo 234. *A test-fit of the roof shows the*
need to provide a short section of wall to fill an
obvious gap.

Do the same to 'room B' and then leave the whole model to dry ready for fitting the roof. It should now look something vaguely like Photo 233.

Unless you are fitting an interior, it is usually worth colouring the visible parts of the card braces with a black felt pen to help render them invisible through the windows. Notice, too, that there is a missing bit of wall above the entrance hall between the rooms (Photo 234), so find a suitable section of boundary wall in the rest of the kit (Photo 235), measure the height (Photo 236), cut out a section to fit and then glue it firmly in place (Photo 237).

You might baulk at loosing a bit of boundary wall but if you think ahead it is unlikely to be a problem: whatever you do there is not enough wall provided in the kit to surround the school and besides, who knows what size and shape the 'plot' for your school is going to be until you decide where to put it? By that time you will probably have lost the remains of the kit anyway, even if there was enough wall left. Of

Photo 233. *Provide your roofs with ample gluing*
surfaces right around the edges.

Photo 235. *I chose a section of playground walling*
and cut a suitable piece from that.

TOP LEFT: **Photo 236.   The length can be marked directly but the height is best measured.**

TOP RIGHT: **Photo 238.   Here's an example of real guttering fixed to a 'fascia board'.**

course, for just a few pounds more you can always buy another kit, cut off the room walls just below the windows, leaving yourself with all the boundary walling you are likely to need – or even cheaper, buy a sheet of brick paper. Or perhaps better still; photograph a nearby real boundary wall, scale it down in your favourite graphics programme and print off your own brick paper!

With this particular kit you may notice that adding that missing piece leaves a gap in the fascia. Being themselves screwed onto the ends of the rafters, fascias are thus always 'proud' of a wall, being placed so as to allow standard guttering clips to support the guttering precisely where it will best catch the rain which runs off the roof (Photo 238). Were you to add this feature – easily done with long, thin rectangles of painted card – then both brick and printed fascias would be hidden. If not, the roof can be allowed to drain directly onto the flat roof and no fascia board would be necessary. Of course, not all building have fascias ... (Photo 239)

Photo 237.   Test fit before gluing permanently.

Photo 239.   Not every building uses fascias however, so it's not a vital component. This guttering is fixed directly to the wall using long iron brackets.

TOP LEFT: *Photo 240.   You will want to model a flat, felted roof so, rather than use a piece of grey chequered card which looks hopeless, paint the roof black with a thick coat of acrylic.*

TOP RIGHT: *Photo 241.   When the surface begins to dry out, sprinkle liberally with cheap talcum powder or if you have it, French chalk.*

LEFT: *Photo 242.   Once dry, blow and brush the residues away and hey-presto! One tarred and felted roof.*

With the additional section of wall now dry, simply paint the surface of your flat roof – I used neat black acrylic (Photo 240) – and sprinkle some talcum powder over it (Photo 241). When it has dried, blow away the excess to leave a quick yet pretty fair impression of a tarred roof (Photo 242).

EXTENDING THE ROOF

Having added extra barge boards, you will remember that the roofs provided with the kit are now too short and will have to be lengthened. We do this by making a butt joint with card of the same thickness. What we are trying to achieve are slight overhangs each end which are parallel to both the original and new barge boards (Photo 243).

If you removed the floor-mounting tabs you'll have plenty of spare card to choose from; if not, there's

Photo 243.   As for the roofs themselves, begin by placing them carefully and ensuring the overhang is both sufficient and parallel to the walls.

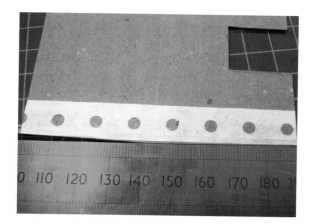

Photo 244. *Having added barge-boards at both ends, you will need to extend the roof, so join on more card using thin paper to strengthen the joint.*

Photo 245. *There is now ample overhang to enable you to trim it to fit.*

always the edging. In an effort to help any such joint remain where you put it while the glue sets, begin by adding a strip of thin paper (i.e. 'copy paper') along the edge to be joined using PVA wood glue. Old 'continuous stationery' for chain-drive printers is of an ideal thickness – or rather thinness – and that's what I've used here (Photo 244).

Now glue two fairly narrow strips of card alongside the original roofs. Use plenty of glue, press together firmly, wipe away the excess which squeezes out and then leave alone to dry hard.

Having trimmed the strip's lengths to match the existing roof depths – that is from apex to eaves – we now need to 'try' the new roof on the gables to see where we cut it off to length (Photo 245). Holding the roof firmly against the gables, turn the whole model upside down so you can see the over-hangs. First check the 'as per instructions' end fits properly (Photo 246), and then check the 'new addition' end (Photo 247). Mark your line with a pencil and cut off the excess (Photo 248). It should now look like Photo 249 and thus match the other end.

Repeat the process with the second roof for 'room B' (Photo 250), only this time you will note that some of the roof is pre-cut away to miss the entrance hall. If we were to match the new roof to this reduced line it would look wrong as roof eaves

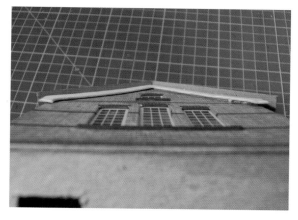

Photo 246. *Having chosen your overhang at the 'front' end, you should replicate that dimension at the back.*

Photo 247. *Hold the roof, mark the line of the barge boards in pencil, and use that to project the roof end.*

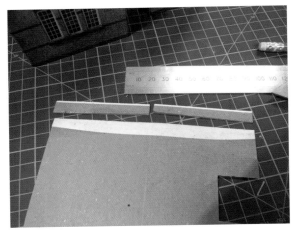

should balance and the overhang beyond the barge board should be equal on each side. Once the glue has dried therefore, leave that side deeper until a trial fit (Photo 251) when you can mark where you want to cut it off (Photo 252). You can now check again for the overall length (Photo 253), mark (Photo 254) and trim to length as previously (Photo 255).

Note that you can use the same process of gluing a joint with thin paper to restore folded joints that have torn (Photo 256), only use less glue so that the paper does not become too stiff. That way the joint will still fold.

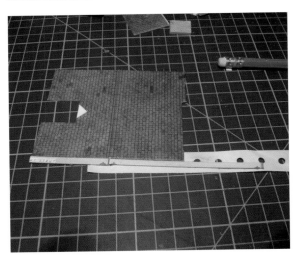

Fig, 250.   *Where the fit is dubious, as by the central entrance hall, it is usually best to cut any additions over-long, then trim them back later.*

TOP: *Photo 248.   **Having provided sufficient offset for the overhang, cut off the excess. Owing to accumulated minor errors, the ends are rarely completely square to the gutters but parallelism between the roof and gable is the governing factor. After all, the gable may not be square to the building's adjoining walls either!***

MIDDLE LEFT: *Photo 249.   **You should now have a good fit at both ends.***

MIDDLE RIGHT: *Photo 251.   **Here the model will look best if the roof overhangs the barge-boards by the same amount on both sides, even if the roof is shorter over the entrance hall itself.***

Photo 252.   *Mark the roof in situ with a pencil.*

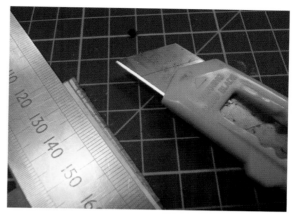

Photo 255.   *Cut neatly on the cutting mat.*

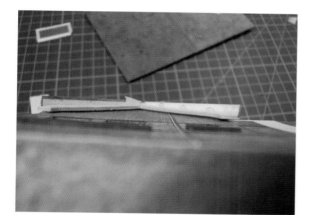

Photo 253.   *Check for 'parallelism'.*

Photo 256.   *Should you tear a folded edge with all this folding and fitting, don't worry: merely fit a paper strengthener, as in Photo 244.*

Photo 254.   *Mark that with a pencil too.*

What you have left when all is dry remains a very weak joint however, and it needs strengthening if it is to last any length of time. A favourite wheeze is to fill the joint with a builder's water-based glue such as 'Instant Nails' (Photo 257), using a scrap of card to force the glue into the joint and yet at the same time to smooth the finish off as if it were caulk (Photo 258). Having carefully filled the joints on both roofs, leave it to 'grab' for a minute or two and then use a damp cloth to wipe away any excess smears on the surface (Photo 259) so as to leave a neat, smooth finish (Photo 260). Leave for at least an hour to dry and preferably overnight to go hard.

Photo 257. Before finally gluing down your carefully fitted roof, you may need to fill the gap where you added the extra card. A quality builder's wood glue will both fill and glue, unlike simple PVA.

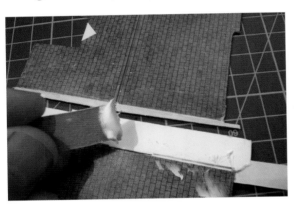

Photo 258. Smooth it into the gaps with an offcut of cardboard to provide a near-perfect joint.

Photo 259. If you moisten a bit of rag slightly once the surface has dried you should be able to simply wipe away any excess.

Photo 260. You should now have a perfectly good joint which only needs colouring.

Photo 261. Glue the main roofs in place one at a time and leave to dry. Nearly there now!

Photo 262. Do much the same for your dormers.

Photo 263. Fit those roofs too.

Then you can safely assemble both roofs onto their respective gables using PVA along the eaves and gable ends. While you *can* use the same glue along the apex, if it is available I prefer the firmer, filler-type consistency of 'Instant Nails' for that job because, being thicker, it makes for a better joint between two surfaces which may not actually be physically touching for much of their length. Add to that the advantage of its being thixotropic so it cannot run away down the inside of the roof!

Your roofs should now look like those in Photo 261 from the one side and Photo 262 from the other. You will need to extend your dormer roofs over their new barge-boards in much the same fashion then, after fitting those, your building should look vaguely like Photo 263.

SQUARING UP FOR A FINISH

While everything is set aside to dry firmly, now might be a good time to make and attach the chimney stack. This is a substantial affair for a boiler to heat just two rooms but still; making it is good practice! You will find the print for its brickwork on the accessory sheet (Photo 264).

You may ignore the instructions again, rejecting

their unlikely, two-flue stack since two open fire-places would both need constant attention whereas a boiler, which could be lit and left during lessons, was the normal installation for a school. Therefore it was felt that a rocket-stick braced, single-flue stack would be more than adequate for one boiler – and far less likely to fall apart if clouted with a passing elbow.

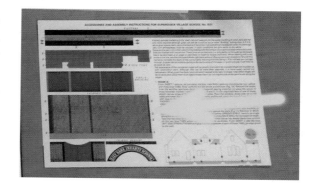

Photo 264.   The kit provides a nice if rather elaborate chimney for the school's boiler. For strength, I found a suitable rocket stick for the core and sanded the sides flat. I used that to mark my corners rather than rely upon the kit's arbitrary measurements.

Having cut out the chimney, including fixing tab, lay your rocket stick across the tab end of the card and mark down the inner edge with a pencil. Then, using a ruler, a new blade and a *very light touch*, ever so gently draw the blade down the ruler just to one side of the line at an angle of about 45 degrees (Photo 265). Turn the blade to the opposite angle and do the same from the other side of the pencil line, thus raising a very thin sliver of card between the two scores (Photo 266). Teasing this sliver away with the point of the blade (Photo 267) will produce a crease which allows you to fold a perfectly neat and square edge (Photo 268). If you do it correctly (practice!), there should be no stress on the printed card and even folded at a right angle it will leave you with an excellent finish (Photo 269).

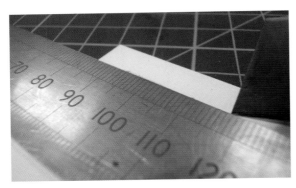

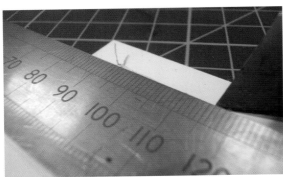

TOP LEFT: Photo 265. *You will need to score the joints carefully.*

MIDDLE LEFT: Photo 266. *The best way is to make two light cuts and remove a small triangular sliver.*

BOTTOM LEFT: Photo 267. *With the basic cuts made, gently loosen any stubborn bits by eye.*

TOP RIGHT: Photo 268. *Done properly you can achieve a neatly-folding corner which will remain where it is put.*

BOTTOM RIGHT: Photo 269. *Proof that this job can be done without cutting right through.*

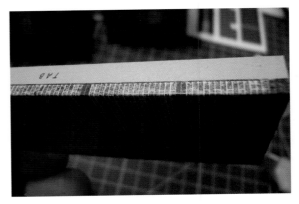

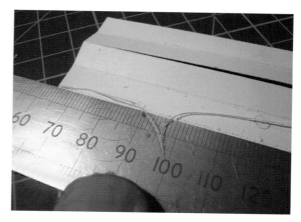

TOP LEFT: *Photo 270.   Sadly, just one light slice too many gives this result ...*

TOP RIGHT: *Photo 271.   Never mind, keep going with the other corners.*

RIGHT: *Photo 272.   Check the fit with your rocket stick.*

This is known as the 'Pendon Technique' because this is how Pendon teach you to carve and fold up entire cottage wall sides. It is a technique worth learning, even though it perhaps ought to be called the 'England Technique' after Roye England who, although he probably didn't invent it, certainly insisted his helpers use it. It certainly obviated untidy joints at corners and in doing so set a new standard for model building construction. There; a bit of history for you!

Now you can replace the rocket stick, mark off the next corner and repeat the exercise but remember, don't cut too deeply: Photo 270 shows how not to do it! Repeat for the third side, and again for the fourth (Photo 271), it's all good practice! Now if you cut right through the spoilt joint at the same angle as originally you will end up with two neat, angled sides. It is probably best to glue these to your rocket-sick former first (leaving the stick 'shy' at the top so it is less visible), and then fold over the tabbed section and glue that too (Photo 272). Continue with the third and fourth sides, gluing the fourth over the tab.

When all four have been glued, the final 'lapped' joint will look like this (Photo 273), while your

Photo 273.   Using an overlap gives a secure joint, but you are bound to end up with a visible edge on one corner.

Photo 274.   Fortunately, colouring the edge of the card to suit goes a long way towards hiding it. Do the same with your 'scored-through' corner before gluing, and that too will become practically invisible – as you can see.

Photo 276.   There are some thickening pieces on the sheet to enhance these: let's use them, remembering to paint the edges first.

neatly-cut joint, after any white card showing has been touched in with a pencil, should look like Photo 274. Properly scored and folded 'Pendon' joints look like that in (Photo 275) – which is why it is worth doing …

Now find the 'chimney banding' (Photo 276), cut it out and glue it on around the top using the same techniques. You may care to add a few small rectangles of card to each 'inside' edge at the top to

increase the thickness to better represent brick. Paint the inside of the chimney black and the top edges red to match the banding and, with a smudging of black as soot where you see fit, it should begin to resemble the one in Photo 277. Your chimney can now be glued onto the building which, we hope, will now look like Photo 278 from one side and Photo 279 from the other, a view which also shows up the new barge-boards nicely.

Finishing this model can be done in several ways, mainly depending upon what you want your roof to

Photo 275.   You will notice some red chimney banding at one end.

Photo 277.   Glue some thin card round the inside of the top of the chimney to represent the depth of brickwork. A cap and chimney-pot are probably unnecessary but you could add them if you wanted. Paint the inside of the chimney black, of course.

look like. You could paint the new roof sections to more or less match the printed ones – the quickest option and fine if the model is to fill a small hole well back in the model (Photo 280). The next option would be to use the card roof as a base for a replacement plastic one – but the favoured option is to hand-make a paper slate, tile or pantile roof and the methods of creating those really belong in another chapter.

As for the other fittings contained in the kit, such as the wooden and brick boundary walls, an odd little room which does not really seem to fit and

Photo 278. So now, apart from roof finish, guttering and downpipes (and we will deal with the various options for those in another chapter), here is your completed school kit.

Photo 279. And because of the work you have put in, the back looks just as good as the front, so you are not restricted in which way round you fit it on your model!

Photo 280.   Placed in a suitable setting it's not at all a bad model.

a few other odd bits and pieces, I consider most of these to be 'optional' fittings which you can add if you want to. In fact most of them seem to be there merely to fill up odd corners of the sheet so the kit looks 'full'; but even if you don't use them, plonk any 'possibly useful' bits in a cardboard shoe box, along with similar bits from other kits, and mix and match these 'extras' as you see fit when the fancy takes you. That's all part of the fun but as far as these instructions go, if you have got this far with a result something like mine (Photo 281) then you have all the skills you need to do the rest beautifully and without any need of another word from me!

Photo 281.   The brick banding is perhaps a bit lavish for a one-room rural school building but even so, you have the basis for an acceptable model for a few pounds and a few hours' work.

CHAPTER THREE

RESIN AND PLASTER READY-TO-PLANT (RTP) BUILDINGS

INTRODUCTION

In this section we will be looking at using or adapting models you can buy already finished and ready to plant in your landscape. To do so we will concentrate on just two complete but very different model railways at opposite ends of the spectrum, starting with this very basic GWR 00 branch terminus which, at the time of writing, could be built for a total material cost of around £100 (Photo 282).

THE NATURE OF THE BEAST

Complete buildings cast in plaster, in a variety of qualities, have been readily available for many years. Largely superseded by cast resin examples, particularly those by Hornby and Bachmann since 2008, pre-finished buildings have now generally improved enormously over the earliest offerings which were too often poorly moulded copies of out-of-scale and shoddily-made originals. Some poorer examples are still offered for sale however, and if trying a supplier other than those noted above for the first time I suggest buying just one or two initially to see what the quality is like before investing in enough for a whole layout. Indeed, even some recent releases by the 'big two' have turned out to be rather poor models so some care, thought, and the study of a decent photograph of the intended purchase is strongly advised before parting with the hard-earned readies, especially at the prices asked for some of them.

Photo 282. Ready-To-Plant buildings are never as good as scratch-built ones but they can nevertheless be very effective, as here, where they are mixed with a few simple plastic kits to provide all that is required.

Photo 283.   Chosen and placed carefully, RTP buildings also have their place amongst more complex kits and scratch-built structures – especially with a little 'tweaking' here and there.

Of course you do tend to get what you pay for in this life and as 'impressions' of buildings they often do fairly well if they have the shape and structure of something believable. Sadly, while some do, others don't, and it really is a case of looking at each item individually and deciding personally whether or not it suits the use and position you want it for.

At the other end of the model railway spectrum comes this large, multi-tracked, highly-scenic, N-gauge, Network Rail layout with its many hand-built and kit-based models. But even here a few modest, cheap, RTP resin and plaster models have their place – and not just as dark, distant corner-fillers, either, as we shall see (Photo 283).

As noted, the more modern examples of the genre generally past muster individually but any attempt to buy terraces of resin structures is probably dooming yourself to disappointment because resin mould-ings will not retain flat, straight edges when released from the moulds too early. Thus if you want, say, a truly straight steel girder bridge, a number of mould-ings for a viaduct or a terrace of houses, you would be well advised to aim for plastic or cardboard kits rather than buying multiple resin castings because the latter just don't fit together realistically. It's much the same problem when joining individual but differ-ent buildings to turn them into rows, although if you join two with different outlines it becomes easier because the sides and roofs don't have to line up; the end of the smaller one can simply be ground down to fit the untouched end of the larger one – as we shall see – although even that's not easy!

Fortunately, fitting moulded N-gauge model buildings together is generally easier because their small size means there is only a quarter as much material to remove to get a good fit. Unfortunately, even with power tools, grinding away the seriously-tough resin material used these days is tiresome and dusty while perfection of fit is often impossible anyway, especially where roof lines are supposed to be continuous, as in terraces. So even N-gauge RTP buildings have their limitations but they certainly have their uses too, not least as temporary 'stand-ins' to complete a scene or to try out ideas. You can always use them and decide later what properly-made prototype you want to replace them with, even selling on what you no longer want; with the usual limited production runs there's always a market for older models. But whoever makes them and whatever they are made from, N and 00 RTP certainly make adding buildings to a 'quick train set' a doddle and in that context too they have much to recommend them.

CHOICES FOR A SIMPLE BRANCH TERMINUS

What you see in Photo 284 is the whole of the scenic part of a very simple branch terminus; indeed the only bit you cannot see are the two or three 'fiddle yard' sidings just below the camera. The design and overall scenic aspects are well beyond the subject of this book but to keep the cost down, both scenery and track have been kept to a minimum while the use of RTP buildings was likewise almost mandatory. Even so, any model railway should be well-designed, lots of fun to use and look fabulous – which is possible as long as one picks the *right* buildings, choices made even more important when you intend to use so few of them. Therefore the reasons behind these particular choices and where they were placed is what we consider next.

THE STABLE BLOCK

I think this '00/H0' stable block by Scenix could reasonably be described as one of the less satisfactory examples of a resin RTP model, not least because I have never yet seen a stables built entirely of engineer-

ing blues! (Photo 285) Colouring apart, no attempt has been made to offer copings to cover the joints between the four planes of the roof, despite the red painted lines, while the upper halves of the apparently-open stable doors are filled in. This presumably saves having to show any interior walling! Added to this is the provision of only one stable door top-half. Obviously a left-hand stable door would have hung over the edge of the model had it been included but why not model it closed? Perhaps the idea is to cut off a horse's head and glue it to the backing but for most model railways the railway horse had long been replaced by an early lorry, certainly in rural areas of rolling hills, even though railway horses survived in some towns and cities until well into the 1950s.

Nevertheless, something was needed to help break up the verdant bank behind the platform so as to add an extra layer of width to a rather narrow model; the whole thing being only 15in (38cm) wide. This stable block – just visible in the first photo – seemed about the right size and came with an office and a simple hut for just £9.99p. But how can we make what turned out to be an unpromising casting into something useful? Could it be rendered semi-derelict – or at least disused – but still be somewhere the local lorry can have its nose parked out of the frost to aid starting on cold winter mornings? Perhaps.

First we place it in situ while we consider what to do with it. It always helps to rough out the situation visually so add a few trees, even if they get moved around later, plonk some vestigial fencing roughly where you think it might go and thus flesh out the scene a little so as to give the imagination something to work with (Photo 286).

Deciding that a dry-brush of red-brown paint would improve the brickwork and 'mellow' the structure somewhat, hiding that very poor roof under a generous growth of weeds also became a 'must', as was generally bedding it into the surrounding undergrowth as much as possible so as to hide it away (Photo 287). Yes you could add cardboard or plastic ridge tiles but the added relief would attract attention and, frankly, the rest of the model's not worth it!

These two minor adjustments only took moments and showed promise. Then it was time to drill out

Photo 284. *A simple layout with a simple track plan can be built quickly using commercial buildings. You can always replace them later with hand-made structures.*

Photo 285. A typical first-generation cast building of poor quality – but very cheap to buy.

Photo 286. Making room for a building can sometimes mean arranging your scenery to suit the model, rather than the other way round.

Photo 287. One way of hiding poor roof detail.

Photo 288. *Setting a poor quality building back into the landscape allows the eye to sweep right on past without particularly noticing it – and yet it adds another 'man-made shape' structure to the background which is, on balance, beneficial to the 'composition'.*

one of the openings and hide the now painted but quite untextured interior wall by planting a vigorous weed sprouting from the inside, the door having presumably been lost long ago.

In sum, these changes managed to give the structure a general air of worn, insouciant decay, creating a 'nonentity' of a building which in this case is precisely the effect desired. Even so, this obviously man-made shape does provide a vital counter-point to the natural greenery draped around it (Photo 288).

Across the road from the stables is an indeter-minate hut, the simpler of the other two castings in the Scenix pack. This was given a coat of fading creosote which helps withdraw it from our attention yet retain its value as another square, man-made 'shape', adding to the general work-place ambience of the goods yard: after all, you can never have enough huts! In fact I would offer a general rule – obviously meant to be broken, of course – that in almost any given situation, if a scene does not look 'finished', either add another tree or another hut or several, or even both: nine times out of ten it works!

Photo 289.   Some suppliers provide rather better quality buildings which are really limited only by the material they are cast in, as with these solid plaster cottages.

CORNER COTTAGES

In a track-less corner of this layout is a cottage. It is one of a nice range of plaster buildings which over the last few years their cottage-industry originator has begun to offer pre-coloured. At around much the same price as the Scenix examples, this 'kit' (in that the chimneys come separately and need gluing on!), offers a much more believable shape, far better colouring and has a what might be described as a 'quality pedigree' in that one feels the modeller may actually have had a particular building in mind when he made it. True, the 'blind' windows will not appeal to everyone now that Hornby and Bachmann fit etched ones over approximated holes but, since the building is positioned at an angle acute enough so as to effectively hide them from the operator, this example in this position could only be improved by something scratch-built.

Of course, neither a cast-plaster nor a 'hand-built stunner' of a cottage improve the operational quality of the layout one iota but the vaguely 'Riverside Cottage' ambience, and the hint of life it gives to this corner, both render it invaluable to the overall atmosphere, which can be no bad thing! (Photo 289)

Incidentally, the roof has been repainted in better

'slate' colours, as was the station building's, and soot stains have been added to provide variety and interest to what was otherwise a rather bland gable end. An access path with a small gate ('Merit', I think), encourages the roving eye back into the model (Photo 290).

Photo 290.   Adding a white picket gate which can only be seen close-to distracts the eye from poor window detail, and with the gate in the railway fence opposite, leads the eye back into the station.

So this plaster cottage ends up having three purposes: it acts as a 'frame' to this end of the scene and stops the eye 'wandering off the end'; it increases the humanity of the scene by suggesting village life; and it ties the whole model together by reflecting the local stonework colours which are repeated on the station building and again on the backscene. Furthermore it frames the railway between itself and the station building, thus including it in the community physically. It also mimics and balances the weight of that building; an effect called 'dualism' by Ruskin, and one which encourages a feeling of repose or peace: surely a desirable attribute for a rural branch terminus! (Photo 291)

STATION BUILDING

The station building itself was one of the first produced by Hornby in its then-new 'Skaledale' range

of cast resin buildings. For this model the gutters, downpipes, doors and window sills have all been repainted in 'GWR Dark Stone', as befits a Great Western branch terminus of course, but the most significant change has been to use a Dremel and a slitting disc to carve away the stepped gables which adorned the original casting: they were just too reminiscent of an eastern style of architecture to be permitted anywhere west of Bristol![1] The raw edges left by this process have been hidden by stone 'drip mouldings' (in plain cardboard), touched in with acrylics.

On reflection I should have made the soot staining of the gable end (as supplied) rather less obvious

---

[1] Yes, you can find stepped gables in Devon but they are not common. When you only have a very few buildings to express character, it is vital to choose examples iconic of your landscape, not curious exceptions.

Photo 291. *Painting the backscene buildings in colours which blend with those of the resin and plaster ones gives a genuine sense of 'community' to a rural village, so making the railway a true part of the landscape.*

Photo 292. A modern commercial resin structure – 'tweaked' just slightly.

Photo 293. Adding small details such as posters and noticeboards is helpful but needs to be done with care and understanding.

by dry-brushing various colours onto the faces of the stonework while painting the dripstones – but I didn't (Photo 292). However, I did add some detailing to the front: the faded poster advertising 'Cheap Day Returns' is an original part of the model but the addition of a 'Tinysigns' GWR noticeboard head and tail, along with other time-table and advertising hoardings from the same company, all help to convey the atmosphere of a traditional country station (Photo 293). More 'Tinysigns' poster boards and railway holiday posters are fitted to the two single-storey extension buildings, whose stepped gables were also 'corrected' before fitting. The GWR posters are carefully selected as being from places other than the South West, the supposed general location of the model. Railway companies tended to extol the virtues of their holiday resorts and rural retreats in their cities but conversely, extol the delights of the cities and large towns at country stations. Thus, if I recall correctly, we have adverts for Hereford, Chester and London.

With the addition of some typically-Great Western pagoda and round-roofed corrugated iron huts (both plastic kits), some Cooper Craft 'cast iron' GWR station seats and platform trolleys (again, plastic kits), and a few lengths of Squire's etched brass 'iron fencing', we now have most of what we need to portray a convincing scene (Photo 294). Adverts, weeds and the other usual items of platform furniture all help, too, but do note the lack of people. Far too

many modellers populate their country platforms with a dozen or more passengers – some of them forever running for a train which would normally wait happily for them, of course; such was the character of quiet rural railways. Unfortunately all this merely advertises the modeller's lack of understanding of what he is modelling because at a rural country terminus, the platform atmosphere for 95 per cent of even a busy summer's day would be total utter inactivity. When a branch train arrived the passengers left immediately and went home. The train was turned and then sat at the platform ready to depart when its time came – but that was usually much later, often half-an-hour or more, the return journey generally being timed to connect with a through service at the junction or a major station some distance away. Thus a few locals might arrive, with ample time to spare to catch their train, and in summer stand on

Photo 294. A number of structures are usually combined to form a 'station'; arranging them to best effect is where the 'art' comes in.

Photo 295.   Another simple resin building which looks poor close up but still serves a purpose in the overall scheme of things.

THE COAL OFFICE

Finally, the third hut which came with that Scenix set is here doing duty as a coal-merchant's hut in the goods yard. It has been slightly 'weathered' but otherwise remains as it arrived in the box. Coal merchants may have had wagons and lorries with their names on them but only in the larger towns where there was competition did they commonly put a large nameboard on their office. Therefore almost any kind of hut will suit most coalman perfectly well (Photo 295).

CHOICES FOR A BUSY TOWNSCAPE

Moving now to the other extreme of modelling, a busy townscape densely packed with buildings, let us consider the role therein of the cheap ready-to-plant model. Look at this little timber hut in the foreground of a modern business park (Photo 296). This corner of my N-gauge model 'Wye Notte' denotes the start of what the local council would probably call a

the platform until it arrived but in the other three seasons nobody would wait out in the cold or rain on a platform when there would have been a roaring fire in the waiting room! So if you want recreate a quiet rural idyll, don't populate it like a city.

Photo 296.   A much better hut fulfilling a similar function; that of adding 'purpose' to a particular space.

SMALL TOWN THEORY

The proximity of very mixed sizes, shapes and types of buildings is very much a part of the ambience of older towns in the West Midlands. They seem somewhat confused as to the precise nature of their locality in that old, 17th century cottages sit next to Norman churches and Victorian terraces (the latter often dating from the arrival of the railway), while modern housing and even glass-walled office blocks all have their place in and around the High Street, perhaps just a few yards away. It is this wondrous, seemingly ad-hoc mixture which give so many of these towns their character and it was one I felt obliged to copy in this model. The reasons for such a seemingly random juxtaposition of uses, styles and periods are simple enough to detect, of course, as each building owes its existence purely to the vagaries of local history.

How does this apply to a model? Well, by way of example, this is the 'back story' to Wye Notte. A hill-top Saxon settlement probably lead to a medieval straw and timber village on lower land at the foot of the hill, where a more substantial half-timbered grange or hall might survive to this day. The church, originally wooden too of course, would have been replaced with a stone one sometime through the centuries and either renewed or, as like as not, 'refurbished' by the Victorians who seemed to have a passion for such things. By that time more traditional stone cottages and shops had often surrounded it. When the railway came the original heart of the village soon became just one part of a larger town and the centre moved down to the station, the approaches to which so often became a new High Street.

The almost guaranteed existence of a gasworks at one time would normally demand a location beside the railway where its insatiable hunger for coal could be easily supplied by rail, perhaps being built in an old quarry dug to supply the stone needed for the railway's embankments or the new town's buildings. The noise of

Photo 297. *It is impossible from this distance to see what is hand made, what is a kit and what is a commercial casting – which is how it should be. Note too, how colours are used in blocks right across the scene with brown, grey, red and beige all playing their part in creating a harmonious whole, an effect increased by repeating each colour as a highlight nearby.*

shunting all night in the goods yard and the smell of the gas works would, in their turn, probably have made this end of town undesirable, (unless you worked at either, of course), and it would have been the need for workers' housing which led to the construction of the terrace of small brick cottages lining the road, probably replacing what might once have been a stand of trees on ground belonging to the quarry. When the gasworks closed after the war, as so many did, the site would have lain derelict for a number of years while people wondered what to do with it, apart perhaps from a single gasholder for local 'peak demand' storage. Eventually, with memories of the smell and taint of the gasworks finally forgotten, a developer came along in the 70s and covered the site with shops and three-storey town housing. A few years later the last gas-holder was probably removed and the rest of the site became a Motel with modern shops and offices in odd corners.

So, starting from the main road we have properties all of differing ages but all with excellent reasons for being where they are. Turn the odd derelict, unwanted corner of land once owned by the Manor into somewhere to put a chapel and, after the Great War, a war-memorial. Build an 'offy' and the beginnings of another brick terrace along the lane, on land probably sold off to pay death duties, then finally turn the old Manor House into a pub or steak-house and there you are; a typical semi-rural, semi-urban slice of railway landscape not too far from the Welsh borders. All it needs is a Morrisons. And it's got one of those too: a backscene behind the station. (You can't see it in these photos but it's there: I supplied the photo of it myself to Jenny, the lady with the patience of a saint who found, adjusted, reversed, mucked about with and generally stitched together dozens of photographs to produce the over thirty feet of very complex and unique backscene. Many thanks Jen!)

Photo 298.   Red brick usually brings an element of 'town-ness' to a rural scene ...

'valuable green corridor and wildlife resource'. It's a cutting leading to a tunnel where once there ran a goods branch. 'The Green Heart of the Town' they so often label such routes restored to public use. What they don't tell you is that much of the line has been bulldozed to make room for factories; nevertheless the tunnel under the main road and out past the church-yard has been de-rubbished and opened up as a walkway to the nearby countryside, so it's not all bad news. More on that section later but a small wooden hut like this might well find several uses in such an environment – it could even be the home of a local model railway club ...

Away in the far corner of the room is a little niche where one of Hornby's latest (at the time), 'Lyddle End' models, a detached modern house, does not look out of place beside a housing estate – except perhaps for the over-ample provision of chimneys and the multi-paned windows. With rooms which would be thought 'pokey' even by today's standards – and positively 'poor man's cottage' by the Victorians – this rather odd little property does not deserve a place in the foreground but, hidden away near the backscene, its small size and pleasant colouring make it a warm, friendly addition which complements the landscape (Photo 298). Fortunately it looks even better from further away (Photo 299).

The 1930s semi-detached houses in the foreground – plastic kits and one of a group of three

Photo 299. ... and you can confirm that impression with a classic 'semi-detached' – or even better, a row of them!

BELOW: Photo 300. On the other hand, a row of disparate stone cottages suggests history, tradition, longevity and village life. What you choose to use matters.

Photo 301. Arlington Row, Bibury, Gloucs. Henry Ford (yes, that one), thought it typified Englishness. With care you can achieve a similar effect.

pairs used here – help depict the confused 'rural but urban' nature of the average small-town landscape where old and new businesses, shopping and housing all jostle together happily, quite unlike either cities or truly rural places which tend to be one thing or the other but rarely both in the same place. This 'melange' is an aspect worth studying if you want to get the atmosphere right on your own model. It is discussed in the panel on pages 114/5.

Moving backwards from resin to old plaster castings, these stone cottages are now perhaps twenty years old and all came from the same supplier (whose name I have sadly long since forgotten). They are all variants of the same basic vernacular but were produced in different shapes and sizes (Photo 300). This, of course, made them perfect to combine in one of those delightfully-if-deliberately varied terraces once beloved by the landed gentry for their

'model villages'. It is a style so often copied, even by modern developers, that today it has become a cliché; however the original of all these was probably this cottage row in Bibury, Gloucs., largely converted from a long barn over 400 years ago (Photo 301).

Note how Wye Notte's row follows the line of the original pre-railway road, now severed: another way of suggesting change and historical progression. From this perspective you can also see how the colour of the cottages' stonework has been tinted with a wash to match, more or less, the colours painted on the railway's retaining walls and bridge abutments (Photo 302).

Naturally the colours of the local stone buildings – especially vernacular and railway buildings which were almost always made of stone quarried locally or won from cuttings – should match nearby rock cuttings, which is why I have included this next photo.

LEFT: **Photo 302.** *Emphasize your contrasts with colour: the red bricks, tiles and truck form a block of colour which contrasts well with the blues and greys of the railway, while they are both bounded by the greens of nature. Now you know why that door is blue.*

BELOW: **Photo 303.** *EWS colours echo that 'town theme' of red and tan, carrying them into the rest of the layout, whereas vernacular stone buildings carry the rock colours of the landscape into the town. All this helps your model become one single entity.*

Photo 304.   The poor window definition of many RTP buildings can often be obfuscated by putting interesting detail close by to distract the attention. Look closely, and the green shape turns out to be a bike under a cover, while the bright garden furniture and 'coloured' fencing also attract the eye, as does the riot of untamed undergrowth nearby.

I know I have the stone colours pretty much bang-on because one of these stones is a real one plucked, by me, from a quarry in the Wye Valley[2]. And yes, I did ask first! (Photo 303).

Returning to the cottages, the backs are very simple and the windows are not particularly inspiring in their detail but, by adding some brightly-coloured features in a few gardens, the eye can be distracted from poor detail which is thus rendered innocuous. Another important job, since it is highly visible, is to replace the rather washy grey, supposedly-slate

colour, of the original roofs with warm reds and browns because that will tie these buildings in with others around them. This cohesion is a vital element if a scene is to look natural (Photo 304).

PUTTING A HEART IN YOUR VILLAGE

This stone cottage row really forms the start of what you might call the 'old village' part of our model town. In wider views you will have noticed the church which sits next to these cottages. In the next chapter we will look at it particularly closely by way of a 'case study' in how to upgrade an old building to meet today's rather different standards

---

[2] It's the big triangular one above the nearest wagon, if you wondered.

Photo 305.　Disharmonious reds can, however, be a bit aggressive; a few greys calm things down a bit and a warm brown here and there helps too. We could do with a bit more brown, perhaps, while some greenery to 'soften' everything would also be good.

but to complete this chapter, let us review why a church was the right choice for this particular location and why a cheap, 20 year old casting became the heart of the project.

The ambience, age and authorities of our model community are gradually being established by a careful choice of available models old and new. During this process it became blindingly obvious that both the fictional community, and the model visually, demanded a focal point at the centre. Put simply, the village needed a heart. Churches make very good 'hearts'.

Theoretically, of course, the manor house came first, then the church, and then a great many years later the Victorian brick replacements for such old, largely decrepit, half-timbered cottages as maybe survived into the railway age. In creating the model scene however, the landscape with its curved, dropping road came first because whatever was modelled had to fit above some electronic indicators over the sidings beneath. The land then had to somehow drop down to meet the High Street below and to the right. To do that without a ridiculously-steep road it was decided to only model half the drop and to infer the rest by curving the road off the front of the model. Doing that also increased the available area of the High Street but that was a bonus, not an original intention!

The long, curving terrace of kit-built brick cottages rapidly followed because they could be made to follow the hill in both slope and curvature and in doing so create a 'signature feature'. Next came the corner shop and its adjoining short terrace, then the manor house, the gables of which so neatly echoed that of the shop's shape, and to balance that, the short end-on terrace completing the far side of that street which, at this juncture, looked like this (Photo 305). All that was needed now was to put something 'interesting' in the foreground to attract attention, although it had to be something with sufficient space around it to let you see the other buildings, which precluded another terrace of cottages!

It is generally understood that in many a medieval village the church was provided for and used by the local gentry, so you will often find it close to the local manor house. A church seemed the perfect answer since firstly, I thought I possibly had a suitable model sitting in a box somewhere and secondly, the low-level nature of a graveyard allows you to both clearly see the buildings behind and to add lots of eye-catching detail. Fortunately, if you look around the western fringes of the Black Country conurbation today, you can still see small areas of old villages which look almost as if they stood as the prototype for this very model. And in a way, they did because the ambience I was looking for, a kind of cross between the suburban city and the small commuter village, clearly still exists today all over the West Midlands and I have no doubt I was influenced subconsciously by what I had seen on my travels. But to get back to the heart analogy, the model church I proposed using here turned out, upon close inspection, to be one which desperately needed a transplant!

In fact, this plaster moulding of a church was already an old casting a the time it was bought and rejected for the original model of Westbury, although it was later included in the most un-Westbury-like village which I added above some hidden storage sidings on the other side of the room. The fact that that same building has once again ended up over more hidden storage sidings I find amusing – obviously the crypt's inhabitants have grown accustomed to the vibrations of trains! Sadly however, the church's exterior – never really up to the standard I was looking for in the first place – was now, some 20 years and more later, decidedly looking its age! No, there was nothing for it – it had to be either replaced or quite sensationally upgraded (Photo 306).

But that left me with a problem. There simply was nothing else available which was even vaguely suitable, either in size or style. Neither, to be honest, has anyone ever made a 148th scale church which has anything like the balance, harmony, proportions and sheer 'believability' of architectural style as this quite delightful model: in fact its only real problem was that it just wasn't any where near the standard of detail demanded of a model today. But could that be fixed? The more I thought about it, the more I thought it could.

Alan Downes once applied 'Windows are the eyes of a building' to models. I know what he meant: I have seen many a good model ruined by poor windows and even though few poor models are saved by good ones, there is no doubt that poor windows always stand out whereas poor walls can usually be disguised. But why should this be so, I wondered? And come to that; is it also true of churches?

Our local village church is obviously a church from any angle and could not be mistaken for a school, a hospital, a house large or small, nor for a fire station or a library – and yet church or no church it's windows are largely hidden by wire mesh grills to either prevent yobs breaking them or birds from getting in through the occasional hole exposed by crumbling lead 'cames'. Therefore, although both the stained and plain glass look fine from the inside looking out, seen from the outside they look dull, dirty and hardly different in tone or colour to the stonework surrounding them. So perhaps it is not specifically the windows which are the 'eyes' of all buildings – or if they are, perhaps churches are best modelled as they are most often seen in the flesh: asleep and with their eyes shut!

In looking closely at a typical village church then, one soon concludes that it is the Norman-inspired components which are probably the really iconic features: the pointed window traceries, the squat, square towers and, in particular, the mighty stone slabs which throw the water off of every wall-top or buttress. Other generally ecclesiastical features, as often as not Victorian additions, are the pinnacles, crosses and weather vanes which are so prominent from a distance because they tower over every other building in our villages. So although one cannot exactly 'ignore' the windows of a church – they must be of the correct size, shape and proportion for the age of the building they sit in – from the outside they are less important in churches than perhaps in almost any other building you can think of, simply because they are not the most noticeable or iconic features. It follows therefore, that if we can isolate what particular features of churches generally are iconic and then reproduce them to our new, higher standard, we can 'lift' our simple casting into quite another dimension despite its poor windows.

With every church in the land being unique there is, of course, no one 'correct' answer as to how you do this: what you see over the following pages is therefore just one way of going about the task. There must be literally hundreds, probably thousands, of other routes to the same effect; all you have to do is to go out and study a few churches and pick your own favourite icons. At least there are ample examples out there to choose from!

Photo 306. *How about a nice brown church? The size and shape are good but it's very drab; it needs some 'zing'. The next chapter shows how we go about adding that.*

CHAPTER FOUR

UPGRADE FOR AN OLD PLASTER MODEL CHURCH

HOW TO REFRESH A TIRED OLD PLASTER CASTING

This dull, solid church is a tired old plaster casting dating from the 1970s and its finish is left far behind by the standard of today's resin models – but don't ignore it completely. With a little imagination and a lot of work you will be surprised at what can be done with it.

The tower, which came as a separate part, has been glued to the main body of the church and the whole thing mounted on an MDF base. This has been let into the landscape to see how it fits (Photo 307).

This is always a vital part of any alteration because it allows you to get an 'overall impression' of what the model will look like in its setting. The colour can be changed but does the shape feel right and is it about the right size? It will, after all, have to fit in well with any surrounding buildings if it is to look realistic and appropriate.

Even at this early stage it will be realized that the church, being approximately 'post-Norman, pre-Victorian Gothic' in character, must pre-date the railway by quite a few years. Therefore the original churchyard can be imagined to have extended over where the railway cutting now sits, even if the

Photo 307. The church, as supplied, is finished in a pale grey wash. An N-gauge plaster casting, it comes in two parts, tower and knave, and has been duly assembled.

cutting itself is already redundant after merely a century's use!

I would like to ignore the Victorians' insouciant demolition – even complete erasure – of what would often today be considered valuable historical architecture. It's a practice still prevalent today as far as many late Victorian and early 20th century 'Metroland' and 'Garden City' developments are concerned, despite their being architectures which tomorrow may well be considered 'lost' themselves. I do not ignore it, however, because there were many instances where the Victorians fearlessly uprooted

A SIDEWAYS DISTRACTION INTO COLOUR

The relative colour of buildings is an interesting aspect, especially pertinant now with the availability of excellent pre-coloured models. Comparing this church with Hornby's 'Skaledale' brown/red buildings behind, and the rather more brilliant red of the printed card terrace to the right, the choice of a warm brown sits comfortably enough with its neighbours, both in tone and 'depth' of colour.

Tone is simple to understand of course, varying as it does between dull and bright, but 'colour depth' is perhaps less so, although some computer graphics users will know the meaning under the names 'gamma' or 'colour intensity'. But whatever the name, colour depth is an aesthetic judgement of the amount of colour on a scale from pure to grey. It is important because it decides whether a particular model suits the position it is to take up in the finished landscape, a judgement which is all but impossible to translate into words. It is true, however, that correct depth of colour goes a very long way to making a model either 'right' or 'not right' in its context, which makes depth-of-colour a crucial decision.

Fortunately, even if models are pre-coloured, depth is one thing which can be modified by either 'weathering' or washing over with a lighter or darker hue, or indeed both. You can also change one building's 'colour position' by careful choice of the colours of the buildings surrounding it and by adjusting the perceived 'depth' of those colours too. If one building's colour is deemed 'too strong', then placing a stronger colour in front of it will lessen the perception of it as being 'wrong', just as replacing a pale colour behind it with a paler one still will make it seem worse. In fact the whole 'perceived distance' of an entire area can be either brought forwards towards the viewer or sent backwards away from them by careful control not only on the colours of the items within that area but of those before, beside and behind them. The experienced eye calculates these variations in a fraction of a second and anything that is wrong stands out instantly, although trying to describe how that works would take a professorial knowledge and language I simply don't have! But work it does, especially if you rely upon your 'inner eye', as it were. By this I mean don't 'look' for the error as such; rather, just gaze happily at the scene for a minute or two and let any errors reveal themselves to your subconscious. Sooner or later they will, I promise!

Understanding the gist of colour depth theory is simple enough, but deciding which way and by how much to 'move' objects by changing their colours is really something only tolerably computed with the benefit of experience. With a thoughtful, prolonged study of the nearly-finished scene however, even the most abject novice can eventually see whether something looks 'right' where it is or not. It should not be too big a step thereafter, to move on to deciding whether the model is physically in the right place or not and if it is, whether the colour needs toning down or highlighting to make it fit better. From that point on, it's down to practice!

church graveyards and their contents in the name of progress. Recent burials were only re-interred – often elsewhere and with due ceremony – but all the headstones recovered had, by law, to be replaced within the boundaries of the remaining land.

With the coming of the railway, the area remaining around our church became quite small. The model topography has already been 'layered' into terraces, which give us several levels, to which we have added an embankment, wall and railings at the front where the path has supposedly been widened and upgraded. Even at this stage I imagined a Yew tree and an early Victorian lychgate to the right, the main entrance being from a 1970s built car park in the triangular area beyond. (Sadly I never did get that yew tree!)

But let us focus on the church first, even though chronologically the fencing, boundary walls, steps and lychgate were done and dusted long before I completed it because those other bits were worked upon as various stages of the church were set aside to cure.

PLANNING THE UPGRADE

The church moulding as it comes in its original condition shows fine, chunky proportions; the square tower on the left delightfully balancing the small chancel to the right in a nicely-stepped progression through the central nave. The dark and pale-grey finish of the roofs, incidentally, is the original colouring of the whole model, apart from some pale brown doors: one which made it look rather wishy-washy – almost translucent in fact – so that it was very difficult to visualize what it would look like once repainted. Giving the walls a coat of a deeper colour made it look far more substantial and revealed that the detail work, though shallow, was really pretty good for its day. Somebody, somewhere, did some excellent work!

With that observation made, let us look more closely at the moulding. If, as I suggest, the overall shape is right what, you might ask, is actually wrong with it as it stands? Well: the door is rather small although not unduly so, especially as it is really the deep, bland expanse of wall above it which exagger-

ates its lack of height and that can be got round by adding a porch. Conversely, that adjacent window is rather on the large side, perhaps more suited to the end of the chancel than the side of the nave where several smaller windows would be more likely; but it is certainly an ecclesiastical type of window and would undoubtedly make for a bright and cheery interior so perhaps that's acceptable, even if one would not want to make too much of it as a feature.

But the real problem with the model is one which is the bane of plaster mouldings of anything: the lack of any prominent details which sit proud of the surfaces of the model. This is understandable, perhaps, because the whole model only cost a few pounds and the designer wanted to get lots of castings from his mould before it became damaged. He therefore omitted any notably proud, thin detail which, being plaster, could be easily damaged, either when releasing it from the mould or during posting. To protect the mould itself, any deep hollow sections which

Photo 308.   The first job is to apply proud dripstones to each 'step' of the buttresses.

might rip were also omitted. Compared to today's resin castings – or even to a real stone church – it is therefore this lack of basic 'relief' which is the most obviously missing feature. Fortunately, this is something easily corrected if one has the time.

DRIPSTONES

You can start to add depth by replacing the flush drip stones on the upper surfaces of the masonry with plasticard pieces suitably filed to shape (Photo 308). These should be fitted wherever they would have appeared on the real thing, so: at every step in the buttresses, along the gable tops and beneath the windows as part of the sills. If I remember correctly I used 40 thou. plasticard for this job, tapering each

BOTTOM LEFT: Photo 309.   Adding gargoyles from Milliput is fun and adds humour and interest.

TOP RIGHT: Photo 310.   All kinds of demonic characters were originally created by medieval craftsmen and copied, more or less well, by Victorians attempting to mimic history.

MIDDLE RIGHT: Photo 311.   All should be quite individual, this one being almost leonine in character.

BOTTOM RIGHT: Photo 312.   Gargoyles are, by definition, designed to support rainwater spouts that throw rainwater away from the walls and footings. 'Grotesques' is the correct name for similar caricatures which do not have this function.

piece slightly so it was thinner at the top than at the bottom, and filing away the existing plaster surface until the new piece fitted snugly against the remaining blockwork: a job simpler in some places than others. With care, though, all can be made to fit nicely into place. To glue them reliably, a drop of quality super-

glue should be dripped onto the clean plaster edge first, being allowed to soak in and solidify. This might need dressing before attempting to glue anything to it but it does create a firm surface to work with. Thereafter, the only things to ensure you get right are to fit all the pieces at the same angle and to 'dress' the edges of the plasticard to make it look like heavy lumps of well-worn stone, not lightweight lumps of plastic! In the detail of the tower end you can already can see the 'life' being added by this simple if monotonous task.

GARGOYLES

The next stage is a lot more fun: Gargoyles! Popular mythology has it that gargoyles were created to ward off evil spirits but I think in reality, at least to begin with, this was just late medieval masons having a bit of fun! Later, gargoyles became far more common, as did 'grotesques', the latter by the way, being the name for fantastical figures without the gargoyle's specific purpose of supporting a wooden or lead pipe long enough to throw rain water well away from the walls – vital for sandstone constructions before the invention of gutters.

As can be seen in the photographs, I have represented the lead pipes with short sections of thin-walled brass tube cut long enough to mount into holes drilled into the tower corners. The four gargoyles – all different, of course – are made with varying amounts of effort from Milliput, plonked on in a firm lump and then worked with knife blades and 'doofers'[1] into four quite different fantastical faces. The first (Photo 309) has pop eyes, a beard and a very long tongue; the next (Photo 310) has a slightly gormless, squashed look about him, occasioned by a deliberately heavy brow and a weak but also bearded chin; the third (Photo 311) is far more normal with deeply sunken eyes but has something of a feline look about it; while the last (Photo 312) might best be described as a frog with a quiff and a ruff – or not, as you prefer!

You will also have noticed how the crenelations have begun to be dressed into something rather more approaching reality with a Swiss file. They were still in 'rough form' when these photos were taken as at that point, no depth had been chosen to align them to: another of those odd 'aesthetic' choices which rather depends upon what abuts them.

ADDING A SACRISTY

Moving on now to a rear three-quarter view, you can see at this same stage a new structural addition the church: part of a Hornby 'Lyddle End' chapel in use as a modern entrance porch and sacristy, the latter being somewhere to lock away the surplice and wine (Photo 313). In fact, I wanted to hide an inappropriate feature on the original casting, which was quite wrong for this model, and adding a new 'wing' was

MENTAL PERCEPTION

Creating physical relief or 'surface undulation' is an issue of 'mental perception'. Real stonework is, in a great many buildings, so carefully brought to a flat surface and so neatly jointed that an accurately printed sheet of paper should, in theory, be the best way of modelling it. Thus photographing a wall and mounting the print should reproduce an Ashlar wall perfectly. Experience proves however, that prints just don't 'work' for no matter how accurate the print, the lack of texture makes it look like the photograph it is. It seems the mind's eye insists stone must have texture and edges and that mortar must be recessed, even though in reality it often isn't. Therefore on a model, even in 2mm scale, a textured surface always looks more like stone than an untextured one, even if the colouring is less perfect than that of a photographic reproduction. Strange, certainly, but I think you'll find in practice that it's true …

---

[1] Doofers: blunted pin-pointed metal rods with handles which will do for this, do for that …

Photo 313. At the rear I added an off-cut from a chapel conversion to act as a vestry. This was deliberately 'left over' from a conversion using two examples of the same model, as shown below.

BELOW: *Photo 314.* Using one and a bit of the same building to enlarge a ready-made model can produce a vaguely familiar yet quite individual structure.

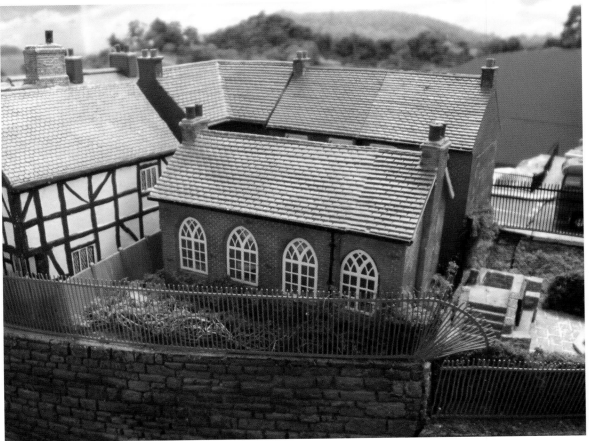

certainly a quick and cheap way of doing so. True, buying a model just to use half of one end is not cheap, perhaps, but I used the other end to extend a second example of the same chapel model to make it bigger – see Chapter 5. You can see the result of that in Photo 314, where you will also see that the third of the four windows is the one you would expect to be present on the far or unseen side of this extension. In fact, I replaced it with a new door, of which a glimpse later. I was therefore being particularly economical, not to say 'green', by using up an otherwise wasted part of a moulding!

At this stage the whole church, with all the flush original drip stone mouldings on the buttresses replaced by overhanging plasticard ones, looks like Photo 315. As you can see, viewing the church from this higher angle still leaves it looking rather bland so it was decided to add more deliberately iconic features to the upper surfaces. These included detailing the tower, by adding pinnacles and a weather vane, and improving the body of the church, by detailing the gables. The first improvement is an obvious one, however replacing the plain drip stones on the gables with more interestingly-shaped ones will also help, because it balances the greater relief of the tower's extra detail with minor echoes at the opposite end. This is important because physical relief or 'surface undulation' is a vital factor in creating visual impact in the smaller scales; probably rather more so than colour.

MORE DRIPSTONES – AND SILLS

The gables have now been given new dripstones, each being tapered to be thinner at the top so that each sits slightly proud of its lower neighbour (Photo 316). There are two reasons for this. Firstly, real stones overlap each other, a method which creates a series of shallow but distinctive steps, in order that rainwater cannot fall into the joint and wash out what would have originally been lime mortar rather than

Photo 315.   Next the castellations around the top of the tower are sawn and filed into a neater, deeper pattern.

Photo 316. Nicks are filed into the apex of the roof and more plasticard dripstones added to the top of each gable.

Photo 317. Sills along the bottom of the windows help provide texture and improve the relief.

cement. Secondly, the notched outline to the gable which this creates not only improves the relief of the model but the distinct 'edges' now present around the bottom of each stone will capture dry-brushed paint well while the rebates thus formed below them will not. This will help considerably when completing the final 'weathering' of the stonework, as we shall see later.

Two further points to note: firstly the edge line of the stonework is deliberately not precise; old stones do tend to settle slightly over the years, particularly when secured with lime mortar; and secondly the dripstones of the buttress may well, as here, be a different width to those used on the gable as a buttress is sometimes wider than the gable it supports. To 'top out' the job, both gables have also been given carefully-shaped capstones. One has a flat top supporting a small stone cross (from a gravestone moulding), another common church feature.

With the gables thus improved, it was time to look at the sides (Photo 317). The addition of sills, proud of the surrounding stonework, will certainly enhance the appearance of the windows but I felt that in N gauge at least, the drip mouldings above the arches probably sufficed as they were. With a similar

example in 4mm scale, I would probably have added depth there too as on a model with four times the face, any lack of relief would have been much more noticeable (a 4mm scale model being both twice the width and twice the height, of course).

As will become apparent, in 2mm scale the minimal benefit of extra depth gained by adding modest drip mouldings to the sides are not worth the time they would take to add, which is the exact opposite of the position with the much larger gable facings in their much more prominent position at the top. Besides, I deliberately did not want to draw attention to those blind windows and prominent arch stones would have done just that.

On the other hand though, all that extra detail up top does need something lower down to balance it or in a low-angle photograph the church's sides will look rather unrealistic and lacking in detail. The new deepened sills help with that, of course, by adding shadows at the base of the wall that make the model seem weightier. Perhaps adding a fancy new porch might be just the thing, too; one would certainly disguise that rather anaemic-looking door! However, you should look at your own model yourself, make your own judgements, and work on it accordingly;

do not simply take my word for what should be kept and what replaced!

Incidentally, the pale patches along the bottom of the walls are where old scenery has been removed. This became glued to the stonework when the church was 'bedded' into the landscape of the pre-

Photo 320. It was mounted on a length of brass rod fitted into a short length of tube – people always want to 'see if it turns' so, rather than have it break ...

Photo 318. Four Victorian pinnacles from scrap plastic sprue were added, along with a brass weathervane structure.

vious model. Most of it just scraped off with the paint but, where necessary, any damaged surface was restored with Milliput epoxy putty.

PINNACLES

We have now reached the pinnacle of the church, in both senses! Pinnacles are such an iconic feature of churches, far more so than spires in my opinion, that they stand out from all angles and shout 'church' to the subconscious whenever you see them (Photo 318). These simple examples were filed up from odd remnants of plastic sprue – of which I have a box stuffed full with different shapes and sizes. Holes were drilled in both tower and pinnacles for short lengths of tinned copper wire, on which the latter were mounted. This is so that they may perhaps remain loosely attached when somebody's careless elbow knocks them loose – as sooner or later it inevitably will! To allow this, while the pinnacle end of the wire is secured with super-glue to ensure it is not lost, the other end is glued in place with a contact adhesive. We can always make another pinnacle if one is lost, but repairing in situ a broken corner of a plaster tower is a far more time-consuming task!

Photo 319 shows a much better view of the weather vane. This can now be seen to be a train; the fat end being obviously some kind of generic steam engine, the other its train of carriages tapering

Photo 319. The weathervane itself was filed up to represent the silhouette of a train in three-quarter view, with the engine prominent and the carriages trailing away to a point.

away into a pointer. One must forgive the blacksmith who fashioned it however, as he is obviously no train buff. The GWR, the original owning company of the nearby station, never had a loco like that as far as I recall … To aid its longevity – because there's always going to be some idiot who pokes it to see if it turns – the vane actually rotates in a short length of brass tube soldered to four brass wire supports, the whole being mounted in five holes drilled in the plaster.

The angled view in Photo 320 shows that the crenelations have now been dressed properly top and sides and the four pinnacles fitted. Note that their faces align with the buttresses, not with the sides of the tower; a subtle but important point! The width of each pinnacle at its base is the same as the stone it is mounted on but while those are rectangular, the pinnacles must, of course, be square in plan or they would look most odd.

THE PORCH

We now move swiftly on to that porch mentioned earlier (Photo 321), comprising a lead roof, timber sides and fancily-pierced planking which makes up a traceried fascia. The whole of the timberwork is mounted on dwarf walls surmounted by stone cappings. It is actually very easy to make from a variety of plasticard sheets, the most difficult bit being to

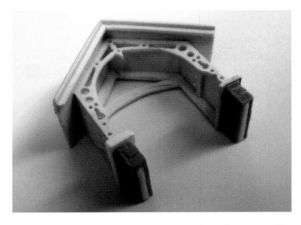

Photo 322. This was mounted on dwarf stone walls and given some fancy fretwork so it looks good in those inevitable photos of the bride and groom at the door. That's my excuse!

keep the fancy pierced work looking much the same on both sides of the arch. Seen from slightly beneath (Photo 322), it is obvious how the rear bracing is plain except for the curved horizontal strut at the back, shaped so as to help it to hide in the shadows. Ostensibly to help resist the whole thing falling apart should a freak wind get inside it, this bracing is actually there to provide a decent surface area when glueing it to the church wall, just as the width of the dwarf walls at the bottom offers an acceptable surface area there too.

READY TO PAINT

The overall impression we have created so far can be seen in the high-angle view (Photo 323), which represents the normal way of looking at 2mm scale model buildings – that is, from above! Before we move on to look at the completed model and its setting, I trust that from this photo alone you can see why I chose to add the detail I did because from up here, almost the only bits you can see which have *not* received some additional detailing are the roofs and you would naturally expect them to be nearly flat in this scale anyway. At this stage it is also worth looking up at it from a much lower angle too (Photo 324). From down here you can see that the porch and

Photo 321. A fair amount of time was spent putting some interesting detail into a plasticard 'timber' porch.

Photo 323. With the addition of a simple cross mounted on the top of the inner gable over the nave, I thought I'd probably gone far enough with the extra detailing.

Photo 324. A good study from a lower angle confirmed my original conception that the church was now ready to paint.

drip stones are doing the same job at this angle as the pinnacles, weather vane and drip stones do from above; that is, distracting the eye from the less realistic details by presenting interesting, iconic church features to look at instead.

THE LYCHGATE

I mentioned previously my desire for a lychgate at the church's main entrance from the car park (Photo 325). These iconic if odd structures (sometimes spelt without the 't' but outnumbered by those with one by around 90:1) were originally somewhere sheltered to stand the lytch, or corpse, while the procession preceded to enter the church. (I suspect, however, that they were mainly used as somewhere for 'his Lordship' to stand out of the rain while waiting for his guests to dismount from the following carriage!) This one is made from more plasticard sheet and no doubt all that needs to be said is to suggest you study the illustrations for technique and a nearby church for inspiration – just like I did! Anyone who's made the least attempt at real-life carpentry should be able to create a plausible structure, although one has to admit there are a lot of bits to fashion for what is a very small model. One point you will notice (Photo 326), is that the gates are brown whereas all the rest is white. This is because they come from a length of commercial picket fencing: with their tall hinge-posts and detached braces they would make a rather odd set of gates for the average house drive but they do work rather well as a pair of lychgates.

Photo 325.   I did want to add a traditional lychgate, however, and made one out of plasticard strip and a pair of commercial plastic gates.

Photo 326. The 'legs' were made long enough to 'plant' into the ground.

Photo 327. Pre-fitting it enabled me to decide to tile it rather than slate it, because the reds would be better visually than more greys.

Photo 328. Finally, with regard to the lychgate, this roof, as with the half-timbered house, is painted with warmer reds which helps balance the colder printed ones of the card kits and resin pre-painted buildings.

Photo 329. When painting the church, the first job is to get rid of all that white with a 'stone shadows' colour ...

RAILINGS AND FENCING

With the lychgate ready to roof and temporarily set in place (Photo 327), you may also care to consider the fencing which surrounds the churchyard. All of it comes from brass etchings; the main 'spear and rail' fencing around the site comes from a range of architectural etchings by Squires, whereas the 'cast-iron pattern' fencing which you will find alongside the paths is supposedly 'old' and provided by the church commissioners. That comes from an etched brass fret of fancy N-gauge fencing by 'Scalelink'. There are short lengths of several different types and small sections from the same fret appear both in the churchyard surrounding various very old graves, and anywhere else where on the model where a bit of 'fancy ironwork' wouldn't go amiss – the reasoning being that since we'd bought it, we might as well use it! Both types were still available at the time of writing.

Photo 328 is another overall view, this time showing particularly where the lychgate sits in relation to the church, but also allowing us to take a quick look at a groundwork modification. If you look back to the first photo (305), you will see I have since added a ply fillet to the church's base so that the path approaching the porch is nearer to the railway cutting. The

DRY BRUSH TECHNIQUE

'Dry brushing' is a technique in which a little colour is mixed on a palette and then allowed to partially dry before use. When the surface of the mixed paint stiffens, a clean dry brush is used to pick up just a little colour which is then worked back and forth on a scrap of paper until only streaks of paint are being transferred, at which point a few strokes are applied to the model; the process being adjusted and repeated as desired.

porch turned out to be deeper than expected and I considered pall-bearers in particular would need more space to turn and enter the church. It also provided more room for would-be wedding photographers and allowed extra space between the path and the church walls for yet more detailing.

The odd-shaped white item on the right of the photo is not a grave, by the way, it is that new door for the Vestry entrance mentioned earlier. The window and the brickwork beneath it were removed from that section of the casting and a new plasticard door and frame made to fit the hole. We will look more closely at the groundwork around the church soon, but by now you will no doubt be keen to know what the thing looks like painted!

PAINTING

Now comes the fun bit! The first thing to do is to choose a background colour which will represent the darkest depths of stonework, in shadows and damp corners. I prefer artist's acrylics and for this type of job swear by Rowney Series III, one of the flattest and most consistent acrylics I've ever used. It comes in several sizes, the biggest generally being the best investment, especially for black and white. I usually find it easier to start natural stone finishes with very dark colours and add successively lighter ones over the top, thus what you are looking at here (Photo 329) is what will effectively become the colour of the shadows.

Despite the prominence of this model right at the front of the layout you will note that I have not used black, which I find too strong for anything in 2mm scale except tunnel mouth interiors. (In fact, I very rarely use pure black in 4mm scale either.) Here I've used a slightly-blue dark brown. Paint all the white plasticard, any chipped bare plaster and any 'damp' places with this colour.

When dry and hard – you will need to leave it for a few hours – you can at last paint all the surface stone its final basic colour using a 'dry brush' technique (*see* panel), thus allowing the base colour to show through in holes, crevices and shadows. A medium brown was chosen for this job because the church would pre-

Photo 330.   ... then a warm brown and paler highlights create the effect seen here.

date the railway and the stone will have been brought by ox and cart from the nearest quarry bearing good quality stone, which may have been some miles away. This ecclesiastical insistence on good quality stone gives us the option to choose a 'distinctive' colour to help the model stand out from its surroundings slightly more than would otherwise be the case if it was completed in whatever the truly local stone happened to be. Of course colour is optional and in another situation I might indeed want to use the local stone colour, as with the GWR branch in the previous chapter. But that is where the art of artistry comes into play; the more you understand of what you are doing, the better the choices you make.

With the first coat applied, you can then add a goodly touch of white to that same basic colour and, while the base coat is still fresh, broadly dry brush all upper surfaces and edges where the sun would reflect highlights, or where rain might wash away dirt and algae, as you can see in Photo 330. When you reach the finer-detailed parts, such as the gargoyles, care should be taken to ensure you do not let the paint clog up your detail or much of your efforts will be wasted! (Photo 331)

Photo 331.   All the upper surfaces can then be further highlighted to suggest sunshine reflecting off the stone, bringing it to life.

Photo 332.   From even a short distance away, the stark contrast of the two colours is far less obvious, but the detail now just cries out to be noticed.

While that dries, the church slates can be painted a blue-tinged grey colour. The ridges tiles are segmented and so would be made of clay mouldings. They are therefore painted in a selection of warm orangey-reddy-brown colours and are presumably Victorian replacements for what may originally have been lead work. At least terracotta adds a splash of colour (Photo 332). The pale green and orange mosses on the slates were added much later when the church was almost ready to position, as were just-off-white droppings from pigeons – unless there are bats in your particular belfry, of course, in which case additional deposits may be required!

Note that although the coping stones on the nave gable beside the tower have not yet been highlighted, the shadows created by adding those individual pieces has already improved the quality of the model. The addition of further, more carefully painted highlights – this time of a slightly yellowed, even paler stone colour – really brings the stonework to life, as you can see in photo 333. It is applied to the gargoyles, pinnacles, dripstones and any upper stone surface deemed to be 'in sunlight', because the yellow tone is intended to show how the sun brings out 'the inner warmth of the stone'; however, do leave some of the previous light brown showing through so you are adding 'layers', not simply replacing the one colour with another. Call it what you will, it works, as you can see!

The plasticard porch was first painted in much same dark grey as the church base (Photo 334). I rarely use neat black on buildings but it can be of value in tiny interiors, as in the upper, rear-most corners here. The lychgate is more open and got the same dark grey all over, apart from the mounting spigots used to hold it by. The roof was formed from 10thou. plasticard sheet, scored into strips the width of a tile so as to 'separate' each one. The sheet was then cut into strips at 90 degrees to the scoring and overlapped layer upon layer, after which the tiles were painted in the now familiar warm terracotta colours (Photo 335).

Note that by adding red ridge tiles to the church and new sacristy, and a red tile roof to the lychgate, we are 'harmonizing' them with the red brick

Photo 333. To make it look warmer from further away, a coat of very nearly neat white was slightly yellowed, then carefully brushed on to the extreme edges of the tower's upper stonework with a few vestigial flecks added to the tops of the gables.

BELOW: *Photo 334. The porch was first given a basic 'shadow colour' undercoat.*

buildings in the background. The linking of colour between buildings helps to establish visual harmony between them, because it helps 'tie' the church in with the surrounding buildings by reflecting their main colours in a minor way, in small but prominent areas. This echoing of colours is a vital factor in 'artistic composition' – Constable used it shamelessly – because it helps turn a disparate collection of buildings into one, visually-unified community. Visual harmony is attractive to humans. That's why they used to put groups of pretty buildings on chocolate boxes, it made us buy them! You rarely see buildings on chocolate boxes today but you can still

Photo 335. *The lychgate was given 'creosote black' timbers and varied warm red tiles.*

Photo 337. *Dark colours highlight interesting shapes by creating dramatic contrasts.*

see the phenomenon at work on Christmas cards, where snow links the buildings.

The porch roof however, was quite deliberately painted grey lead to echo the house-roofs behind (Photo 336). This view shows not only the proto-typical detail of air holes in the planked sides (to allow the movement of air which helps prevent the wood from rotting when damp), but the roof of 'lead' dressed over rounded battens. These last are

formed simply by cutting rectangular strips of plas-ticard and then drawing the knife blade along two adjacent edges with the blade angled at some 100 degrees to the plastic, which draws away the edges. Repeated a few times this action rapidly produces neat, rounded corners: a technique which has many uses when trying to make scraps of plastic look like other materials! A slightly lighter browny-grey was then dry brushed onto the outer and upper surfaces, highlighting the detail and leaving the internal struc-ture dark, as if in 'deep shadow' (Photo 337).

GROUNDWORKS AND GRAVESTONES

While these various coats of paint are being allowed to dry, it is now time to turn from the church, which we will see in all its completed glory shortly, to the groundwork into which it is embedded. Starting with the wall behind the church, we see how it sup-ports the adjacent road (Photo 338). It is formed from a few off-cuts of a very poor quality, vacuum-formed, rectangular stone sheet by Squires but only because it saved wasting a better-quality product where it hardly showed! To be fair, by the time

Photo 336. *The supposedly lead-covered porch roof was given a slightly drybrushed coat of medium grey.*

Photo 338.   *The gravestones and grass-covered graves behind the church are simple, but you do need something there as people often look to check!*

Photo 339.   *The steps are a simple moulding from Squires.*

one has painted it, added greenery and a row of dishevelled head-stones, this quick 'impression' of what you would expect to find there is more than adequate for our purposes and after all, it can only be seen by people deliberately peering over the church's roof to see what's there, and satisfying that kind of curiosity is of course the only good reason for bothering with it in the first place.

The first of what became a considerable number of gravestones have been painted and fitted, along with a quick coat of glue and some grass scatter material. The fencing is etched, as previously noted, and has now been sprayed with matt black car paint. Where the clergy would need to get down to the vestry, a gate (Scalelink again), and some stairs have been added (Photo 339). The fine corner posts are just tinned copper wire with rings of the same soldered near the top but the more substantial hinge-post is brass tube, soldered to the fencing and held in place with a large pin through it and down into the foam base beneath. An 'iron' handrail was made from a length of tinned copper wire, the wooden steps are another Squires product – actually an architectural

moulding to 1:100th scale rather than the 1:150th or so we would prefer – but again, this is not particularly obvious and it passes muster perfectly happily: indeed, if I hadn't mentioned it, I doubt you'd have noticed the 33 per cent discrepancy, even though you can see it very clearly in this photo! It just goes to show that for the majority of a model landscape, 'scale' is probably less important than 'proportion' and if the depth of the tread is reasonable compared to the width, then the eye accepts it, whether the treads are a separated by a scale ten inches or

Photo 340.   *Commercial gravestone mouldings in plastic and castings in whitemetal were mixed with simple sheet plasticard shapes to increase variety and provide ample numbers without too much repetition. Colours, of course, just have to be grave.*

Photo 341. With some carefully chosen walling, a fair representation of a cobble path can be quickly effected. The trick is to shape the edges carefully.

an out-of-scale fifteen! The rock face around the tower is very simply done, too: just a smear of car body filler carved with very little detail – it just isn't needed!

Another row of grave stones stand in front of those stone cottages (Photo 340). Some come from a rather expensive packet of cast whitemetal examples, the rest being either from plain plastic card or two cheap but effective packets of moulded plastic shapes. Many of these last are cut roughly in half; not squarely, you'll note, but at a greater or lesser angle to represent the way very old headstones always seem to settle into the ground more at one end than at the other – although only heaven knows why, of course. The majority are in fact simple rectangles of 20, 30 and 40thou. plasticard, snapped from a rectangular matrix of lines, scored to roughly match the mouldings in size. That pack of cast whitemetal crosses and sarcophagi was used to ring the changes and add a little 'depth', as well as a few odd lumps of real stone – choice examples from the chippings in my front path – intended to represent headstones so old they probably pre-date the church! From memory, even in so small an area there are some 70-odd headstones but in either shape, size or colour they are all quite different; as individual, in fact, as the real thing!

There is one other point worth mentioning. Obviously a church yard dating from the middle ages (even if the church itself does not), will have existed

long before the railway was carved through its graveyard. When this happened, although old bones were often carted away with the earth as 'spoil', the headstones had, as previously noted, to be reinstated in the same ground. This is why once-larger churchyards beside railways or canals often had serried ranks of old, generally illegible headstones set in rows around the circumference. Here they are but a single row, but in at least one churchyard I have seen them standing four deep. Of course, these days old headstones are as likely to be laid flat as found upright – fear of prosecution being all too genuine these days – but I find the 'Health and Safety' argument over this quite contrary to the religious doctrine of accepting moral and physical responsibility for one's own actions. As far as I'm concerned, therefore, if God wants to Act by dropping a religious symbol on to the toe of somebody who, from His point of view may very well deserve it, who am I to argue? So I will have none of that nonsense on my models and some of my headstones may thus be found to be 'sublimely in decline': that is, angled and threatening to adopt the horizontal long before those final trumpets sound. In having them thus I am deiberately contrasting them with a modern 40 tonne truck easing past sarcophagi half a millennium old. It is precisely these very Ruskinian contrasts which give a model 'depth' and reality, as well as indicating something of the modeller's personal perceptions: at least, it does to the curious …

PATHS TO GLORY

At the opposite or choir end of the church is something completely new, the churchyard's main approach path. I wanted to suggest the use of well-worn small stone slabs, elongated cobbles really, and the type of Squires' stone walling seen in photo 341 seemed to fit the bill very well. Certainly some of the slabs are far too long for stones one would find in a path but I was convinced that would not matter; the 'impression' of stone, rounded with age and use, being all that was really important – a characteristic that this sheet offers in abundance.

I cut out a single piece to fit from the lychgate to both church doors. Then all that was necessary was to file each individual stone at the end of every row to a rounded shape, thus losing those plain-cut lines, one of which is so obvious on the upper edge of the lower curve, the only bit which here remains to be done. This is a simple job with a triangular Swiss file. Given an undercoat of dark grey/brown, like the church, and allowed to dry, it has now been laid in place and given a first coat of pale brown where people are most likely to walk (Photo 342). The colour will be 'tickled' to precisely the right shade later, once the greenery is in place. To the right, watered-down wood glue is being added before scatter is sprinkled around where the tree will be 'planted'.

To prevent anyone falling off the path, Scalelink do a delightful range of etched brass fencing; one N-gauge sheet containing that 'fancy' variety of etchings mentioned earlier, which are eminently suited to a location such as this (Photo 343). At least they'll draw attention away from that ghastly, over-blown, 'picture window' with its rather soft cartoon mullions, supposedly representing ecclesiastical masonry. They do actually look tolerable when viewed from an angle acute enough that the precise pattern is indecipherable, and we can prevent people seeing that

Photo 342. Again, a dark browny-grey provides the mould and fungi which tend to collect in the joints, while the oft-trodden bits begin with a much lighter colour to suggest wear. The wood glue is to secure some texture where I want to plant a tree.

angle by adding a tree — and of course every churchyard should have one of those, preferably a yew!

Note the simple edging to a bed of ballast above the burial on the right, while three of the stones of

Photo 343. The reason for the tree is this rather poor-looking window which has somewhat idiosynchratic 'tracery' of a strangely 'soft' character. It needs to be hidden, from this angle at least!

Photo 344. *The side windows are not exactly brilliant either, but if you can't hide them you can at least distract the eye with some fancy tomb-work.*

the large sarcophagus beyond it are simple rectangles of card, albeit one trimmed to a slight point at the top. Nevertheless they all look acceptably 'real' because of their lack of precise alignment, as if they had indeed been there for several hundred years, which is exactly the 'history' one is attempting to illustrate.

DEAD AND BURIED

The space created by moving the path further out from the church walls allows us to add this fancy 'tomb' with its own tiny wrought-iron fencing, more grass and more gravestones, the rather more nicely-proportioned stonework on these windows now becomes an asset rather than an annoyance (Photo 344). The knightly character carved in stone on the top is a plastic figure filed flat at the back, while another figure with a pair of added wings creates a bronze 'guardian angel' at his feet.

With the stonework on the lower porch now painted to match the walls, our path is supported by more Squires' embossed stonework, this time of

BELOW: **Photo 345.** *Increase the depth of any scene by adding layers of groundwork or fencing and by alternating structures with greenery.*

Photo 346.   Finally, break up any larger stretches with draped greenery hanging over the edges – just like the gardening books tell us.

the 'squared' type (Photo 345). A variety of clump foliage fills the odd gap left by the intrusion of the railway cutting into the church-yard – and it's all beginning to look quite good, really.

You can see how the introduction of the porch has gone a long way towards hiding the problem of the casting's rather too-small side entrance door. It's still far too small, of course, almost as if it were partly down a step, but the porch does an excellent job of disguising it and, despite mentioning it earlier, I suspect if I hadn't brought it to your attention again you wouldn't have noticed the discrepancy. Do you see how the two 'real' stone, heavily weathered, railing-protected old graves instantly distract you? This is precisely why they're there: the door is now in shade and these bright points distract the eye time and time again; you have to make a conscious effort to look at that church door now and even so, the eye wanders the moment your attention does ... one interesting solution to a difficult problem.

Moving for a moment to the nearer boundary wall, again completed using stone walling, but this time made by Wills. This is a 4mm-scale product but with the very largest stones divided into several smaller ones, it still makes excellent 2mm scale walling (Photo 346). The coping stones along the top are a feature I've mentioned before, being filed

up from 40thou. plasticard, but do note the strand of stretched tinned copper wire soldered to the upper edge of the fencing. Not only does this give it some much-needed relief, it also adds genuine strength which will help the very thin brass survive the odd sleeve caught on its spikes a lot better – and, positioned so close to the front edge, that event is merely a matter of when, not if!

Photo 347.   Just a chip of stone found wedged in my sole, but it had interesting shape and texture. Seen with a 'scale eye' and given an etched border and some grass, it becomes an ancient headstone.

Photo 348. Most model graveyards are too neat and too empty. Ensure that yours is well populated – the residents won't complain, for sure.

The bottom edge is soldered to short L-shaped lengths of tinned-copper wire every four inches or so. These are let into holes drilled into the filed-edge plasticard coping stones which top the wall. Should an elbow snag and catch the fence they will, with luck, just lift out without being bent and damaged.

Note also how several lengths of well-teased-out foliage mat are used to drape over the wall before the fence is added. Breaking up the otherwise long hard edge of this tall, very solid wall with foliage is vital if it is not to dominate the scene; with so much stonework in evidence, a bit of nature's softening caress really helps, just as it does in a garden.

Returning to the church yard proper (Photo 347), this tiny 'ancient grave' was quickly created from a corner of left-over etching, a selection of scatter materials and a bit of natural stone I found in my shoe one day. Any local Lord or Lady worth their salt would have been buried inside the church, assuming they could afford it, so it is difficult to say precisely who is buried here. It must be somebody important, of course, to be so close to the church and

surrounded by fancy wrought ironwork: perhaps a local man who made the exalted rank of bishop or the like a few hundred years ago. We'll never know now, unless we ask a local, for the dedication on the headstone has long since worn away …

This might be pure fantasy but the point is, if you dream up such ideas in your model community you will find ways of expressing them in the model, as here. It all adds character, interest, gravitas and a sense of history to a model, a sense of 'past lives' leaving their echo in the present. Here you can see that the churchyard boundary is now entirely lined with old headstones, with further rows descending in serried ranks (Photo 348).

PRAISE THE LORD

With the groundwork complete we can now see the results of our 'upgrade' to this 'fine old Norman church' which, I think you will agree, has been well worth the effort (Photo 349).

Once all the pathways, steps, walling and copings are done and dry, and once the church is securely

Photo 349.   The finished church. See how the highlit verticals draw the eye, as does that chip of bright stone. Even the porch roof distracts the eye from the windows when seen from up here. Job done, I reckon.

stuck down (using two large dollops from a hot glue gun), the final greenery can be added. This consists of various scatters: mainly fine green foam for the grass and a variety of tufts, clumps and heaven-knows-what for the unkempt areas. I tend to just open a few packets of likely-looking textures and colours and throw them free-hand onto deeply

wood-glued areas, starting with the largest pieces and working down size-wise: what sticks, stays; what doesn't gets hoovered off. I never know quite what it is going to look like until the glue is dry and the loose bits are hoovered away but it's usually fine! If not, I just pick a 'better' colour/texture for any 'missed bits' or sections I don't like and glue that

Photo 350. Roofs, especially old ones, tend to attract lichens and mosses. A little careful drybrushing with brilliant greens and oranges reproduces the most common types, while the odd speck of white will not need any explanation ...

BELOW: *Photo 351.* From lower down those windows are slightly more obvious but at least they are vaguely ecclesiastical, while that stone chip battling with the dark depths of the porch and the pinnacled and gargoyled outline of the tower compete to attract the eye away.

Photo 352.   Seen from here the tree – a commercial product – both neatly separates the church from the row of cottages behind and adds some nice, natural colour and foliage to prevent the view becoming too 'urban'.

over what's already there. Alternatively, use the cheapest, nastiest, smelliest hairspray you can find because it's usually the stickiest and therefore ideal for our purposes. The smell's a bit unpleasant for a few minutes but it soon disappears. Can confuse the wife, though, so do 'show her how you do the green bits' the first time you use it. Saves that 'thoughtful look' which closely follows the wrinkled nose when she comes home with the shopping …

The close-up of the nave roof shows how the new plastic drip stones and cross on the gable apex look when painted and weathered (Photo 350). Bright lichens not only soften the rather cold blue-grey of Welsh Slate (none of your Spanish slate when this was last re-roofed), but help bring out the relief of the slates, too. Adding a few pigeon droppings is fine but don't over-do it; this is not Trafalgar Square!

Note, too, how the touch of blue in the church's slate colour makes the roof slightly more intense than that of the printed slates on the terraced

housing to the right and the plain grey wash over the resin 'Lyddle End' row on the left. This is another example of 'scale colour', where the intensity helps position the model correctly in its surroundings. The cross is so placed to be overlooked by the manor house behind, at once reminding the local 'lord and master' not only that he had spiritual as well as pastoral duties to perform, but that there was a higher authority to which he, too, had to answer one day. I wonder if it helped?

The side-on view in photo 351 shows how effective all this extra work has been in 'lifting' the model to a new level. Standing back a little, as it were, the three-quarter view in Photo 352 shows how churchyards tend to cope with ground on a substantial slope: they make terraces. It also shows the effectiveness of all that wrought iron fencing rather better, too. There are four types, all etched brass and all 'mounted' on those tinned copper wire 'legs' soldered to the bottom edge. These are very tall

Photo 353. The same tree also usefully separates the 'olde worlde ecclesiastical' of the church from the 'post-2000 era' car park. Only a hint of the lychgate peeps around it but partially hiding something simply makes you want to look at it more closely …

Photo 354. ... and when you do, it becomes obvious what it is, while the new vestry stops the eye wandering into the distance and highlights the row of gravestones.

'L' shapes, the short arm of the L being soldered to the etch, the other being left long enough to use as a handle when spraying. A simple matt black car paint is ideal; you can always weather it down with a subtle 'drift' of red-oxide undercoat if you want to make it rusty but I am assuming the parishioners have been round with the paint brush. I used pure black for two reasons: such railings are often painted black in reality but moreover these are very short models (some of them just 6mm high), and being very fine they would be quite invisible if they were not painted in a stark colour. I averred that I never use plain black even in 4mm, never mind 2mm scale but I lied. I do. This is the exception which proves the rule and you have to admit, even seen as closely as in photo 344 it does not look at all wrong,

does it? Despite the colour, from a couple of feet away they still almost vanish, so do look at your details carefully from several different distances: do they all fit in place as they should? If not, it's probably the colour that's wrong so experiment – that's half the fun!

After all that work the lychgate is perhaps rather hidden behind the tree (Photo 353), but you can see how that odd triangular corner left over has been turned into a small car park. The lychgate still looks excellent from the right angle, as in the view in photo 354 which shows it from a position in which the gates are more obvious. Yes, those tiles are over-scale in thickness but strangely, from a distance of only a foot or two, they look perfect whereas tiles the correct scale thickness would

Photo 355. That large end window, whose tracery looked so odd from square on, looks fine from this angle and is exactly what you would expect to see on the end of a church – so that's another problem area dealt with.'

BELOW: Photo 356. From the visitor's perspective, the church's unique and original angle – it faces due East, of course, as it has done for hundreds of years – becomes more obvious, so adding a further sense of history by illustrating that it was built before housing re-defined the shape of the road.

look too flat. Strange, certainly, but exaggerated relief is sometimes a necessary ploy in modelling!

This view also shows the main village street as seen from above the control panel – if you lean forwards far enough! The bright red lorry is there largely to prevent the eye 'escaping' into the wallpaper behind it. It does so because who could look at that view and not wonder whether the truck was going to squeeze past the car or not? This brings the eye down to the road to judge the gap and then the light-coloured pavement draws the eye forward again: it's called 'composition'.

Note how the large size of the tree is perfectly acceptable from this angle. Seen from the front in photo 355 you can see how the gap between it and the church allows the eye to lead you right through to the manor house and yet its bulk really helps

balance the scene when looked at from outside the layout where, with the curving row of cottages, it forms a natural, soft backdrop to the drama of all those pinnacles and castellations (Photo 356). Seen from rail-level however (Photo 357), the same church fades quietly into the background, its mid brown colour allowing vivid greens to dominate the foreground. That 'green way' along the disused railway line looks to be an inviting walk …

Finally, photo 357 is a view which shows the whole of the 'old village' part of the townscape, proving that although the church is now the desired focal point, it is the wood behind which dominates the scene, not the buildings, in the same way as nature predominates in the real Wye valley. To complete our 'old village centre' story, those other buildings to the right of the church are dealt with in the next chapter.

Photo 357. *Standing back from the panel to take an overview, the church and village settle back nicely under the sylvan background, and even if no trains move to distract the eye, that brilliant yellow cement lorry draws you back to the railway, just as it should do.*

CHAPTER FIVE

CONVERTING KITS AND COMMERCIAL RTP MODELS

You will appreciate by now that I am perfectly happy to use commercially finished 'Ready-To-Plant' buildings more or less straight from the box if they are right for the job. True, these models have a short shelf life so there has to be something appropriate available at the time you want it but, better still, if there's something which with a few minutes' work can be converted into something more individual then I will opt for that. Major conversion work is rarely worth doing but sometimes the exception comes along which proves the rule, as I have just illustrated with that church! But, familiarity being a counter to reality, it will come as no surprise to learn that if I can produce a slightly different model by 'tweaking' a common commercial item, then I will. Using something ready-made as a basis for a different building is really just a sensible way of saving some time on basic construction.

But why, you may ask, would you want to convert a perfectly good finished model into something else? It's called history. Sometimes you find you need a particular type of building to suggest you have modelled a particular area and yet are unable to find anything suitable 'off the shelf'. If so, you will either have to build an example yourself from scratch or, if you can, take the easy path and convert it from something else. This chapter is all about the latter option: conversions.

MODELLING HISTORY

PRETTY AS A PICURE – AND A DISUSED STATION

I deliberately begin this chapter with a classic 'chocolate box' image of a pretty cottage model in a sylvan setting; after all, everyone has plenty of old choco-

Photo 358. A well-placed cottage in a sylvan setting can both define your landscape and create interest; interest suddenly diverted by the movement of a passing train.

late boxes, jigsaws and biscuit tins around the house for inspiration! This particular example began life as a simple cast plaster garage; another of the 20-year-old models from the original layout 'Westbury' but a repaint, some chimneys and a fine new bay window covering the old garage doors made for a cheap but very pretty building to both fill a corner and help explain the setting (Photo 359).

Creating the half-timbered walls was just a case of studying the arrangement of a few suitable images and painting in the timbers with a very dark grey. The chimneys were simple embossed brick plasticard fabrications snuggled well down into the tiles. The bay-window roof was precisely similar to that of the lychgate only with hips, while the window itself was an assembly of black and white plasticard sheet over 4mm etched brass diamond fencing which, sprayed dark grey, passed muster nicely as leaded lights. The only 'fancy' idea was to file a small rectangle of 6mm black ABS sheet into a bold ogee shape on one edge and then saw it into strips to create the series of deeply-carved,

ogee-shaped dentilated timbers along the top. This gave it the necessary 'weight'.

But creating 'reality' in a model railway involves a bit more than just going for the obviously pretty. I have mentioned the use of 'themes' before and to persue Wye Notte's general one of the chang-

TOP: **Photo 359   The half-timbered cottage is absolutely typical of the rural West Midlands – yet you can't buy one anything like it. I find that surprising for such an attractive and common type of building, especially one reproduced across the land in almost infinite variety.**

RIGHT: **Photo 360   The ugly also has its place on a model railway, especially the nostalgia aroused by creating a derelict or disused building.**

ing face of the landscape over time, a little bit of Ruskin's 'sublime decrepitude' was very much what was wanted to offset the 'pretty-pretty' image of two black and white half-timbered buildings: the cottage and the manor house. Just over a low hill from that cottage, this semi-derelict disused station is therefore an important part of creating balance in the model (Photo 360).

This started life as one of the very first cheap, cast-plaster models you could buy. Sold as 'N-gauge', the brickwork was formed from 00-scale sheet, the windows were badly done and the grey-washed slates were as thick as your fist! But despite its faults I felt it could still make a fine an old abandoned station since the overall shape was good and it had stone quoins on the corners to add interest.

Ignoring the over-scale brickwork, I hid the offending windows behind plasticard 'plywood' sheeting and added a simple, if somewhat damaged, canopy to the front using plastic canopy edging mouldings and more plastic sheet. I then tidied up the chimneys, repainted it completely and added a few hints of old noticeboards. Sorted! The stone walls along the back of the platform are commercial resin castings and all I had to do then was to add a section of partially-removed paviours under the canopy and model the 'cut-back platform edge' so common these days.

Returning for a moment to Ruskin: one of his theories, put into less flowery language, proposes that 'total dereliction cannot, by definition, be "sublime"', whereas something rapidly approaching ruin, but still serviceable, can be. Thus, according to Ruskin, what

Photo 361. When modelling modernity, it often helps to design in, right from conception, some long-gone junctions and other historic but disused features. Redundant routes or bridge structures are an excellent means of both providing history and opening up interesting views.

at first looks like an attractive but unremarkable near ruin can, in fact, prove worthy of a little study for it should tell us something if we only look at it with a little understanding. So it is with this building. Its presence unmistakeably defines a station which once was but is no longer: a victim, like so many stations on still-open lines, of a determination to speed up the trains by limiting their number of stops. The railway may still exist and still carry passengers but purely local travel is now discouraged to save the seats for longer-distance travellers because they will pay more for that same seat. So things have changed, changed again and are still changing.

This physical depiction of change in progress is *the* recurring theme on Wye Notte. There are the obvious examples: the disused railway buildings, bridges over long-lifted railway lines and tunnels once full of smoke now used as public footpaths. There are more subtle remains: bridge abutments now missing their bridge and an embankment cut off abruptly short (the remainder bulldozed for a new housing estate); and the minimalist, disused iron and stone features in old railway walling and access paths now leading nowhere, these last suggestive of lost structures or lost purposes (Photo 361).

The point being made, for those who have the wit to notice, is that nothing new is made without being built on its past. Railways are a fine example of that, for even our newest lines are built to a gauge used by Stephenson's Rocket and to clearances which Brunel would have considered miserly – but such is progress! It is with this theme in mind that one can begin to understand why I wanted to cover a wide range of time periods in the buildings I chose to model and yet in doing so, attempt to create an entirely believable and realistic 'as-it-is-today' townscape to enhance the purely 21st century model trains.

MORE 'OLD VILLAGE'

Our 'old village' part of the townscape really is just one small part of that same intention, albeit a fascinating and fun one to reproduce, which is why it is in such a prominent position: a lot of work goes into making such a scene and one wants to put that time and effort where it can be best seen and appreciated, right under the visitor's nose! To complete this 'conversions' chapter therefore, we will now look at how we can believably travel from a 15th century half-timbered manor house to a 21st-century concrete office block in less than two feet!

The first requirement of the site was to visually link the road overbridge (the one with the red articulated truck on it), to the station underpass some three feet or so away. A direct road would have given too steep a slope, besides which I also wanted to separate what was to become the 'old village' from what was to become the 'High Street' by visual as well as spatial means. By not having the two roads actually connected, that is by merely inferring a connection somewhere just off the baseboard edge, I could get round both problems so this provided my starting point for the entire scene.

THE CHAPEL

It was while setting out an approximation for the industrial units of the proposed 'business park' on the other side of the High Street that I wondered if these two chapel castings shown in Photo 362 might make an old 'meeting house'. Simply mated as shown, the result would be too long but I thought it might work if shortened, and then the thought occurred that I might use the door end off one model for my church upgrade. Although I replaced this building in that location with something else, if I pinched a large chunk of one model for the church, could I still re-use the remainder to advantage? Well of course it all got used, as you have already seen, ending up next to our manor house (Photo 363). The roof joint is sadly less than perfect but, despite being blatantly obvious here, it is actually far less so in the flesh while on the other, more commonly-seen side, the roof joint is merely a 'shake' in the straight line of the slates – caused by a dodgy rafter no doubt!

The war memorial is a whitemetal kit with extra stonework behind it and two extra bottom levels added to its base, so creating an interesting corner out of space which was otherwise difficult to find a use for (Photo 364). The grey-haired lady is pre-

Photo 362.   With a collection of suitable buildings to hand, there really is nothing like laying them out on the actual site to see what they look like. Move them around until the scene 'feels' right, and if a particular building doesn't suit, find another one! This pair of chapels was 'wrong' singly and 'wrong' together, but there was a third answer ...

Photo 363.   By taking the end window off one and adding it to the full length of the other, a nicely balanced building resulted, even if it did 'move' half a mile up the road!

Photo 364.   Every British village worthy of its name has a Great War memorial: here's ours.

sumably a Granny, perhaps with a family name on the obelisk, but any sadness is instantly removed because she's waving to a young child, probably held by her daughter, so what might have been a maudlin scene – the representation of dead ground in two senses – has been changed into one of a cheery nature just by adding three suitable figures carefully positioned.

You might also, bearing in mind the thematic sense of applying layers of 'history' to the model, note the faded but still recognizable 'Spratt's Dog Biscuits' advert adorning the end wall of the adjacent house; just as it does to this day on an end-of-terrace wall in Yeovil from where I copied the idea! It was applied with a well-worn but useable No.2 sable and some nearly-dry acrylics.

THE MANOR HOUSE

How the mighty have fallen! A wonderful, possibly 15th century half-timbered manor house survives a few yards off the old road, the frontage carefully placed facing a view which would have been magnificent before the railway arrived! (Photo 365) Again this is a very old plaster casting (bought at least 20 years ago) which, other than the original windows, has been completely repainted with an off-white and a 'warm' black, along with some very 'warm' tile colours, but ones which set off the starkness

of plain black-and-white walls very well. It is shown in Photo 366 partly done, with the model's original too-creamy white and anaemic-brown colouring on the right-hand gable for comparison.

Incidentally, this also neatly illustrates my point about 'colour depth' bringing a model forwards or sending it backwards. The originally grey-washed roof has had a 'wash and splodge-up' to try out the tones. Fair, but as the reds around it turned out to be equally dull these tiles were later brightened up a fair bit to increase interest.

THE 'OFF LICENCE' GROUP

Next come three modern resin models, all current when this scene was built in 2008. Firstly, one left and one right-handed cottage (Photo 367), intended to be joined as pair or row, then a corner shop model which had then been recently re-released as an off-license. Note the subtle change I made to the colour of one of the cottages' roofs, suggesting the slates had been replaced at different dates and thus both explaining the slight line where the tiles meet and expressing the individual ownership of the two properties, despite their matching features.

Although these are completely new, modern releases the windows are obviously far too heavy in section, despite being etched brass, which is a

Photo 365. The only alterations made to this side of this model were to repaint its walls and roofs.

Photo 366. Here the right-hand gable is in the original colours, but the roof's first colour looks too dull and too stark, especially compared with the final finish offered in the previous photo. It is surprising how a lick of paint can 'cheer up' an old, bland model.

shame since the doors and porches are excellently produced. Sadly, one just has to put up with these things sometimes.

Another problem was that although these models are sold with the idea of combining numbers of them into a terraced row, they are cast in a very hard resin and it took quite a lot of machine sanding of the ends to get them to fit even tolerably well. It was not a procedure I want to repeat too often; not least because the resin dust is probably carcinogenic! Fortunately the joint of the outer wall against the shop moulding was a lot easier to get to fit as the roof line was slightly different and could therefore overlap.

As to selecting this particular version of a model sold in several guises, I felt that an off-licence – colloquially known as an 'offy' – would be an interesting choice as they are another 'vanishing trade' these days having been decimated – indeed, all but eliminated – by the supermarkets (Photo 368). To make a bit more of it, two actual window displays were photographed in a real off-licence (the last 'offy' in Telford, as it happens), then reduced and printed to fit behind the model's windows. Both are illuminated at night using 'surface mount' down-lighters glued

to a 'ceiling' which prevent light escaping into the bedrooms above.

To my mind these Hornby and Bachmann brick reds are a bit too brilliant or fierce to be 'proper' brick colours, especially in 1:148th scale. Victorian or older bricks are usually much warmer – and often

Photo 367. This pair of Hornby cottages are nice enough but they are difficult to join into a terrace with both themselves and the corner shop from the same stable.

Photo 368. Hornby's off-licence is a nice enough model but it cried out for a bit of detailing in the shop windows. Having produced that I decided to light it too, to add interest to the night scene; but that's for another chapter!

browner – in tone against modern standard bricks which latter tend to come in particular colours and these days, as often as not, have carefully falsified 'mixed' colour faces all represented on the same brick! I have therefore 'tickled' these buildings by adding a warm, tan-coloured 'mortar' colour wiped in here and there to tone the brightness down a bit, although I still find them too stark. Perhaps it is because these models are made in China where the colour red has an entirely different history and meaning. Never mind; the printed brick red of the cottages across the street is not a lot better – and just as uniform – but, considering these model's minute size in the overall scheme of things, I can put up with it and balance them by painting much warmer reds on adjacent roofs. So I accept it and use it – but I don't have to like it!

Before we move onto describing the obviously-Victorian terraced housing which rambles down the rest of the street, we must take a final glimpse down the cul-de-sac (Photo 369). By making the roof colours of one building reflect those of the buildings around it you add cohesion to the group. If you want to create the impression that a building has long been part of the local community, it will be strongly enhanced by placing it very close to, and having its roofs line up with, the adjacent properties. The old manorial family probably sold their whole estate to the railway company when it came through in the 19th century and their house probably became a pub/hotel a hundred years and more ago. But no pub-sign, no beer adverts, no nameboard or land-lord's name above the door all indicate that it's been sold off privately. Sadly, this is a typical fate for so many pubs these days. Calling 'time!' on this one reflected the age and also spared me the trouble of adding lots of signs and advertisements.

The grey box under the eaves, incidentally, is a spare surface-mount light emitting diode portraying a 'floodlight'. It creates a lovely bright little corner in the night scene, highlighting the etched brass 'carved wood' band added between the floors. Compared to the earlier part-painted photo, you can also see how a lighter warm-red wash has really tied those various base reds together into a single, believable roof.

CHURCHILL TERRACE

Having now dealt with the variously-cast buildings which make up the entire group in the foreground of this photo (370), the next important area is the curved terrace of cardboard-kit built housing in the middle distance. Why is it important? Because it forms the main link between the road by which the red truck has just crossed over the railway and

Photo 369.   By carefully mixing printed, pre-painted and re-painted colours, resin, plaster and cardboard buildings can be made to sit harmoniously as a 'group', as this side street shows.

'HISTORY BEGINS TODAY'

Reflecting trends which are current when the model is built is, of course, yet another way of adding history to it because as a friend of mine says, 'History begins today'. When I built this model's predecessor 'Westbury' I had Jean Hunt, that late arboreal mistress of scenery's sylvan side, make me four specimen 'dead elms' because they were so very much a feature of the early 1980s. Unfortunately we still forget just how much of what we take for granted today will be gone tomorrow; who now remembers how different so many pastoral scenes once looked when they were framed by huge, magnificently-proportioned elm trees, now long dead and gone? In similar vein, in 25 year's time, will anyone remember the days when people 'popped down the offy for a packet of 20 and a bottle 'o beer'? Perhaps if you model one, in a generation's time your grandchildren might look at your model railway and ask, 'What was an off-licence, Grandad'?

the much lower 'High Street' which crosses under the railway in the background, as indicated by the blue bridge girders. It also represents the coming of the 'railway age' to a tiny village community: a time when terraces of small, two-up, two-down houses replaced rambling thatched cottages with gardens; a process which, less the thatched element, continues to this day. The group also form a specific link between the 15th century manor house and the post-2000 shops at their far end.

Here we see the terrace from the operator's perspective where it looks its most effective (Photo 371). These are simple card kits which come in 'pair' and 'single' formats. My customer had already made two 'pairs' and a whole row of 'singles' ready for me to use – but, as you'll have gathered by now, I rarely use things 'as they come' because, like any modeller

Photo 370. The cheek-by-jowl nature of the typical 'nucleated village' is well represented in this 'old town' part of the model, although concrete modernity is its immediate backdrop.

Photo 371. When you build a terrace on a hill, using kits is a very easy way to quickly build the multiples of individual properties needed. They need to be individual so you can fit one to another around a curve and down the variable slope of the landform.

RIGHT: *Photo 372. The entire 'village' area seen from the operator's viewpoint.*

BELOW: *Photo 373. This low-angle view with its interesting roof-line shows just how effective a curved, sloping row can be. Undulating curves are always a dynamic art form, sweeping the eye up the road and into the scene.*

worth his salt, I want my town to look different to everybody else's.

Faced with the particular problem of how to visually link two quite disparate road levels within half a metre or so of each other, how was I to do so without introducing unbelievable road gradients? This curved, gently descending terrace was the answer. Standing back a bit with the camera and looking down you can see how the curve of

the old road coming down the hill will meet with an imaginary continuation of the alignment of the High Street if both are projected into the operator's area (Photo 372). This, allied to careful management of the gradient, immediately infers in viewer's minds the conviction that the two roads will meet just 'off scene' and thus the believability or 'integrity' of the town is assured, even though they never really get anywhere near each other. This proves that if the mind's eye can be led to visualise how it all fits together, then the 'illusion of reality' can be maintained, even without actually modelling it.

The two pairs of cottages mentioned are to be found at the top of the slope at right-angles to each other; the upper pair in the cul-de-sac, sitting on their own dwarf stone walls, and the lower pair facing the street. Obviously as the slope increases (deliberately so, of course), pairs have to become individual houses to accommodate the increasing variety of levels (Photo 373). This is easily achieved by glueing each house to its mate at the appropriate height. Keeping the doorsteps at pavement level is relatively simple by arranging them all as 'left-hand' houses, that is with the doors at the higher end, but the slope then caused a gap under the ground floor windows of each

Photo 374. Adding some indeterminate 'wild weeds' and grass to the verge helps soften the railway retaining wall. The 'mended' road surface duplicates the flow of the pavement, restoring 'restfulness' to the dynamic curve.

cottage. To cope with the curving road, however, a small slice had to be trimmed off the front of each cottage to produce the slight angle required and this involved carving the left-hand end wall off each cottage. (At this point I took the opportunity to fit 'lighting tubes', false floors and room dividers; these last to prevent anyone looking straight through from one side to the other – often a problem with build-ings which are supposed to have internal walls!) I was therefore able to 'rescue' enough spare brickwork to 'fill in' under all the windows. There was ample left over for the new, longer garden walls imposed by said curvature, which also increased the width of each plot at the rear.

Viewed from up here (Photo 374) the slightly curving alignment through each cottage is obvious as is the variation between chimneys, very few of which would serve 'working' fireplaces in these days of automated central heating. See, too, how the width of the already-narrow road would have been intolerably constricted had the retaining wall and tunnel mouth continued at their true alignment. Not wanting to move the cottages backwards, this puzzled me for a while until I remembered the 'squinch': an accepted architectural form which allows one to bridge an internal corner with an arch, as shown here (Photo 375). It was invented in pre-Roman times to support round domes built over square rooms. If this one looks vaguely familiar, it is, because having already created master, mould and castings for two single-track tunnel mouths, I merely grabbed another casting and used it here. This saved resorting to the only other option, that of having to move the tunnel mouth another couple of inches to the left which, as you can see in the next photo (376), would have made the painted edge of the baseboard a lot more obvious. The height of the ground here is necessary, incidentally, because below it are the printed circuit boards and sensors which provide the train indicators for this end of some hidden storage sidings.

RIGHT: **Photo 375.** *If you look hard enough, there's usually a prototypical 'form' which can help solve a space problem – as here, a very particular arch called a 'squinch'.*

BELOW: **Photo 376.** *Without modelling the cutting and tunnel mouth, from this angle there would have been more baseboard edge than model – a common problem with the smaller scales.*

Photo 377. To look effective, tunnel mouths should be properly 'dark', whether in railway use or not!

VERTICAL PLANNING

One of the joys of a layout with a continuous circuit is that now and again you can just sit down and watch the trains roll round. By sitting on a low stool, as opposed to a high one, on *Wye Notte* there are several places where the trains are at about eye level and so look more realistic, partly because you are closer to them but also because the viewing angle replicates that of seeing real trains. With high parts of the layout, such as our 'village on a hill', any excuse to replace the bland, painted baseboard edge needed by the landform with something scenic which can add to the overall effect is to be heartily embraced! Look at photo 376 and imagine the view without the cutting wall relieving the baseboard edge. There would be more wood than model!

To prevent a huge expanse of painted wood spoiling this view, a long-closed railway is supposed to have once forged its way through the hill. Now cleaned up and re-opened (it was either that or fill it with discarded junk), the track-bed today provides

what one imagines to be a public footpath through a deeply-walled cutting. The alignment to the operator's left follows that of track properly drawn up (but never actually laid) so as to believably approach what was once a supposed junction with the still-used lower main line.

Where this cutting leaves the baseboard edge is therefore already established by this alignment but the section to the right (where the line climbs to reach what was once a goods yard and exchange sidings), was always going to look its best if the tunnel mouth could be placed as close to the edge of the control panel as possible, thus removing every possible inch of plain baseboard edge. A 20-year growth of trees (about forty feet or 80mm in 'N'), helps to break up the equally large expanse of wall while the large tree in the churchyard and the greenery trailing over the top edge both help to soften the hard but interesting surface of the masonry which is itself enlivened by the architectural features. So with care this scene can work from very close up, from further away, and from several angles. It was adding the squinch which allowed me to achieve that.

When ambling idly around old buildings, observing and mentally noting obscure architectural features might seem a strange way to pass the time but an

Photo 378. People often peer around the back of models out of curiosity, so where they physically can do so, give them something to look at.

inquisitive mind is bound to wonder how apparently-hanging architectural loads are supported. Such curiosity, followed by a little research to find out what some particular feature is called and how it is used, can sometimes be repaid by the chance of using that particular form in a model: which just goes to prove that close observation of even the more esoteric aspects of real life is rarely wasted! The squinch's general form was quite deliberately mirrored in the tunnel mouth below it, another example of using 'dualism', while the repeated pattern of the cottages is also restive (Photo 377).

BACK YARD FUN

Whereas the front of a terrace of simple brick cottages is always going to look repetitive – all the more so if one only uses the windows supplied with the kits – then it is round the back that one can, and should, provide those individual details that turn a bland, boring row of house-backs into individual homes lived in by people with different characters. That is precisely what happens in real life, of course, for while there is little an owner can do with the

Photo 380.   I'm not sure I would choose yellow guttering with a blue door, but some people would!

front of a house if it's listed (and these look as if they might be), round the back almost anything seems possible! The owner of No.9, the first house, for instance (Photo 378), appears to have both a log burner and a job in the timber trade; either that or he knows someone who can deliver unwanted off-cuts because that's what he collects in his back yard. His neighbour in No.8 obviously has the plumber in fitting new central heating because the old water tanks, piping and fittings are all lying around in the back yard, waiting for the non-ferrous metal dealer (Photo 379). There's even the packaging for a new boiler lying in a corner, so one can almost hear through a window the sound of a blow-torch soldering up joints ...

Such simple work is easy enough but a bit more complex is next door, a home obviously established much longer, with its single-storey kitchen extension in the same style as the original house, complete with floral patio. By looking at the yard before the railings were added we can see a bit more of how it was done (Photo 380). As it happened, I had a spare house which had been somewhat squashed but was

Photo 379.   A heap of timber for firewood, some old plumbing fittings awaiting scrapping or a garden full of patio pots – or all three. The choice is yours, of course.

TOP LEFT: *Photo 381. A 2mm-scale cat is a very small item, so give it some striking fur if you want it to be noticed. Here it is in black and white.*

TOP RIGHT: *Photo 382. Most Victorian yards would have had high, claustrophobic brick walls but these days people often open up their yard to gain the view, so why not model some of each?*

not required anyway, so it was a handy source of bits for several extensions including this one! Road, yard and path surfaces are achieved with spreads of car body filler because it sets quickly, lasts well and is easy to work, accepting carving and scoring perfectly well when dry and hard, so carving in a few paving slabs takes but seconds. Also to hand were some 'clump foliage, green, small' and some 'flower heads, foam, various' which were immediately put to good use. 'Milliput' two-part epoxy putty, once mixed, can be formed in seconds into round, tapered forms which can then be sliced off as flower pots. Slice a larger one down the middle and you have two wall-mounted plant-holders! A shape spotted in a bit of plastic packaging made a nice roll-top bath and there you are: several easy ways to create a cheery, colourful floral patio.

One little detail which I couldn't resist was a knocked over, broken pot with its plant and soil spilled over the flagstones and the culprit, a black and white 'moggie', standing on the neighbour's wall above. Pest! (A few bits of wire and a blob or two of solder gave a vague shape, a few dabs of black and

white paint, especially highlighting the pointed ears and tail, and those blobs become recognizable as a cat, even though it's only about 5mm long from nose to tail! (Photo 381)

The next two gardens are similar but No.6 has small beds with tall plants and retains the original

Photo 383. And instead of making all the kits precisely as per the instructions, why not add the occasional modern extension, as here: a two-storey one with its flat roof.

Photo 385.   I have no idea why this station fencing was moulded in red but it makes great modern 'trellis'.

Photo 384.   Normally the extension is hidden from view, so painting it white not only prevented having to match the existing bricks but made it more visible at a glance. Note the simple plumbing details thrown together from a few offcuts of tube and wire.

brick wall and outside toilet, now probably just used as a shed, while No.5's owners have removed their outside loo and replaced the brick wall with traditional slat fencing: less private but creating a much lighter and airier space to look out upon. No.4 has decided to completely replace their extension by building a new, longer kitchen and adding a third bedroom above it (Photo 383). With such a large

MAKING FENCING

This area uses '12mm Post and Rail fencing' from Squires and is finished in both traditional black and modern grey colours in different locations (Photo 382; *see also* photo 392). To make long sections, the end vertical strakes of two adjoining pieces are cut off and the remaining horizontals bent slightly and soldered together one over the other so that a continuous strip is formed. As previously (see p145), the entire strip is then given 'L'-shaped tinned copper wire 'legs', the short base of the 'L' being soldered along the bottom horizontal stretcher – clearly visible in the photo – so as to provide both a strong joint and visual subtlety. Any necessary bracing should be added before the entire strip is removed from the layout, sprayed and put to one side. It should be about the last thing you fit in place.

Such fencing is probably best not glued down, because if it should be knocked out by a misplaced elbow it can be carefully replaced, rather than fixing it so firmly that it gets bent or mangled. Particularly vulnerable sections should be left separate from longer, more protected pieces (less to replace should the worst happen), while fencing so positioned that it is almost bound to be damaged is normally best protected by clear plastic protective screens.

Photo 386. Lean over the control panel and this is the view, the tall white extension creating a natural stopping point for the eye which can then take in all the detail instead of speeding straight on to the half-timbered building and missing all your hard work!

extension – made from embossed plastic sheet, with brass tube and copper wire 'external plumbing' – the 'yard' becomes little more than a paved area letting light into the original lounge window: somewhere to let the dog out to 'perform' on the plain, yellowstone flags (Photo 384).

No. 3 have removed their old khazi (note the hint of whitewash where it once was), and used the new extension next door to add climbing frames for their plants (Photo 385). No doubt there will be something colourful climbing up there next year, if not sooner. And I *think* I painted that paving before I fitted the fencing …

It is, of course, by means of form, structure and colour that real gardens are created. In models too, the different types of fencing, walling, building height and shape, open and closed areas and the varied decorations, all help to enhance the individuality suggested by the kit's ludicrously primary back doors colours (Photo 386).

The area behind and below these cottages once housed the local gas works. Such relatively small

works were decommissioned not long after World War Two and, after these 'brownfield sites' had typically lain derelict for perhaps 20 years, the pressure for new, high-rise housing, more shops and other facilities brought about a typical 1970s Georgian-styled shop-and-housing development. This is what we shall study next.

THE 1970s HOUSING DEVELOPMENT

The first thing to notice about this area, (seen in photo 387 under construction) is the creation of a footpath right through the site from the village centre above, down past all the housing, to the High Street. This deliberately gives metaphorical access (model people don't actually walk, of course), from the new development up to the local church, pub and 'old village' amenities and down to the nearby High Street. It is probably also used as a short cut by

Photo 387. Linking parts of your model with roads and walkways is an important encouragement for the viewer to 'look around'. Etched fencing is easily 'tweaked' to suit any undulations.

Photo 388.   A simple plastic kit of a pair of three-storey, semi-detached mock-Georgian style town houses so typical of new 1970s developments.

Photo 389.   The same manufacturer (Kestrel), did a shop version, too. Adding the top third of one to the lower two-thirds of the other makes a nice four-storey building.

noisy drunks making their way home late at night but whether or not, its importance is as a visual device to 'draw the viewer into appreciating the detail of the model': artistic clap-trap for simply giving the eye a route to wander along and then modelling something interesting for it to look at when it gets there! Do note how the broad window sills of the first story have been extended into a proud stone band right around the building. There will be questions later …

Held in my hand in this next photo (Photo 388) is the basic kit as made up according to the instructions. My customer had made four 'residential blocks' and a shop version many years previously. He later found them in a box and offered them for

Photo 390.   'Kit-bashing' a few more of the same model in various ways makes creating an entire development a simple and rather enjoyable task!

possible use. As you can see, they are fairly bland models but with their reconstituted stone façades, concrete string courses, the occasional Georgian pediment and 'underground' garages beneath 'aerial walkways', they are absolutely typical of the watered-down period architecture favoured by developers in the 1970s.

In fact, they fitted in very well with my overall theme of land being subject to continual re-development and I felt that suitably 'doctored', they would introduce a fresh, different and rarely-modelled building period to the town that would offer a distinctive look, even though it was one already historic and out-dated in its styling. As they stood, however, they were neither imposing nor distinguished enough to be 'interesting' as models in their own right; they were missing that 'certain something' we call character.

After 'roughing out' the general layout of this side of the High Street I felt the shop might be OK if it were taller, an adjustment which led to the idea of raising the rest of the buildings behind to match by fitting garages and a service floor beneath, the latter under one of those elevated walk-ways.

So now you can see why I introduced that distinctive string course – to disguise the joint between two, two-story sections of model so as to make this four-story building facing the High Street (Photo 389). A village near me has a similar structure as its

Photo 391. A suitable road layout was created around the finished building; here the loosely fitted paving sheet is being marked up for the garage approaches.

Photo 392. Having used up all the available window panels to make the model taller, the back wall was made from plain card. This needed some detail, so why not a huge poster? They are common enough these days opposite stations. This one came from a Sunday supplement.

Post Office with the owner's flat immediately above the shop, general lets above that and a sorting office, now disused, behind.

With large parts of two models used for the shop, two more had their backs and one end wall each removed. The two fronts were then butt-jointed with plastic bracing behind, the spare central chimneys from the shop kit providing the missing third 'pair' at the new roof joint (Photo 390). The two 'rescued' ends were used for the extra plain walling needed to support the walkways over the garage approaches and flank the plasticard steps. Bits removed from the back of these houses were used to create the detail of the garage and utility room level, the doors and their adjacent windows providing individual 'service entrances'. The finished walkway is seen here being used to trim the 'road' sheet to size (Photo 391). This new taller group of four houses was then joined

Photo 393. The completed 1970s development waiting for the roadwork. Now what to fit along the nearer part of the High Street?

Photo 394.   As it happened, the customer had provided me with a hotel model he'd built many years previously and it fitted in here rather well. It needed its own secure car-park, of course, with barriers between the car-parking area of the hotel and that of the housing.

to some 3-storey store rooms for the shop. These used the 'waste' rear ground floor of the shop, cut out, turned through 90 degrees, and then given a new top floor from the upper shop section. The stores was completed with a flat roof.

The railway embankment behind has a sloping retaining wall. This was trimmed slightly to accept the finished housing at the left-hand end but the remaining, narrow area tapering outwards towards the street was retained as a fire brigade access and dustbin area and was therefore walled off and gated.

With a missing rear wall to replace and disguise, and that only because it was just visible from the visitor's area, I felt something more interesting than white card was required so I did a trawl through the weekend's Sunday papers and found this excellent advert for New York and its skyline which fitted perfectly (Photo 392). Not an unusual use of a long wall opposite a railway station you will agree.

Photo 395.   The typical concrete and glass hotel with its delightful wing roof lurks nicely behind a new Japanese 'multi-kit' dressed up as offices, these two completing this entire area.

The fourth house (behind), was used largely 'as is', except for the addition of the broad concrete banding. Being further up the hill it sits higher above its walkway and oversees the rest, despite only being 3 storeys. The small green area beyond that is the only bit of the village not under concrete, apart from the graveyard of course, but sadly there are 'no ball games allowed' here either.

The re-construction and layout of the new development was completed by: adding three more lock-up garages, two for the pair of houses above them with one for that nearest the shop, which lost its garage to the approach steps, along with a curved sloping access to the aerial walkway for push-chairs and the disabled (Photo 393). It was now time to add one of those paviour-clad 'aprons' which are supposed to make roadways look like pavements so as to make people drive more carefully. To add interest, I used up an off-cut of rounded stone walling to create a few feet of 'original cobbled road', a last vestigial reminder of the gasworks. Further raised areas of kerb and paving were later added to prevent vehicular access from the garage approaches to the hotel's car park.

This next 'fisheye' view shows the finished parking areas very well, from garages which will not accept today's MPVs to the now-tired coloured paving once used to make 'North Sea Close' look attractive (Photo 394). The barrier allows access to the motel car park – but for paying customers only, naturally! A rather drab corner then, but oh-so-

Photo 396. The 'country end' of the new 'green way' created along the route of the disused railway. Despite the period church and cottages on the skyline, the walker here would be only a few hundred yards through the tunnel from a busy modern High Street.

Photo 397. Fortunately, since they would make a very large model, modern supermarkets tend to be found away from the High Street but we've still got one, this Morrisons appearing on the backscene just behind the station.

Photo 398. The other side of the High Street was finished with a well known kit for a car showroom. The old railway cutting has been cleaned up and now provides access to a 'green way' out of town.

typical of the genre that it almost has a charm of its own. Doesn't it?

THE HIGH STREET

The High Street was completed by adding the owner's 1970s concrete and glass Motel, with its dramatic gull-winged roof, and a recent Japanese kit for a modern, brick-fronted, post-millennium office block, both coincidentally finished largely in that now-familiar tan concrete colour. The former, made by the customer himself many years ago, has darkened glazing so was merely given a few subtle interior 'glows' but to the latter, it being so prominent, detailed, well-lit, cafe and office interiors were added. These new buildings sit happily side by side forming a pleasant 'full stop' to the old village area behind them (Photo 395). In a space less than half a metre square, therefore, we have buildings from the 15th, 17th, 18th, 19th, 20th and 21st centuries that all look perfectly at home together and between them reflect perfectly the centuries-long develop of so much of the West Midlands.

This is the 'busy' view from the control panel, one which contrasts nicely with that from the other end of the 'green walk' and tunnel, as seen from outside by the visitor (Photo 396).

Incidentally, the model being set 'today', you might wonder why there's no supermarket. Well, there is, but as it and its large car parks would make a rather boring model they are perhaps best kept on the backscene. So that's where we put ours ... (Photo 396)

Final detailing of the modelled High Street was completed by adding a road surface and markings, some traffic, the odd street light and a coach-load of business-people arriving for a conference. This completed the left-hand half of what is in fact a lid over those hidden storage sidings (Photo 398). To the right is the first building of the 'business park' and behind that, but still prominent, the railway with its freight yard, platforms, period station buildings and canopies, all ready to serve this thriving community. Mission accomplished, I'd say. I can only hope you agree!

CHAPTER SIX

SCRATCH BUILDING FROM CARD: WALLS

PLUCKING UP THE COURAGE!

There's no doubting it; taking a pristine sheet of pure white cardboard and attempting to start laying out thereon what you hope will be your first stunning cottage is an extremely daunting task. That huge expanse of white space, those hundreds of stones or thousands of bricks which await individual marking, carving and painting to look 'just so' ... What about the corners, how am I to do those? Should I leave a base below ground level for handling? How high do I take the walls, exactly? The intention is to 'really do it properly this time' – an intention somewhat dented by the sinking realisation that you have absolutely no idea where or how to start the job in the first place. It therefore takes a brave man – or woman – to pluck up their courage and reach for a

3b pencil and a reference photo – and hardly surprising that most of us then decide to cut our teeth on something simpler!

Here I admit that was my route some thirty-odd years ago: I started with a sheet of what was then 'Bristol Board' and a photo I'd taken of Prince's Risboro's delightful market building (Photo 401), and just 'set to'. The result (Photo 402) once had the bell-tower on top: it was a sliding fit into the clock tower so as to later admit of a grain-of-wheat bulb for illumination. Sadly, that is now missing, although I still harbour (probably forlorn) hopes of finding it in another box somewhere, someday ... That was quickly followed by another model, this time of the library a few yards up the street (Photo 403), although now I used a mixture of Bristol Board, artists mounting board, Pyruma fire cement and embossed plastic

Photo 399. A cruel close-up (the track in the foreground is N-gauge), of a terrace of tiny stone houses built in perspective. Perspective allows you to suggest far greater depth than actually exists and this helps disguise the straight line which normally forms the rear edge of a baseboard.

Photo 400. Every now and again the opportunity arises to really let your hair down! It was in my very early professional days that the chance arose to create an entire rural hamlet. It was to be on a hill some six feet from front to back which hid six return curves at the end of a huge public model railway at Poole, Dorset. The result, seen in this tinted black and white photo, was 'Foxes Farmhouse' and its surroundings. These included a huge but dilapidated barn and a row of half-timbered thatched cottages, complete with bee hives in their front gardens. I cannot remember now how long it all took but my staff and I coloured, cut, and laid thousands of individual tiles on the two major buildings alone. All but the farmhouse were built in perspective (something I still use today), as was the landscape behind in which the lane continued for a quarter-of-a-mile before ambling gently over the brow of a hill, even though there was only a foot of space left. This hill was complete with miniscule hedgerows and a clump of trees, with a hint of a building of some description lurking within. It wasn't perfect then, and I can pick even more faults with it now, but it was done thirty years ago and represented what was, even then, a long-lost rural idyll. As such it was much appreciated by those 'of a certain age' who saw it, and I trust it still is an image which can inspire you to emulate something like it because the relaxed epitome of a rural English village is the perfect foil to the brief but insistent roar of a passing train.

Photo 401.   The market building of Princes Risborough, Bucks, photographed in the 1970s as a possible subject.

sheet; just to try out different techniques to see how I got on with them (Photo 404). As you can see, it all came out fine, which just goes to show that any novice could do what I did, given the right determination! The original photos of the real Risborough buildings date from the late 1970s, before the days of yellow lines and excessive street furniture, but I took the models out of their storage box and photographed them anew just for this book, so you see them here after thirty years of existence. They are both in need of a little touch of repair, certainly – mainly in the gutter department – but the idea of fitting 4mm scale structures with gutters was a novelty at the time so I make no excuses. I would certainly do it rather differently now, of course!

I accept that to start this rather odd hobby of ours by building a fancy brick struc-

Photo 402.   The resulting model building, now over thirty years old and missing its bell-housing and weather vane, has survived the test of time well enough, even if the card used to support the guttering has separated under handling. It would probably have survived better if used on a model.

Photo 403.   Another Princes Risborough subject, the library, taken at the same time.

ture from scratch, carving all the bricks by hand and cutting and gluing individual tiles, is a formidable proposition and probably *not* the best way for every novice to get great results first time! On the other hand, if my first attempts produced results which both look like these and have survived more or less intact for over 30 years, so can yours. But enough of this encouragement: let's study some actual methods, shall we?

SIMPLE CARD CARVING

More recent examples of simple card-carving are the station buildings produced for Tupdale, my 4mm scale odyssey on the Yorkshire Dales. Tupdale was, among other aspirations, a deliberate attempt to see if one could make a truly representative model of a place without actually going there. It was an excellent choice because there have been literally dozens of books published on both the railway and the landscape, so all the information you could possibly want is freely available in print. The buildings, for example, are detailed and beautifully drawn in the late David Jenkinson's 'Rails in the Fells' (*Peco Publications* 1973), wherein you will also find track plans of all the stations, a brief line history (already very thoroughly covered by other books), a useful general appraisal of the line and its traffic, and some really useful photos of the kind only an experienced modeller would select. As you can gather, I heartily recommend it!

So, armed with a photo-enlarged copy of David's plans of the 'large' station building and waiting rooms, I sat down at a table and began drawing and carving (Photo 405). The first thing to decide is where to put the joint when you fold up the walls (usually an unseen corner at the rear or, if possible,

Photo 404. The model of it, only a few weeks younger than the market building, has also survived quite well, all things considered.

Photo 405. The drawings, reference book and cut-out walls of, from the bottom up: Tupdale's goods shed, the 'down' platform's main station buildings and the 'up' platform's waiting room.

an internal corner where it will not be noticed), and then working from there, draw each of the sides in turn, in outline, upon your card. As can just about be seen in this detail photo (406), the major stones of the quoins at the corners are drawn in next including, where there is sufficient width of material, the stonework of the reveals' inner edges

Photo 406. A detail of the previous photo showing the next stage, that of drawing in the 'quoins' or large corner stones.

by projecting them across the openings. Draw in a few millimetres of the interior too, if there's room; enough to produce an edge and a surface to glue to (bottom left-hand corner). Then the excess card in windows and other openings is removed and the whole building cut out from the sheet.

The next step, *before* you begin carving individual stones, is to turn the card over and carve away some three-quarters of the depth of the card so that the corners will fold easily to 90 degrees. This is achieved in precisely the same way as when scoring to fold the chimney for the Superquick school, except that this card is a lot thicker so there's more to carve away. But if you can do it with card a few microns thick, you can certainly manage it with card some 1.6mm thick, since there's more to spare! With this done, the work can be reversed and the stonework of the quoins carved in, although care and a sharp blade is needed at the corners or the joints can fracture, as can be seen with the waiting room walls, top middle!

But as it says in a certain handbook; DON'T PANIC! Whereas with a Pendon-type building (which would be painted using watercolours), you

Photo 407.   One of the most satisfying moments of creating any building comes when you begin to turn a flat sheet of material into a three-dimensional model.

would have to throw the bits away and start all over again, by using acrylics you can simply wait until you need to assemble the pieces and then glue them together with wood glue. The only concern is to ensure that each stone is neatly pushed flat before the glue dries. You might have to leave that joint a bit longer to 'take' and then handle it more carefully until you've glued it to a base – but waste all that effort for a mere fractured corner? Never! No professional could afford to do that and neither do you. A coat of acrylic will hide a multitude of sins and if the worst comes to the worst and you make a real mess of it in one area, you can either hide it under a rambling vine or cut away the messed-up surface,

Photo 408.   The completed shell with booking office floor and 'wings' added. Behind it is the goods shed, the walls strengthened with rocket sticks as it is a large building with a removable roof and only a partial floor.

give it a coat or two of 'Tippex' to restore it, let that dry thoroughly, and then carry on. Incidentally, liquid correction fluid makes a good substitute surface under watercolour, should you decide to try that painting route sometime. With the carving of the quoins completed, you can then carve in the rest of the stonework and create whatever surfaces best suit your prototype.

At this stage I mark and cut out bases of 3mm mounting card – just as with the school – and begin to turn the building from the flat sheet into a 3D model. A very satisfying moment! (Photo 407)

Photo 409. Soffits are now being added underneath the archways to give depth to the model. They are carved to match the exterior stonework, before fitting, and they sit behind the walls so as to disguise the inevitable joint as much as possible.

Photo 410. The office end of the completed goods shed.

The central area floor, entrance lobby and outer wings are all added next. The goods shed is treated in much the same way except that, not wanting an entire floor of cardboard, the upper and lower edges of these long walls are stiffened with more rocket sticks (Photo 408). Depending upon your preferences, and whether you intend fitting interior lighting at some stage, you may now add any soffits to the tops of your arches if you want them (Photo 409).

My next stage is painting the walls in hues appropriate not only to the prototype (Photo 410) but, by actually putting the model into its final location (Photo 411), ensuring that the depth of colour you are using is correct for its location within the landscape. You might care to consider whether you need to model the back or not – as you can see from this view (Photo 412), I gave it a miss to save time, although I did fit and glaze the rear windows and provide sills as they might have been visible through the front windows (Photo 413). Some might say 'Ah, but I would *know* if it's not there'. Of course, it's your hobby and so it's your choice, but why build three four-sided buildings when you could build four three-sided ones in the same time? I know my Black 5s run on electricity not steam but it doesn't stop me wanting a steam outline model on a 1955 layout! So think through your attitudes carefully: your time is valuable, make the most of it.

Continue by adding any interiors you want (Photo 414), noting that anything beyond the simplest coat of paint is probably best assembled on sub bases and

TOP: **Photo 411.   *Before fitting the details, check the depth of stonework colour achieved against the surroundings to ensure proper balance.***

MIDDLE: **Photo 412.   *The rear of the shed shows how it is only modelled on three sides: why waste time building something you can't see?***

BOTTOM: **Photo 413.   *The shed's interior, showing its lighting.***

Photo 414. A cardboard 'dado' rail helps define the edges of your painting, while a few posters and notice boards create instant character.

glued in lightly during final assembly (Photo 415). As to how far you go with the detail, there really is no point in adding anything which will not be seen through the window. 'Getting it all right' only to hide it away is, let's be honest, also a waste of one's time! What is worth doing however, is to flesh out basic shapes such as the table, fireplace, chimney-breast and mantelpiece, along with any visible seats or benches, of course (Photo 416). Adding a few appropriate posters is also worth it, as you can see

Photo 415. More complex interiors are best built separately and glued in during final assembly.

from this illuminated night shot (Photo 417). (Yes, it's an LMS poster on a BR period layout but old posters often lasted for donkey's years at out-of-the-way locations.)

Famously, Tupdale only has one solitary passenger; here he is reading his paper (Photo 418). The paper is two rectangles of bent tinplate soldered together and the figure is one from that early Airfix 'platform figures' range, for which I still find many uses (Photo 419). In BR days, stations like Tupdale did well to sell 6 tickets a week so he is likely to be 'it' for the day. Hiding him away in the waiting room, to be pointed out only at night, helps reinforce the fact that for 99.9 per cent of the twenty-four hours in a day, many stations like this were an entirely passenger-free zone. No wonder Beeching closed them!

Returning to the unfinished booking hall (Photo 420), the rail side was furnished with a ridiculously elaborate glazed screen, presumably erected to protect the interior from the infamous Helm wind. This was not an appropriate detail for cardboard. Yes, it could be done but I felt plastic did it better (Photo 421). Even so, to achieve the right effect meant cutting the glazing bars out of black 10 thou.

Photo 416. *If you keep your shapes bold yet simple, an effective interior like this can be knocked up in half an hour or so.*

Photo 417. *A single point of illumination in a corner is perfectly adequate – which is why he is sat there to read his paper!*

sheet (easier to see against the white of the 'glazing'), adding the rest of the panelling and, the whole being supported by metal columns, making some representations of them from stretched sprue. The whole

was then coated with 'RTV' rubber and a copy made in clear resin. At the same time I made one off, and then cast, some six 'cast iron' corner brackets, added a single door (the other one's opened wide), and then painted the completed screen (Photo 422) before fitting it. Glazing all the other windows and fitting lighting tubes, ceilings, bracing and a roof (see Chapters 7 & 8) completed the basic structure.

Finishing is now simply a matter of adding the final external details. Precisely what these are will depend upon the prototype but do not be tempted to rush them, just give them the same attention

LEFT: Photo 418. *The figure is an old plastic one with the arms and legs 'broken' and reset to suit. The paper is bent scraps of tinplate.*

RIGHT: Photo 419. *The same figure in side view. His hat has been carved down into a cap, and a mounting peg of tcw 'inserted' ...*

Photo 420. The booking hall interior is a simple affair; bare floorboards, several doors, a ticket window and a few posters/notices are more than sufficient.

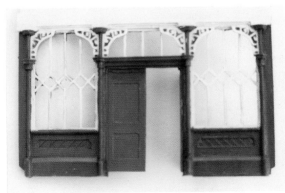

to detail as you gave the main structure when you started and all will be well. Far better to do it once and do it right than spend the rest of the building's existence on your railway rueing the fact that you rushed something just to get it finished quickly! (Photo 423) The barge boards, for instance, are complex and come in three different sizes. I made originals in plasticard and moulded copies, of which you see both sides of two 'partial failures' here: a bit mucky after 10 years in a box but still useable as 'spares' if one got broken (Photo 424). These, being both exposed and fragile, were added right at the end of the build to save them from being damaged.

So, a lot of work just for a smallish station but I trust you will agree that the result was well worth the effort (Photos 425 and 426).

MIDDLE: *Photo 421. The glazed screen is too complex a job for cardboard: assembling a master from plastic is quicker and neater.*

BOTTOM: *Photo 422. The finished screen is a resin casting with 'cast iron' brackets (more resin mouldings) and plasticard doors added, all painted appropriately.*

Photo 423. Final detailing includes a small 'way out' notice, flowers in tubs, more period posters, wrought-iron and timber Midland benches and some more home-cast resin, this time in the form of the very fancy barge-boards.

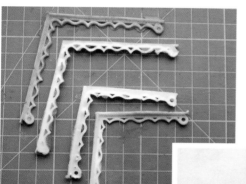

LEFT: *Photo 424. By way of illustration I found these 'failed' castings in a box. Now ten years old, although slightly discoloured they, too, have survived in perfect condition. The originals were fettled from plasticard.*

RIGHT: *Photo 425. This 'vernacular' rubble stone walling requires a very different modelling approach to that just used for 'architectural' work.*

Photo 426.   The station seen from a different angle. The lack of raised individual stone detail just isn't an issue – there's no mistaking what you are looking at.

COMPLEX TYPES OF WALLING

DIFFERENT STONE TYPES IN CARD

There are, of course, a great many different types of stone used for building and many need different approaches to reproduce. Slicing simple outlines of squared-off stonework into card, as with the Settle and Carlisle buildings, is one thing; the non-Masonic stonework of vernacular cottages however, can be very different (Photo 427).

Take this example of a local house wall in sandstone, where the left-hand part has recently been re-pointed but the right was at one time rendered

Photo 427.   This 'vernacular' rubble stone walling requires a very different approach to that used in 'architectural' work.

Photo 428. An example of a 'vernacular' wall of rubble stone 'brought to course'. The left-hand side has its joints neatly 'pointed' in a coloured limestone mortar, which makes them easy to see!

or possibly whitewashed (Photo 428). Note in passing that the originals of the models in this chapter come from South Perrott in Dorset, whereas the photos of real walls show subjects some 30-odd miles east of there in Somerset. Living in the area for a quarter of a century tells me that there is little difference between the two limestones, either in texture or colour, other than a general tendency towards a cooling of those very warm tans both northwards and eastwards, although in any one village, local variations resulting from the depth the stone was quarried from are actually far more significant, especially for the colour. Methods of

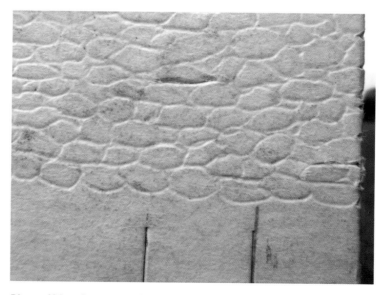

Photo 429. A section of model cardboard wall indented with the ball of a used-up biro pen. Try to ensure that each stone has a plausible shape!

Photo 430.   The unmortared section here shows how very simple variations of colour can be achieved in a few seconds, which will look fine when the mortar colour is added afterwards.

Photo 431.   Here, the use of semi-matt acrylic allows you to add the mortar in enamel as a simple wash. Remove this thin layer with a thinners-dampened rag after letting the enamel dry, but before it goes hard. This, timed correctly, will take the paint from the stone's faces but leave it in the indented mortar courses.

Photo 432. A real 'coursed and snecked' stone wall shows how subtle the colouring changes can be.

construction have always been very similar across the entire arc of the Limestone belt, with local traditional variations changing more from one end of the arc (Dorset) to the other end (The Wash), than across its width.

To achieve this particular look, cut your walls to shape and remove your door and window openings, but do not trim away the insides of the corners yet. Lay out your walls in one long piece and, using an empty biro, indent your stone shapes into the card face, here representing the much more curvilinear shapes of rubble stone walls (Photo 429). Mix up an appropriate paint colour for your period and locality using acrylics, including some minor touches of variety as you paint. Cover your walls with it, as per the small un-mortared section in photo 430. (This whole area is to be covered by ivy and a tree, which is why it was a good place to hide a joint!) Leave it to dry thoroughly, at least overnight. These vague shapes can then be turned into individual stones by using a fine brush to paint around them.

Quicker, if you are brave, is mixing a mortar colour in enamels, letting it down to the consistency of single cream, and then washing it over the

stones to fill in the troughs. Leave to dry for an hour or so then clean any excess off the stone's faces with a *gentle* rub over with a cloth slightly dampened with thinners. This should give you a finish like this next building, which has 'coursed and snecked', dressed hamstone for the main house but rubble-walled outhouses (Photo 431).

'Coursed and Snecked' walls have stones of approximately the same size, laid in rows of approximately the same height; called 'courses', of course! (Photo 432): it's a kind of rural version of 'posh' sawn stonework.) Where a height adjustment is needed, a small squared stone – called a 'sneck' – is inserted to make up the correct height (Photo 433). To achieve this look, again cut your walls to shape and remove your door and window openings but again, do not trim away the backs of the corners yet. Where you have stone mullions, as here, use a new, sharp blade to cut the card at about a 45-degree angle so as to form a chamfer down the edge of the reveal (Photo 434).

Then add any proud 'dripstones'. These can be complex but perhaps the easiest way is to take a strip of perhaps 40 thou. plasticard and, using the

Photo 433.   As shown on this model example, when stones of a particular height run out, a small one-off stone called a 'sneck' caters for the necessary change in height.

Photo 434.   Another wall on the same model shows how to create raised 'dripstones' by shaping long strips of plasticard and cutting off sections with angled corners.

edge of a knife blade, scrape a long strip to the profile of your prototype. Individual pieces are then cut off and glued with Evostick to form the required outline. Try to ensure there are no gaps between the various parts and wipe away any excess glue before it goes hard. In the larger scales, pre-formed hardwood strip could probably be used to advantage.

For any stonework 'brought to course', indent the horizontals first, here done freehand (Photo 435), then add in sufficient verticals to achieve the look you require. I tend to work in fairly small areas at a time, working along the wall in sections perhaps half-

Photo 435.   Curved dripstones and pediments, whole or 'broken' as here, take longer to make but add character. A few will suffice, just as variety from the simpler strip ones.

Photo 436. The completed cottage is basically just two colours, but the subtle variations therein create age, depth and vitality.

an-inch high. In that fashion, work your way around the entire building, gradually moving upwards one 'step' at a time. That way your work will tend to remain the same throughout the job, rather than changing slightly as you progress around the building: a problem which is hardly noticeable until you get back to where you started! A few simple errors are generally acceptable (a dab of neat acrylic here or there can hide many sins), but do try not to get a 'noughts and crosses' effect by over-running your horizontals with too-long verticals.

MIDDLE: *Photo 437. This local hamstone cottage has rubble walls with 'neatened' quoins (as I call them), while the extension is stone 'brought to course' – the opposite to what you will normally find but, as usual, there's a prototype for most things if you look hard enough!*

BOTTOM: *Photo 438. I suspect the choice between coursed and rough stonework was largely dependent upon who was building the wall and with what kind of stone. Stone hewn from beds which split fragmentally into odd shapes (often called 'walling stone' today), demanded the latter but was cheaper, whereas stone which split neatly into rectangular chunks was more expensive to buy but easier to work with. People who built for themselves' time was 'free', therefore they tended to buy the cheaper stone, while builders preferred more expensive 'split-parallel' stone because it was quicker to build with.*

With this mixed-media method, the use of acrylics is very helpful as it adheres to most surfaces. Paint everything, including dripstones, mullions and any other 'stone' features, such as pediments over doors. Apply relatively thinly so as to cover all the surfaces, yet without filling the indentations. This particularly warm tone is largely ochre but it is mixed wet, on the palette, with some umbers to give just a touch of variation here and there. Do not overdo the variety, especially in the smaller scales; change it just sufficiently to look natural and of course if you can, work to a colour photograph. Leave it for a day or two to dry and harden somewhat.

To complete, simply give your card building a pale grey/cream wash of lime 'mortar' colour, (dark-looking, coloured mortars are generally a recent phenomenon). As before, use spirit-based enamels but this time try reducing it to the consistency of single cream and 'flooding' the mortar courses, the paint being worked outwards with the brush until all the joints are coloured. Any slight over-wash can be left to dry, then removed as previously, although with this method you can be a little firmer with your rubbing since the enamel thinners, applied fairly briefly, will not affect the acrylic paint underneath. As with the stone, a slight variation in the colours of mortar used is a help but not vital, merely reflecting different mixes of mortar and different levels of dirt

and algae, as on the wall of the toilet in the photo of the back of this property. The final result of either method can be very effective (Photo 436).

Look closely and you will find buildings where the wall changes from 'coursed' to 'rubble' (Photo 437). This often occurred as families expanded, needed more room and so extended their homes. Sometimes another complete house got added between two other buildings, as at the old bakers in South Perrott where the original house is on the left, the bakery on the right and a new, additional cottage, in rubble-work, has been added between them (Photo 438). See that extra depth below the eventual ground level? It is a very handy device. An extension of the walls downwards towards a nominal flat 'base' for your scenery makes fitting a building in place so much easier. Where you have old cottages you often have land around them which varies considerably in height. Roads may have been built up or worn away, gardens and accesses all tend to be at different heights, while outside steps down to cellars or up to different levels are also fairly common-place.

Starting from a lower 'base line' allows you to choose a variety of surface levels around your building, supporting these on cardboard formers. Also, by allowing an inch or so around the base of your walls and painting the stones just slightly further down than the intended ground level, you need never suffer from 'black line all around the bottom syndrome' again! You might find it a helpful place to mark any changes of finish before you begin defining your individual stones, too (Photo 439). A base also makes a very useful 'handling strip' both when creating the model in the first place and when decorating it afterwards. And if you change your mind on the height of the surrounding land, just add a few more stones to your wall …

Now let's look at a few notable 'real' walls. Here's one once-whitewashed – but not recently (Photo 440). Note that hydrant sign picked out in yellow and black; that's a detail I added to my market building even all those years ago. Photo 441 shows an interesting joint where an outhouse wall meets a much rougher garden wall. Look at those neatly-

Photo 439.   It is probably best to note any changes of finish directly on to the model itself, the handling strip around the base being the ideal place.

matched vertical stones along the top: not all walls have the castellated appearance known as 'Kings and Queens'. More common these days, although period photos suggest the idea certainly dates back donkey's years, are walls with either flat stones, a cement crust or even a mixture of both (Photo 442). Barns and outhouses generally are made from much smaller rubble, the best stuff having been saved or used for the house, while faults in roofs or pipework often result in stains here and there. Generally speaking, the finish of non-domestic walling is flatter and there is often as much, if not more, mortar to be seen as there is stone (Photo 443).

Two more details worthy of note are shown modelled – perhaps two more reasons to follow a prototype rather than your imagination. The first of these is the Western face of this cottage wall which has been rendered as protection against the

Photo 440. *A nice example of a local hamstone barn wall that was once whitewashed. It sports two nice details: a fire hydrant sign, and a neat damp patch where perhaps an internal pipe is leaking.*

Photo 441. *Photographing simple things that you notice while out walking helps you make better models, such as this junction between a shed exterior wall and a drystone one on the same boundary.*

Photo 442. *Even the humble garden wall can have ample character: mortar, mud, lichen and variations in stone type and colour all offer considerable variety, so don't make all your walls the same, but go and see what's really out there!*

Photo 443. *A barn wall showing the smaller, rounder stones used for its construction, leading to more mortar showing between them, which, along with typical features such as water stains and a much flatter finish, makes this wall quite different to that of house walling.*

Photo 444. *While it is impossible to tell the colour of a rendered wall in an old sepia print, the prototype for this model certainly had the dark tone of a road-side wall stained for years by passing horse-drawn rural traffic. Therefore, unless it was painted red (which registered on old film as black), a well-weathered earthy colour seemed the best choice.*

driving rain (Photo 444). Note how mock squared stones have been incised into the render on the ground floor in an effort to improve the impression it projects. I found that perhaps a quarter of all the old properties in South Perrott either had rendered walls or double-thickness westerly gable ends as protection against the prevailing conditions. Certainly the village's location just north of Toller Down makes it a real trap for micro-weather systems!

Just round the corner of the same building, and for similar reasons, is another feature worthy of note: the photo showed that rainwater, running down the inside of the stepped gable end, had

washed some of the lime mortar out from the top corner of the wall, an effect easily achieved with a few strokes of the scalpel (Photo 445). Perhaps they should have rendered that edge too! You will not have to walk far to find a real building with a similar problem (Photo 446). I note bricks have been inserted to replace missing stones at eaves

Fig 445. *It is easy to incise deeper lines with a scalpel should you wish to show areas where the mortar has washed away.*

Photo 446. *The end wall of this barn has very little left now to hold it to the side wall. Note, too, how while the mortar is practically flush with the stone surface, this is not the case at the corners, although whether this is deliberate or just weathering is always difficult to tell.*

Photo 447.   'Nicked' corners are a great way of suggesting surface relief on largely flat card walls, and are very easy to effect.

Photo 448.   Hand-carved rubble stonework on the end of the South Perrott post office. Had I known I would get this close with a camera, I might have spent more time removing some of those too-pointed ends … The sunflowers are nicked tinplate circles soldered to tcw, with lozenge-shaped tin 'leaves' – shown here twice their actual size.

level which, presumably, have also been washed away! Note the 'toothed' edge to the corner of this building's walls too: another task for the scalpel (Photo 447). Despite the flush cement rendering obvious on many real-life corners, separating each stone visually from its neighbour on a model tends to make it look more realistic, for some reason. Odd, but true. Perhaps the subconscious expects stone buildings to project 'rough' outlines rather than smooth ones but, whether so or not, slightly serrated corners to model stonework always looks better to my eyes.

It may be for similar reasons that deeply-carved, dramatic stonework is so inherently satisfying to produce. Taking a painted card cottage and then carving out each individual rubble stone of the wall can be a delightful way to spend a relaxing hour or so (Photo 448). A decent play on the radio or a fine CD in the machine and creating while you listen seems to achieve two things; great walls and total relaxation!

FLOORS, DOORS AND WINDOWS

In olden days, flooring was either beaten earth or stone flags, both inside (Photo 449 – biro) and some-

Photo 449.   A dead-biro indented cardboard 'flag floor' given a coat of acrylic paint then, when dry, 'washed' with a very well thinned mix of black enamel – little more than dirty brush water really.

Photo 450. This path of large outdoor flags (similar to those in Photo 449 but rather more weathered) was given a bit more ochre to show a nice colour where many feet have polished the stone, while the edges are rather more stained. Add ample 'weathering' washes, only wiping clean the 'well worn' areas.

times outside too (Photo 450 – carved). Note also the parcel the postman has left in the porch – another way of adding 'life' without needing an ever-static figure! Other interior finishes might be bare boards, linoleum (which tended to have had patterns so small as to be not worth attempting), or carpets, which are ever-changing although remember they only became 'fitted' to cover the entire room from about the 1970s onwards. Before that carpets were rectangles bought in set sizes and a cottage might often only have a small one in front of the hearth to rest your feet on, the chairs being placed on the stone or wood floor around its perimeter.

DOORS

I am very fond of 'weathered' old wooden doors so was delighted to find this modern example at a local farm (Photo 451) which amply shows the reality of the effect I've been modelling for years (Photo 452). Incidentally, the mortar is too dark and uniform on this model but that's because it's not finished as yet.

Photo 451. A real door with rotten timbers at the base: nineteenth-century 'Tom and Jerry' cat and mouse flaps, perhaps?

Photo 452.   *A similar effect is easily achieved with a few nicks from a sharp blade.*

Photo 453.   *Classic 'ledge and brace' door framing. Note the diagonals always rise up from the hinged side to the outer edge so the joints rest in compression. Built the other way the door soon falls apart!*

If the door is to be viewed from the inside through an opening, as here (Photo 453 – same door from the other side), then you will need to model it properly, along with any other interior detail you think appropriate (Photo 454). Even if you don't intend to fit full interiors, a jar of pencils or the odd ornament always helps give 'life' to a window (Photo 455), as does fitting interior shutters or representing the thickness of the walls of old stone buildings with card off-cuts (Photo 456). The steel pin body you can see projecting is my quick way of representing the traditional, round bakelite door knob (Photo 457). Brass ones can be either painted or made of brass, as seems most appropriate to your prototype. I once modelled a scale 'Norfolk Latch' but, I'm sad to say, it escaped the camera …

Making panelled doors was covered in Chapter 2 but traditional cottage doors are 'ledge and brace'. These have an exterior of simple planks of wood best created, for 'quality' doors, by carving thin lines in sheet card at an appropriate but equal spacing (taken from your prototype door, of course), and then painting. Older or more worn examples, or

Photo 454.   *Who knows what those rectangles are? Parcels or packets of some kind probably – but who cares as long as what you fit looks 'appropriate' for the supposed interior. It's called 'impressionism', it takes five or ten minutes to do, and it's far better than an empty shell – provided you can actually see it, of course.*

TOP LEFT: **Photo 455.** *A few simple, window details give life to any building, whether or not you go on to fit a full interior.*

TOP RIGHT: **Photo 456.** *Window sills from the inside. Fitting sills, with knick-knacks on them and a suggestion of thick walls, is another job which takes but a few moments. The 'pot of pencils' is a trimmed bit of 7/0.2 electrical wire, partially stripped.*

MIDDLE LEFT: **Photo 457.** *A simple household pin makes a nice cast iron or 'bakelite' door handle, but remove the point by snapping it off with pliers. Try cutters and you'll just dint the edges!*

BOTTOM LEFT: **Photo 458.** *These are some Yorkshire bank-barn doors I made earlier: about 100 years earlier ... The barn is due to feature in another book.*

barn or outhouse doors, might perhaps require deeper slices so that more 'muck' can be allowed to accumulate between the planks when painted, or you may even have to resort to slicing away thin slivers to achieve the effect you want. It depends upon how decrepit you want your door to be! Photo 458 shows a fine example of a pair of old barn doors, from which you can see that it is the painting, as much as the carving, which creates the desired effect, while you might find a little 'artistic exaggeration' helpful in establishing character!

Photo 460. Plastic windows in some kits are tolerable, others less so, but glazing plastic windows neatly is often problematic, as with this old Airfix engine shed.

Photo 459. Etched brass windows are expensive but ideal for larger windows where their sturdiness and accuracy pay dividends.

WINDOWS

Some kits provide printed glazing sheets for windows, the fitting and fixing of which were covered in Chapter 2, but of course you can both buy from other sources or even make your own. It is still possible to obtain sheets of 'Downesglaze'; simple rectangular windows printed in white on clear sheet. These have their uses, and they are also most amenable to tinting with watercolour pens but, as with so many things in modelling, it is again a case of 'horses for courses'. For large, industrial-sized buildings – and some goods sheds, of course – etched brass is favourite as being strong, well-detailed, neat and long-lasting (Photo 459). Plastic windows are available in many forms, white metal ones less so. Plastic vary from exquisite to poor – vide Airfix, now Dapol kits, where you will find examples of both (Photo 460) – and while the former can usually be worked on to improve them enough to use, whitemetal ones are generally execrable!

For older or smaller buildings, especially cottages and the like, home-made windows are probably best. Most shopping trips for almost anything these days produces excellent sources of glazing material, from fruit containers to bubble packs. If you look carefully, you can even spot suitable moulding pips which can be used as 'bulls-eyes' in your old (or new), cottage windows, although I find a small dollop of wood glue will normally dry clear enough for the purpose and is easily pushed off the glazing if not. So keep your eyes open when shopping and start hoarding.

My favourite small-window framing material remains thin cardboard, which can be bought by the sheet from art shops or salvaged from packaging, wrappings and business or the larger Christmas and birthday cards. Again, its use is as described for doors in the chapter on the school. A favourite way of adding 'life' to any building – and an extremely common practice on upper floors in the days when bedrooms were 'aired' daily – is to create opened lights. A frame extended inwards into the room and glued to the wall with a triangular fillet is the easiest and most reliable means. If that would be too visible then frames can be extended, bent and glued behind the wall but the without support the joint can fail over the years. Making the glazing material the full size of the opened light helps its strength,

while painting the edges as part of the frame adds depth and also disguises the thickness of the glazing (Photo 461).

For the glazing bars themselves there are several methods, sometimes chosen on a whim but more often to use whatever is to hand. The simplest is

Photo 462. Tupdale's 'Quarry Signal Box' is another ex-Airfix kit and uses the original window frames thinned down but with triangular plasticard inserts added in the top corners to create the distinctive 'Midland' look. I tried both cotton and 'stretched sprue' bars – the cotton won.

to include them in the frame by leaving a cross of card in the middle, as in photo 461. For fine iron or wood bars or lead 'cames' (the grooved lead strip which is used to fabricate 'leaded lights'), cotton, strung tightly across the inside of the frame and glued, is ideal. Any 'hairiness' can be flattened by pulling a length of cotton between fingers smeared with wood glue just before use. The glue will also stiffen the bars so they don't bend as easily when painted (Photo 462). I have also tried making my own pre-shaped plastic glazing bars by filing spare sprue to shape and heating and stretching it into a long thin strand. This didn't work for me, but perhaps I wasn't doing it correctly! (In these signal box windows in photo 462, the black glazing bars are glued cotton, the white ones stretched plastic sprue. The cotton was a lot stiffer!) Shutters can be made from cardboard with hinges from either business card or bent, shaped tinplate where required (see Photo 435). Cleaned, hoarded tin or jar lids are a fine resource for that!

Another option is to paint your bars directly onto the glazing itself (Photo 463). That way you can pick the colour precisely, and use the same one for doors and door frames if you want to. I mention this because a lot of estate properties – and I mean

Photo 463. One option is to hand-paint your own glazing bars. No good for illuminated interiors but otherwise they can look good – with a bit of practice!

the gentry's estates, not the council's – have traditionally been painted in a particular, and often rather odd colour, to denote ownership. Examples from my area include a cool blue-tinted medium grey, an all over mid-ochre and a sharp reddish brown not far removed from scarlet. These once-definitive signals of wealth are less obvious today, but examples often survive in cottage side windows or those of out-

houses and sheds, and for sentimental reasons are still today retained here and there around original country mansions if they once owned large tracts of land (Photo 464). In the main though, window lights, glazing bars and main frames are painted white, even if sills, transoms and mullions are another colour. A fine brush, some slightly-thinned enamel and a steady hand are all that is required to paint a cross (Photo 465); paint a dozen or two and you'll soon get the hang of it and later, when dry, just throw the failures away; the material's cheap enough!

Also notice in photo 465 that because the window frames were flush with the surrounding stonework, they were carved beside the stones into the card. This would have left them being far too thick but by carving lines half-way through the card from the inside, half the depth of the card can be peeled away to let the glazing sit closer to the outside. With really thick stone walls where the windows are rebated, this is not required, of course, nor, as we have seen, is it with stone mullions; however, this technique remains a useful 'cheat' for many buildings.

The final glazing method is ideal for larger leaded lights. Glazing material is grooved with a file by placing it over a drawn 'plan' of the window concerned and drawing the file's tip up and down against a straight edge (here removed so you can see what

Photo 464. This small gate is typical of those found on 'Gentlemen's Estates' and is painted in this owner's traditional estate colour. Historically it would have been found on all the woodwork of properties the estate owned, including cottage doors and window frames; sometimes even on the glazing bars too.

Photo 465. To reduce excessive depth of wooden window frames, pare away some of the interior card wall before glazing.

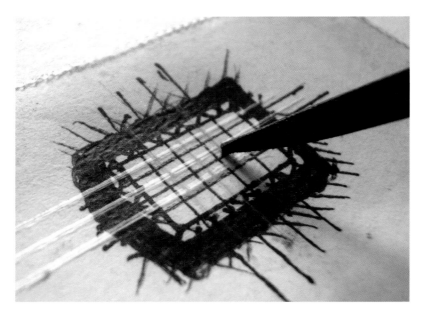

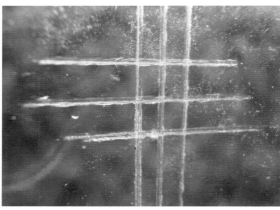

TOP: **Photo 466.** *For windows with lead 'rames', try etching the bars into the glazing sheet. Use a drawing as your guide.*

BELOW LEFT: **Photo 467.** *The completed glazing looks like this.*

BELOW RIGHT: **Photo 468.** *Deeply etched lines allow the 'panes' to flex and so offer interesting and realistic reflection variations in a finished window.*

I'm doing! Photo 466). After completing the shape, just hold it up to the light to ensure the 'bars' are parallel and deep enough. Here the one on the left is only partially filed to width (Photo 467); just file it again until it is deep enough to have two neat edges and if you do go right through, just start again. Done well, the glazing actually crinkles and reflects the light as if you had indeed made the window from individual panes of glass, as shown here on that old Princes Risborough Market Building (Photo 468). Paint with a thin coat of enamel, wiping clear the lights ten minutes after the paint has dried; that is, before it gets hard.

BRICK FINISHES

Returning to those models from oh-so-long ago allows me to complete this chapter with a few words on representing brick (Photo 469). Hand-carving bricks into card is a slow, laborious, tedious job but it does allow you to recreate precisely the correct 'bond' of 'headers' and 'stretchers', complete with 'closers' – half-bricks which enable you to complete the pattern properly at corners and jambs. This is hardly a good use of limited spare time, though, especially on larger buildings, although it is probably more successful than creating walls out of various

Photo 469.   Hand-carving brickwork allows you to create the correct patterns of headers, stretchers and closers, of which there are dozens of named variants.

kinds of 4mm scale brick mouldings. There was a plaster version you moulded yourself, which always looked wrong, and a plastic 'Bayko' type brick which one company marketed some years ago, which I tried and didn't like.

There are of course a great many patterns of brick bonding – far more than can be described here – but the common varieties are English, Flemish and Stretcher Bond, although there are more esoteric examples such as English Garden Bond, where

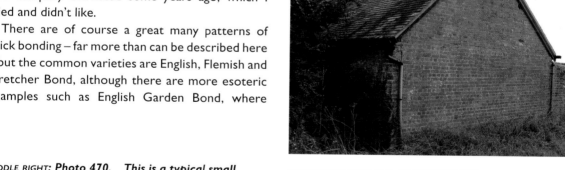

MIDDLE RIGHT: *Photo 470.   This is a typical small brick barn most people would pass by and not look at twice. But pause and look closer ... For further details of brickwork, see Appendix II.*

BOTTOM RIGHT: *Photo 471.   Now you can see it is almost a 'prentice piece – a delightful mish-mash of varying rows of different bonds. The bottom of the wall is laid in 'Dearne's Bond', where the bricks are laid on edge, with one row of stretchers and one of headers, but the upper section is in a kind of 'English Garden Dearne's', with three rows of stretchers – except for one row of two! The stagger on those stretchers is worth noting, too, so altogether it is quite a curio!*

Photo 472.   Commercial N-gauge printed papers can be rather brightly coloured but with layering and weathering they are usable – just!

three rows of stretchers are topped with a row of headers, and 'Dearne's Bond', a kind of English bond on edge (Photos 470 & 471). English is alternate rows, one of just headers and then one of just stretchers, and it is very common in some parts of the UK but almost unknown in others! Flemish consists of rows of alternate headers and stretchers, each stretcher in one row being placed above a header in the next, an effect often exaggerated by laying the headers with different colours of brick; while stretcher bond is just rows of bricks laid end to end. This last is almost always the type portrayed in brick papers but nearly all the commercial varieties seem to use entirely unrealistic colours; either too red or too grey, and entirely uniform across the sheet. Bricks are just not like that, not even

machine-made ones! The only 2mm scale brick paper I could find does the job neatly enough but the colour really is unecessarily bright. However, if you do need to use it then it is quite possible to add relief, by way of depth, by layering the card; and by relieving the colour by weathering, both useful ploys in N-gauge (Photo 472).

A few specialist suppliers exist producing rather better papers in 00 (Photo 473) but they are difficult to find and not always available. The major advantage of brick papers however really comes to the fore with this particular type of building: producing all those right-angled corners neatly in embossed plastic sheet would take for ever and drive most people up the wall! The only alternative to embossed sheets or hand carving for large

Photo 473. Hand-carving bricks for large buildings is highly impractical, of course, and for these, printed brick papers are entirely appropriate, as with this 4mm industrial building.

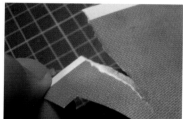

Photo 474. By tearing brick papers rather than cutting them, the joint between sheets can be disguised.

Photo 475. A wipe down the back of the edge with an appropriately coloured felt-tip pen works wonders.

Photo 476. The felt-tip pen removes every last vestige of white paper which, along with the 'waney' finish of the torn edge, makes the joint almost invisible.

buildings is to cut out huge cardboard 'doilies' and wrap them in brick paper, which is precisely what I have done here. (I am not covering bridges or large industrial buildings in this volume but whilst on the subject of papers …)

If you need to join two sheets, just overlap and tear both edges. Tear the topmost sheet backwards, away from the printed side, so as not to leave a white edge (Photo 474). Any slight whiteness can be removed with a wipe of felt-tip on the back (Photo 475), which neatly gets round the problem (Photo 476). Then merely line up the bricks on the two

sheets properly and glue the torn edge over the previous sheet, thus adequately disguising the joint.

Some of the better cardboard kits also use quite acceptable printed brick sizes, shapes and colours but not all, so do be wary! If you want to use a really accurate brick paper, one answer is to find a good 'source wall', photograph it, edit it in a graphics pro-gramme to fill an A4 sheet and then print off your own! Photo 477 shows an example.

So brick papers certainly have their place, espe-cially on large buildings, and where the mortar is generally supposed to sit back slightly from the

Photo 477. A photograph of real Victorian brickwork, digitally expanded into sheet form.

brick. Unlike stonework, I never find the lack of relief to be a problem with brickwork, although some people do. Perhaps they've not looked properly: my house's mortar is 2–3mm behind the brick face at most, while a lot of it is actually flush. In 1:76th scale, 3mm is a scale depth of a fraction over one *thousandth* of an inch – quite un-modellable! Despite that, embossed card and plastic brick sheets have long been available and I have certainly found the latter very useful over the years. The best way of getting the colour as you want it is to paint your own, as in this perhaps rather exuberant, early example from circa 1980 in photo 478.

To use, merely paint the whole sheet the colours you want (slightly brighter than finally required, preferably), leave for several days to harden off completely, and then wash over with your mortar colour. This should tone down the brick colours to what you want. Paint enough sheets at the same time to cover the building you propose making at least one-and-a-half times over; if you make any mistakes you'll need them and if you don't, you'll soon find uses for the leftovers anyway!

To assemble these now pre-finished walls use an impact adhesive, spread first on the support card and allowed to dry, then spread *thinly* on the back of the walls, which can be slid carefully into place and then firmly pressed down. Chamfer any outside edges where they meet at a corner *before* you try to glue them down and when dry and firm, tease away any glue residues from the corners.

Slater's produce popular but lop-sided brick sheets which are perfectly useable in some situations but, as the last photo shows, they are not suitable for buildings with tall joints because their 'less-than-ninety-degree right-angle' becomes horribly noticeable as the bricks stagger further and further away from the corner! Fortunately there is also some excellent stuff available from South

Photo 478. Embossed plasticard can make excellent brick walls. When properly – even exuberantly – painted, even fairly plain walls can be made interesting.

Eastern Finecast which I highly recommend, not least because it comes in bigger sheets sizes, which helps considerably with larger buildings. They also do a range of curved brickwork for arching over windows, although you can use the standard sheet: merely cut it into vertical strips, scraping clean the edges which always get thrown up when styrene is

cut, and then curve and fit one row at a time, as in photo 479.

For all but very particular purposes, I find the Wills brick sheets unsuitable: they are too thick to pierce easily for doors and windows, too small to use on buildings of any size without trying to fudge an inordinate number of joints and, above all, I find them to be some 25 per cent over-sized for 4mm scale, the measured brick size being nearer 5mm to the foot scale. This is ideal for the S-gauge boys, however!

The only 2mm scale embossed brick sheet available, Slaters, is useable but only just. Neat it makes nice 'new' brickwork, as with the beautiful power signal box seen in photo 480. (I can say that because I didn't build it!) It can be also useful painted, if the rest of the model is interesting enough to distract from its poor surface detail, as with the scratch-built 1904 standard GWR platform buildings seen in photo 481.

I have always found it best to mount all except the

ABOVE: Photo 479. Strips removed from the edge of the sheet can be nicked and curved to be used as brick arches.

Photo 480. Slater's 2mm-scale pre-coloured embossed brick sheet can even be used neat with considerable effect.

Photo 481.   It is also tolerable painted, if the rest of the building is interesting enough to distract the eye.

very thick Wills sheets on a base of cardboard, not styrene, as closed styrene boxes warp. Mounted on card they can be easily adapted to work with other finishes, which enables you to try different effects on what can otherwise be totally cardboard models, such as this experimental wall of brick infill, noggin and 'herringbone' on a half-timbered building (Photo 482). Here the sheet was painted and 'mortared' first, and then individual pieces cut out to size. (My favourite is the simple squares laid on their points in a diamond pattern but all the variations here show promise.)

You might also care to notice the hand-cut and individually-laid roof tiles, individually coloured with wood dyes. Those were the days! There is more on roofs and chimneys in the next chapter.

Photo 482.   Slaters again but 4mm scale this time, chopped up and used in a variety of ways as 'noggin' infill for a timber building. It can be very effective, as this experimental piece shows.

CHAPTER SEVEN

CROWNING GLORIES!

GUTTERS, DOWNPIPES, CHIMNEYS AND ROOFS

When the structural part of any building is accomplished, you can move on to adding the roof and any external details you need to finish it. To do so, you will need reference materials but you should realise that 'external details' can mean anything, large or small. I'll give you a 'for instance'. Having stopped to photograph that neat little market building at Princes Risborough all those years ago, thinking, 'that would make a nice model', the half-timbered

Photo 483. The roof-tops of Notte-on-the-Wye start right at the front of the model, trail up the hill and along to the station, then leap via the station canopies to the rest of the town beyond and a mile or two into the landscape behind that. The railway is thus established as being in the midst of a community which it was once brought here to serve and, a century or so later, it still does. The townscape has given the railway its purpose.

Photo 484. The library, Princes Risborough, circa 1975.

library a few yards away also grabbed my attention so I photographed that too. Sadly, good film was never cheap, nor good processing, and the then-modern shop it was partnered with at the time – all machine-made fawn bricks and huge plate-glass shop-fronts – had considerably less appeal and so escaped my camera ...

The theory was that the library would do perfectly well enough on its own but somehow, as I was building it, it just didn't look right without something to 'lean' on. Obviously it wasn't *really* leaning on the building next to it but the entire character which that timber-framed building exuded was that of a 'rake' waiting for a bus, just slightly the worse for a liquid lunch, and so leaning almost imperceptibly on the fellow in the queue behind him (Photo 484). I think that impression is created because the library roof's apex continues beyond the main structure

Photo 485. My late 1970s model of Princes Risborough library; an early 'serious attempt' at artistic model making.

Photo 486.   *Creating your own stonework on plain card means that it is easy to include other features such as old timbers or brickwork, as required for this model of a gable end in South Perrott, Dorset.*

Photo 487.   *A simple timber porch and lean-to shed on the side of the same building. They all appear in plan form on an Edwardian OS map of the village.*

and into the roof space of the building next door. This gives you an 'extra bit' which, rather like an elbow on a bar, genuinely is leaning on the roof next to it. Perhaps that's a touch of über-personification but put another way, the library just looks better placed in the shadow of a larger building. So I needed to find one.

An old brick workshop was found lurking around a nearby corner and, although impossible to photograph (I couldn't get back far enough across a narrow street for my camera to record anything worthwhile), when I came to recreate the library, the memory of it provided sufficient inspiration to add the simple building you see it 'leaning on' now (Photo 485).

Of course, not all your buildings will need a complete additional structure made especially to partner them, but most buildings worth making models of have some quirky feature which catches our interest: if they didn't then they wouldn't be interesting because the common-place never is. That's why 'generic' modelling rarely satisfies; a model full of common-place houses would need quite phenomenal artistry to make it work as an attractive model with lots of atmosphere. Therefore, if you want people to believe in the scene you are spending so

much of your valuable time creating, then help yourself achieve that end by choosing to model buildings which have a particular appeal all of their own. Blindingly obvious, really, but perhaps only so when you stop to think about it …

When it comes to 'detailing', the opposite of making a second, entirely new building is, of course, to make no building at all – merely providing the 'ghost' of a long-lost one instead. Take this wall, for example (Photo 486). Look at it carefully and it tells us a story. At one time there must have been a timber-framed building on the site, probably the original owner's first house. One day he finds himself able to extend along the road in stone and, to give himself as much space as possible, the end wall of the old building was partly incorporated into an interior wall of the new one. Then one day the timber-framed old house was pulled down, leaving that inner wall exposed, and so revealing these ghostly reminders of its existence.

Using card as your medium makes modelling really flexible; adding old timbers to a stone wall is as simple as thinking to mark them in before incising your stonework, as is replacing stone with brickwork for the chimney stack at the top. Part of creating realism is simply to provide your model community with a sense of history: that never-ending story of the extension, conversion and renewal of properties.

Other old timber structures have lasted to this day of course, as this porch demonstrates (Photo 487). A simple effort in card-carving, something of the ilk makes another great 'first project', as would the simple wooden, creosoted shed next to it. Incidentally, the corner timbers here are more matchsticks.

This next, rather fragile-looking porch wasn't, in fact, as ephemeral as it looks for it lasted on the Post Office at South Perrott for many, many years (Photo 488). It is made of some 'pre-crimped' corrugated aluminium I purchased many years ago, and which I

LEFT: *Photo 488. Another South Perrott original, this is my model of the old Post Office as it was between the wars, going by a local postcard.*

BELOW: *Photo 489. Back gardens were practical spaces for work, food and storage sheds for most country folk, and this is a typical example.*

BELOW: *Photo 490. On the end of the same building was once this half-timbered storeroom, cantilevered out over the nascent River Parrett.*

Photo 491. A common West Country feature was to build an extra or thicker wall at the gable end facing a locally forceful prevailing wind. It is by noticing and modelling such local curiosities that you create a sense of 'location' for your model.

found knocking around in the bottom of a scrap-box, but I gather similar is available today if you look hard enough. The curved thing at the top of the entrance is soft metal from a toothpaste tube but was, on the original, a brace of wrought iron. Sadly my porch has not survived poor packing as well as I would have liked and a simple 'tweak' for the photograph was not enough to restore it but, rather than risk a major rebuild by getting tough with it, I decided to leave well alone for now! Fortunately, once you've built a model or two, repairing them is easy enough should the worst happen.

Peering round the back of the same building we find a delightfully rustic timber construction, simple but solid (Photo 489). Note the besom broom leaning by the back door, hinting at human habitation. Beside it, and under the same extended roof, are a store, probably a log store, and a general shelter formed by raising the garden wall and adding a roof between it and the house; a common feature of older country properties all over the South West. It is seen from the other side on the left of the next photo (Photo 490).

To the right, beside the main building, is another, almost unique, construction. In reality now a shadow of its former self, the wall below this extension curves around to follow the course of a stream which has by this point passed two sides of the property. The main building was, sensibly, built a few feet back from the stream but later the space was needed so this wooden outhouse was built on timbers which, at one end, used to overhang the stream! This kept the room square but they must have been substantial timbers as the framing was infilled with bricks, instead of the wattle and daub one would expect for such a jetty. Nowadays the room, probably once a pantry, has been cut back to the edge of the stream, thus losing a lot of its charm, but in spite of that, it remains an interesting and unusual feature.

At the other end of the cottage, which faces the prevailing wind (and rain), instead of a coat of render we find another means of attempting to keep the weather out of a damp building, that of building an extra, much thicker, wall beyond it (Photo 491) as modelled here. The lower portion has been turned

Photo 492.   To keep everything within boundaries previously established, the whole river area and its adjacent buildings are drawn full-size on a plywood base. The bit for the garden was first cut to fit the shape of the river, then to fit the outer edge of the cottage as built, the unwanted bit being removed so the garden can be glued to its cottage. Only then was the garden and its detail added.

into a shed, of which the central missing section of stonework will be covered by the village notice board. It is not visible from this side, but the vertical stones are there to keep down the edge of the corrugated iron sheet roofing which, presumably, was prone to lifting in the wind …

Of this group of four buildings, (all the originals of which are to be found within 50 yards of each other, apart from one demolished when the road was widened c.1925) this is the only one which so far has had its curtilage completed, with a garden added to a wooden base (Photo 492). I made this of 6mm plywood because it is strong, will not warp and gives a thick enough edge to be able to glue it to the building as a butt joint. It has been much handled over the years, through not yet being placed in its finished location, but that joint remains perfectly sound, so the idea must work!

Completing the garden has an added advantage in that the walls can be 'decorated' with less risk of damage, in this instance by the addition of a tin bath, a common adornment of cottage walls during the chosen period of these models (Photo 493). It

was actually made of tin, the sides being a single bent piece soldered to a base cut to shape. The rather over-scale joint is hidden at the bottom and the inside has rather too much solder but despite being slightly lop-sided it looks the part and only took a few minutes to fashion.

Note too, the open window. Like the broom, the parcel and the odd open door here and there, I am much fonder of *suggesting* human activity than of including model humans. If a human is modelled, the illusion is spoilt if they haven't moved once a train has gone by. Now somebody having a nap, or a couple of people standing nattering is fine, they are not likely to move much, but I never did understand the logic of the person on the platform with one leg in the air forever 'running for a train'. It looks odd in a photograph, never mind when looking at a real model.

There is no need to add people to create atmosphere when, as noted above, there are so many other ways of doing it. If you look at one of Pendon's gardens closely enough (in the Chapel group), you will find a pot of creosote with a brush draped across the top. Behind it, while the fence to one side is creosoted, that to the other has been weathered to look like old, bare wood. I thought the job half-done looked better than an old worn fence or a

Photo 493.   The tin bath was a common adornment of outside walls during the Victorian and Edwardian eras.

Photo 494. Odd remnants of card, from window openings for example, can easily be carved into chunks to make 'capping stones'. Painted at the same time as the walls, they can be individually added later; simple but very effective.

Photo 495. A slightly better effect can be achieved by chopping up pieces of old roofing slate with hardy cutters, as shown here on a stretch of Tupdale's dry stone walling.

newly creosoted one as again it suggests life, even though the painter has obviously nipped inside for a 'cuppa'. The powers-that-be at Pendon must like it too: that tea-break's lasted over thirty years already! So before you start adding lots of people, think about whether there's another way of suggesting human activity. If not, try to find something static they can be 'not doing' so that it becomes unsurprising that they have not moved since you last looked.

Again from that same South Perrott model, one more small detail should be noted while we are at ground level (Photo 494): the garden wall has vertical stones laid along its top where their weight helps to hold the wall together and keep the rain out. These are made of off-cuts of cardboard and while they are perfectly acceptable, I turned to using chopped up bits of roofing slate on my Yorkshire walling and thought that looked rather better (Photo 495) though to be honest, there's not a lot in it.

GUTTERING

Reverting to our cottage with the rendered gable end, the old cast-iron downpipes are simply added using brass tubes of various thicknesses, allied to a little tinplate here and there (Photo 496): a simple soldering job, if rather fiddly. The 'mounting clamps' are two single strands of wire, each twisted together at the back, and then the two twists themselves twisted together and soldered together to produce a single 'mounting peg'. This is pushed through a card mounting 'pad' to represent the bracket's base, then through a hole drilled into the wall; thus an almost

Photo 496.   Tinplate collection boxes soldered to brass tube downpipes used with half-tube guttering can provide accurate and durable detailing.

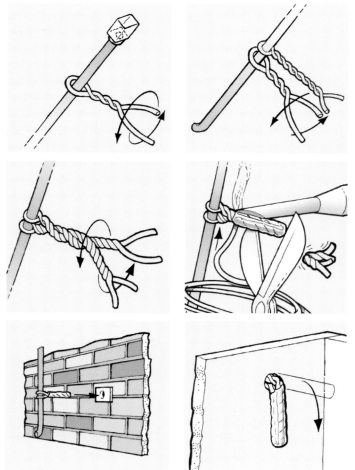

Photo 497.   The formation of downpipe clamps: 1) fold a bit of tcw around the downpipe and twist loosely; 2) repeat; 3) twist the two tails together; 4) solder just enough to hold the 'wrist' of the clamp, then cut off any excess; 5) insert into a hole in the wall; 6) fold the loose ends over inside and glue in place.

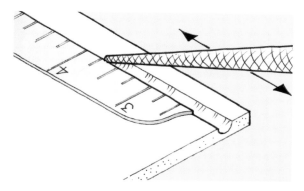

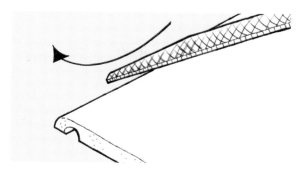

Photo 498. *Make your own plastic guttering from sheet by gouging out a semicircular rebate with a round file ground flat at the end.*

Photo 499. *Finish by turning the sheet over and rounding off the lower edge, then cut sections to length as appropriate and to a width to suit the overhang.*

perfect rendition of a cast-iron clamp is easily and cheaply achieved (Photo 497).

Guttering can be made in several ways. Wills do an excellent, if rather short, version in plastic with large, deep backing strips which can either be mounted *into* a wall, the rest of the wall above being made as part of the roof supports, or shortened to lie against it and mounted on staples, poked through holes in the wall and glued firmly inside. You can also make guttering yourself from 60 or 80 thou. plasticard using a round, tapered file with the end

ground flat. Use this to carve out a channel near an edge of the sheet (Photo 498), followed by rounding off the outer lower edge (Photo 499). Finally, file the ends of the supporting strip back some 5–10mm or so, depending upon the viewing angle, and attach as best suits your model.

More accurate guttering for models immediately under your nose can be made from suitable thin-walled brass tube sections cut in half length-ways, (I use a razor saw), or with thicker tube just file half away. You could also use lengths of tinplate or brass

Photo 500. *One older type of roof had an overhang sufficient to throw rainwater well clear of the walls, which enabled the owner to dispense with guttering.*

shim rolled around wire. All these are 'mounted' by soldering to flattened tinned copper wire 'brackets', which again are poked through holes drilled in the wall. Metal fittings are easily painted, are almost impossible to break and enable you to accidentally handle the model carelessly without necessarily removing the last row of your carefully-laid tiles! Incidentally, the tiles in question in photo 496 are in fact stone flags. Two or three rows of these old stone roofing flags atop exterior stone walls remain a common sight in hamstone areas, even where the rest of the roof has been replaced with slates. This often happened when the support timbers needed replacing because slates need far less substantial timbers and were thus both cheaper to buy and quicker to fit.

Of course, not every house had gutters; some just had extended roofs which threw the rain well away from the walls (Photo 500). (Any passers-by not in a carriage were probably only peasants and it didn't matter if they got wet ...)

ROOFS AND CHIMNEYS

And so, after all that preparation work, we finally get to the crowning glory of your model: expansive

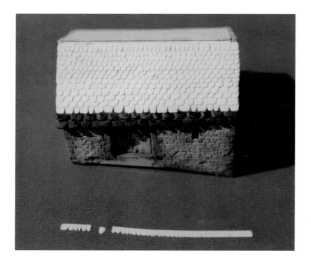

Photo 501. **Stone roofing flags can be filed up from strips from styrene sheet. If the occasional tile breaks away, just glue it on separately.**

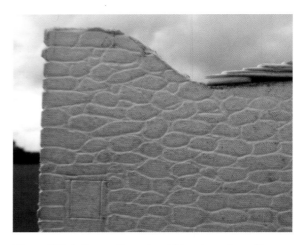

Photo 502. **Stone flags should be sloped to allow the rain to drain off, so do keep an eye on the side view as well as aligning them carefully from above. Here I notice they slope backwards, which is entirely wrong and something I need to rectify!**

angular roofs and, of course, their perpendicular counterpoints – chimneys. These are, in fact, the most important aspects of many model buildings since, if you think about it, most model railways are viewed from above. Roofs, being sloped to throw off the rain, are often actually tipped towards you, so becoming the only part of the model perpendicular to your eye-line and therefore the most noticeable surface. This makes them more prominent than the rest of the building, so roofs *matter*.

It is worth taking pains to get them right because they form such a large percentage of the 'first impression' any visitor gets of your entire model railway and that, with the rest of the general scenic impression, will create interest before you get the trains running. So get your roofs right and a visitor will want to look beyond them, to look more closely at the modelling skills displayed because your roofs have set a high standard. Get them wrong ... No pressure then!

So let us look at a few different types of roof and see how to model them although as always, there's more than one way to do any job so just pick a method that suits you or, more likely, suits the particular job in hand at the time.

TOP LEFT: **Photo 503.** *A stone flag roof finished and ready for painting.*

TOP RIGHT: **Photo 504.** *A similar roof painted and weathered. Flag roof colours tend to be far more consistent than those of stone walls because the former are worked along 'seams' while the latter are won from 'faces' which can vary from top to bottom.*

RIGHT: **Photo 505.** *The 'heap' in this corner is the base of the bakehouse chimney; a typically 'vernacular' mix of wall and roof flags arranged to support the chimney while throwing rainwater off as efficiently as can be devised with the materials to hand.*

STONE FLAGS

Those stone roof flags we saw in the last photo (500) are rather time-consuming but, as you can see, very effective. They are probably best made from rows of 'teeth' filed from strips of styrene sheet (Photo 501). They are carved in rows, each row getting slightly smaller and more numerous as you progress up the roof. Here the two black rows are hewn from some 3mm ABS sheet I had to hand (tough work!), while the next couple of rows are from 80 thou., then 60, and so on up to the top row, (shown at the bottom before fitting), which was carved from 30 thou.

After checking to see that each row sits 'nicely' over the row beneath it – that is, without any huge gaps – and while noting in passing that there is a double row at the bottom (as with all roof coverings except those using the overlapping types of tiles), each layer is then best secured to the one below it with a decent brushfull of liquid cement, normally 'Butanone'. The stones can then be firmly bedded down before the cement evaporates, which should leave them firmly attached from end to end. Note that if you are not careful, your stone flags can end up too thin and look like rather rounded slates, so

Photo 506.   A real Somerset flag-stone roof, albeit using thinner flags than many.

do check the side elevation as you go, especially if it will be plainly visible, as with the South Perrott bakery (Photo 502). In case you are curious, by the way, that rectangle towards the bottom left-hand corner will be painted as an iron access door so that the baker can clean his oven's chimney!

A roof completed and ready for painting should look something like that in photo 503, while after painting you might get an effect like photo 504. With so much filing going on you are almost bound to end up with a few odd bits of waste plastic glued firmly to your flags here and there, especially in corners,

MIDDLE: *Photo 507.   A new slate roof from the first decade of the twenty-first century.*

BOTTOM: *Photo 508.   In the foreground is an old slate roof, mainly from the end of the nineteenth century, going by the colour of good old Welsh slate and its moss, with much younger probably Spanish replacements clearly evident. The roof behind is more recent: the colour is slightly less blue and the mosses are different, which fact reveals the different chemical composition of the slate.*

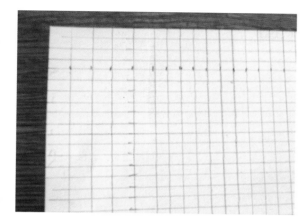

Photo 509. Hand-ruled slates on A4 paper. The main body are rectangles measuring 4mm by 5mm but wider slates are deliberately drawn at the ends.

but leave them be; just paint them as bits of moss and people will think your attention to detail is awesome!

By way of explanation, the 'heap' of stones and flags in the corner of photo 505 is the top of a baker's oven and the base of its chimney. The thick depth of stone helped retain the heat in winter.

Flag roofs are no longer common in my area but I did find the one shown in photo 506. Going by the colour, the stone was not local but, being located just yards from the old Somerset and Dorset Railway suggests it was probably quarried in the Mendips where there are odd pockets which split thinly and neatly, just like this. Such thin ones are rare, mind, and thicker flags are the norm. (For more examples, see Appendix III.)

SLATE

Slate roofs both new (Photo 507), and old (Photo 508), are simply made using paper, noting that where reduced bricks are used to make staggered-joint patterns in a wall, roof joints are normally staggered by slates specially-cut to be half as wide again. (Replacements are commonly half-slates; however, study photo 508 ...)

The easiest method of making these is to buy a pad of feint-squared paper, although it does not take long to draw up half a page of ink-drawn rectangles, perhaps 4mm by 5mm (Photo 509), (remembering

to leave one-and-a-half width slates at the edges), then to scan and print off as many copies as you need. Adding a few spare wide ones at one end of every row means that when you cut a short strip off to length, you have spare single 'wide' slates handy to complete the proper pattern. Just think ahead, that's all!

Slates certainly come in many different sizes, generally called by ladies' names – Countess, Viscountess, Marchioness and Duchess, for example and, amusingly, 'wide Countess', 'wide Duchess', etc. – but while few are 5mm (or 15inches) wide, there are plenty about a foot across. You can be as precise as your prototype, of course, but old slates high on old roofs are not always easy to measure ... However you get your grid, and whatever size you make it, cut up each line about a tile-and-a-half's depth all along one edge, making every cut a double one and removing a very thin sliver of paper from between each 'slate' (Photo 510). Real slates abut, of course, but single cuts will vanish when painted so the wider gap is vital to retain the effect of distinctly separate slates! Paint will largely fill the gaps anyway but with a double-cut, the effect of separation will remain perfectly visible.

Depending upon the intended 'age' of your model roof, you may care to 'distress' a few slates by

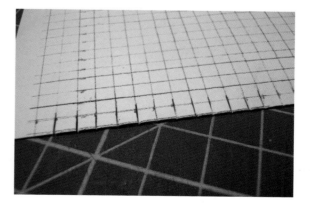

Photo 510. Unlike real slates which are closely butted side by side, paper ones are best 'double cut' to leave a gap if you want to get the correct effect in a small scale. Sometimes you have to 'cheat' to get a model to look right!

Photo 511.   *Carefully space your tile strips so you get a full-depth tile right along and parallel to the apex of the roof.*

Photo 512.   *This GWR station building is cobbled together from bits of the old Airfix (now Dapol) kit walls but with new windows and doors, although the roof is precisely as it comes in the kit.*

'breaking' the odd one or cutting a corner or two off here or there. As elsewhere, you can add as much detail to your roof as you see fit; possibly including 'hooks' – strips of lead or galvanized strip, bent to hold in place slates whose nails have rusted away

– or merely leaving odd gaps to fill with a 'slipped' single slate as you progress. Cut off the slates along the second line from the bottom to leave a neat row, all held together along the top. Having previ-

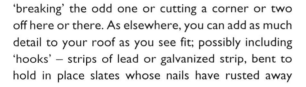

Photo 513.   *This signal box of Midland Railway origin is also adapted from two Airfix kits (to increase the height) but although the ends and windows have been heavily modified, the roof and its finials are straight from the sprue.*

Photo 514. The roof of this permanent way hut is made from single strips of paper which, being right under the viewer's nose, are individually coloured.

ously made a 'roof former' from substantial card, add another single strip of thin card along the bottom edge to start the 'slope' of the slates, then glue your first strip down. As with the flags, and as with plain tiles too, add a second full row, staggered, directly above the first so the rain could not drip between the gaps.

You may find that owing to a conglomeration of minor errors, your ridge and eaves are not quite parallel. With tiles you can fudge it but with slates, either admit the mismatch and line each row up on the drawn line of your previous row, until the last row which you angle, or draw radiating lines across your roof former and use those as your guide so that each row has a very slight but matching taper to one end. Continue until you reach the top (Photo 511).

When the glue is dry you can paint them and add a row of ridge tiles along the apex from card. These varied considerably in length and size and used to be baked clay, like tiles, although these days they might be concrete castings or even mouldings. Generally speaking, ridge tiles are an inverted V-shape and, compared to the roof, raised slightly to an included angle of 90 degrees or so. Others are 'half-pipe' in shape. Angular ones are quickly made from card

strips folded down the middle – great practice for folding cottage walls – while halved cotton-bud stalks are one option for half-round ridges.

Slate strips are all very well for tiny cottage roofs, and even for small town shops and houses, but for really large roofs, or roofs located some way into the model, all that is really required is an impression. However, despite being right under people's noses and a vital element of the scene, the station building for 'Upper Isis' uses the roof moulding which comes with the Dapol (ex-Airfix) kit exactly as it is (Photo 512), as does the first of two signal box roofs on Tupdale (Photo 513). Two roofs were cut-down and joined together for the larger 'Tupdale Quarry Box' (Photo 560); both boxes themselves being made from standard kit parts, adapted and upgraded.

You will have noted Tupdale's various railway buildings in previous chapters. The roof of the permanent way hut (Photo 514) and that of the small station building (Photo 515), being further away, were given similar strip roofs but, to save time, they were cut from 5mm squared paper and so are probably somewhat over-sized – not that anyone has noticed! The main station building, engine shed lower roof (the upper one is from the kit), and the

Photo 515. This small station building's roof is made the same way but, being a couple of feet back into the model, needs more subtle treatment. It has therefore been given an overall 'slate colour' with just the occasional touch of slightly different colour here and there.

Photo 516.   This huge goods shed roof is different, being made from a single sheet of thick card with the slates' edges carved into the surface. Even in this close-up photo the lack of relief is not immediately obvious.

goods shed roofs are merely 1.6mm solid card upon which parallel lines were carved horizontally, with the blade held at a slight angle so as to raise a card edge on one side only. Then vertical nicks were made throughout to hint at separation, producing an impression almost as effective when seen from a slight distance. The card was given a coat of acrylic

Photo 517.   A real roof, newly-laid but using old tiles.

paint to hold the raised edge in place and re-seal it to exclude damp: given card of sufficient thickness, properly braced, this works well and has lasted for twelve years to date without warping (Photo 516).

PLAIN TILES

Plain Tiles (Photo 517), can be produced in a similar fashion, except that they are generally smaller and thicker (Photo 518), so draw your lines closer together and use thin card, which will look much better than paper. It is preferable though, to cut them out and stick them on individually, for the simple reason that they look so much more higgledy-piggledy and there's no other way of achieving that 'individually-laid' look. However, if you are going to all that trouble you might as well make life as easy as possible, so here's a tip!

These individual tiles on the Risborough library were cut from several sheets of pre-dyed thin card (Photo 519). Several A4 sheets were cut in half and each was dyed with a different wood dye. Lines were then drawn about 3mm apart on a sheet of paper and the whole stack taped together at one end. Slices through the whole stack, every 3mm, were then carefully taken most of the way along so that each sheet was now a series of strips held together by several untouched inches at the taped end.

The ruled paper was removed, then a steel ruler was then laid across the end of the stack of coloured strips some 5mm from the end. It was held down very firmly while a number of light passes with a sharp knife cut off dozens of individual tiles, each some 3mm wide and 5mm or so deep. After several passes, hundreds of tiles littered the bench and, with a small trail of glue along the bottom edge of the roof, these were picked up on the point of a scalpel and placed onto the glue. A touch with a cotton bud pressed it into the glue sufficiently to hold it, then another tile is likewise pricked and placed. After a dozen or so, another application of glue is needed, and so the work continues.

To get the 'sagging roof' effect (shown in reality here in photo 520), the position of the trusses is marked and, between them, the supporting card is carved to slight curves along the apex. Before

Photo 518. *A long-established roof of hand-made tiles. Note the slightly differing thicknesses and the fact that they are not all entirely flat, some having 'warped' in the kiln.*

the under-roof is glued to the trusses, the curved top edges are pushed together and glued with a reinforcement of strong paper, thus providing the ready-sagged base. Guide lines are then drawn every 10mm or so up the roof, each line increas-

ingly adopting the shape of the sag as it gets higher, until the apex is reached. Naturally you have to lay by eye, only using these lines as a guide, but it really is not worth attempting to studiously draw in every row of tiles and then lay to these precisely, not least because timber doesn't sag precisely! A slow job, but you can certainly expect to get both faster and better with practice.

For the more 'ramshackle' effect of some really ancient roofs, lay your tiles in triangles instead of rows. Lay a row of perhaps a dozen, then eleven above those and ten above that. When you have your initial triangle, merely add more angled rows of tiles; first to one side, then to the other; until you reach the apex. Continue both ways along the roof until done. This is a method which juggles up the horizontal lines of your tiles more comprehensively and, if not overdone, gives a pleasingly decrepit effect.

For really neat or new roofs, working in straight lines is preferable – the fact that you are laying them singly in rows will automatically introduce sufficient variety of colour by itself as in photo 521, although in this instance, further variety was introduced when my assistant of the time, Sheila, offered to finish the roof for me. Despite being a raw beginner, you can

Photo 519. A model tiled roof made of pre-cut individual tiles glued on one at a time: a painstaking procedure but a very effective finish.

Photo 520. Real old roofs often sag as timbers warp, a characteristic easily reproduced by curving your roof support between its 'truss' formers.

see that she did a pretty good job, so if she can do it … To finish the colouring, merely wash another layer of wood dye over the entire roof to tie the colours together. Precisely which colour dyes you use and in what strength depends upon the finish you want to achieve, of course. Experiment! (Photo 522)

CURVED INTERLOCKING TILES

Familiarly known as 'Pantiles' (Photo 523), these reversed-curved, moulded tiles are not very common in the South West, being more familiar in the South East and East Anglia. Doon 'ere we generally use the flatter, ridged 'double romans' (Photo 524), and sometimes even 'triple romans', as shown behind more doubles in photo 525. All are known as 'mathematical tiles' in that they interlock with their neighbours and are thus more secure in a wind. They also need less overlap so that while per each they

are more expensive to buy, far fewer are used, so on balance there's little in it. Here you can see plain tiles and 'Bridgewater Double Romans' side by side for comparison (Photo 526).

Colours vary as much as with any baked clay product, as you can see, although when originally laid they would have been very similar in tone, being generally from the same clay and made by the same tile maker. These days, most are second-hand or 'reclaimed' – often being mixed from several sources – and thus colours can be very mixed indeed!

Wills do a pantile, although you might find it rather large for 4mm scale, so try modelling both pantile and roman types by drawing horizontal lines across the roof supports as normal, but then glue lengths of tinned copper wire down the roof at intervals of around 2.5mm for pantiles and 2mm for double romans. You can then lay strips of paper across the

Photo 521. 'Foxes Farmhouse' shows the delightful effect of laying rows of individual tiles cut from sheets of thin card coloured slightly differently. By using dyes instead of paints, a further overall wash of a particular dye can 'harmonize' the various colours while retaining the individuality of every single tile. Slow, perhaps, but very easy to do!

Photo 522. In the detail shot here there are a number of points worth making: the porch is supported by etched brass brackets and its diagonal corner is tiled using square tiles bent in the middle. Similarly shaped tiles are available in reality, although ridged hips are far more common. The walls are Slater's embossed brick – cut into lacing courses after painting – glued to a card wall into which the window and door openings were cut, these being provided with thin card frames and 'Downesglaze' bars. Note the curtains! The infill between the bricks is just ballast laid in thin puddles of Evostick, while I think a 'warm oak' finish wash was used to pull the individual tiles into a harmonious whole.

roof into wood glue, using a screwdriver to poke the paper down firmly between the lengths of tcw. For double romans, merely ensure that each strip is firmly prodded down into the gaps, pressing equally on both sides (Photo 527). When the glue had dried hard, it might have been worth running a knife blade down the right-hand side of every second wire to suggest the gap between individual tiles but it was

Photo 524.   Flatter interlocking tiles, ridged down the middle for strength and again at one side to hook over their neighbour, feature more in the south-west where they are commonly known as 'double romans'.

Photo 523.   Reverse-curved interlocking tiles, commonly called 'pantiles', are most common in the south-east of England but can be found elsewhere if you look hard enough.

Photo 525.   A motley collection of 'double romans' and beyond them the rather rarer 'triple romans'; spotted on the same barn roof in Somerset.

Photo 526.   'Bridgewater [a size] double romans' on the roof on the right, plain tiles on the left.

not something I felt was necessary at the time. For pantiles, poke equally firmly but on the right-hand side of the wire only, allowing the paper to flow rather more gently up the left-hand side and over the wire. This will create the 'lop-sided' look of the type (Photo 528). You, of course, may judge the results for yourself and proceed accordingly!

One final comment about this last photo is that it shows four types of roofing on the one model: from the left; double romans (on the out-house), pantiles, thatch and finally slate (below the little attic window). This is entirely prototypical I assure you, having studied large blowups of this, the one-time village Post Office, but such variety is hardly something someone is likely to think of putting on a 'generic' model – which only goes to prove that reality is usually far better than your imagination!

THATCH

Thatch is a subject all its own. The complexities are legion: given that it has a wide variety of base materials (of which long-straw, wheat-straw and reed are only the most well-known), that almost no two houses have precisely the same shape of roof or detail of feature, and that over the years, thousands of thatchers have each added their own subtle differences of method and decoration to their work, not to mention the innumerable regional differences in

ABOVE: *Photo 527. Model 'double romans' made by laying horizontal paper strips over tcw verticals and pressing down firmly between each wire with a flat blade.*

BELOW: *Photo 528. These pantiles, to the left of the thatch, are created by pressing the paper down on one side of the wire only.*

style and nomenclature, all of which makes it quite impossible to generalize on what makes the ideal model thatch! (A few of these variations are illustrated in Appendix III.) If you want to know what thatch looks like in the area you are modelling then you just have to research it by finding old period photos of the location and copying what you see. For colour, go and have a look at what's left! What you will find suggested in this book is therefore (horror of horrors) a generic thatch! Well, almost.

What you see in photo 529 is tealeaves glued over a well-rounded ply base. It is a fair replica of the thatch used on a cottage in Ablington, Wilts, the prototype for the model, while the Poole Quay thatched cottages, seen in photo 530, came from a drawing of a row in Wherwell, Hampshire. These used finely-sieved sawdust. I would admit that the

thatch on the rearmost row does not quite 'swell' as much as perhaps it ought to near the ridge but I suspect the cardboard supporting it got wet and 'sagged' as it dried. The answer was to use something stronger the next time, hence the sanded ply!

The old Post Office at South Perrott, Dorset, will be familiar to you by now (Photo 531) and again it is tealeaves glued to a rounded plywood base. The 'cap' however (as many thatchers call the ridge), is plumber's hemp, with 'liggers' of cotton which has been drawn through wood glue to stiffen it, then held in place by u-shaped 'spars' of tinned copper wire pushed into individually-drilled holes. Finding these holes under all that 'hair' was somewhat troublesome, but without actually pegging the thread down, the hemp would not stay flat while the glue dried! Perhaps next time a balsa-wood-based apex

Photo 529.   A quick thatched roof in a Wiltshire style: tea leaves on a 3mm plywood base with the corners roundly sanded.

Photo 530. Some early thatches of mine which used finely-sieved sawdust glued to cardboard. The latter unfortunately sagged slightly as the glue dried, thus loosing some of its 'fatness'. Tolerable but far from perfect.

former might be more efficacious, allowing the pegs to be just pushed in. In any case, whether you look down on it, as in photo 531, or up at it, as in photo 532, it seems to be tolerably acceptable, so why not try it and see how you get on? As for ply bases, sanding MDF might be quicker but as its dust is a car-cinogenic it would be far more dangerous to health. Definitely not recommended!

Odd-shaped Thatch

Plywood however, is really only practical for properties which have relatively flat thatches such as that

Photo 531. A better effect; this time with tealeaves from a tea-bag, glued to a ply base and with a ridge (newly replaced, going by the golden colour), formed with plumber's hemp and cotton 'liggers'

LEFT: *Photo 532. Looking upwards at the same roof it is equally effective; the very small bits of leaf you get in the basic tea bag look, from any angle, very much like the ends of straw thatch.*

BELOW: *Photo 533. A real thatched roof in North Dorset. Being almost flat, plywood would make an excellent base for a model. Do note, however, that it is steeper than most thatches — more akin to one from the New Forest than the Somerset/ Dorset borders.*

Photo 534. A model of an old thatched bakery, cottages and stores complex. From an original in South Perrott, Dorset.

shown in photo 533. More complex roofs are difficult, for example the old bakery in South Perrott is made up of four or more different buildings (Photo 534). Few of the walls line up, only the elevation facing the road is straight, and its thatch is made more complex still because the two main roofs are not at right-angles and because the dormers (see photo 536), are also entirely dissimilar. It is, simply, an attractive-looking glorious confusion of a thatch which, in reality, must test any thatcher's prowess to make look attractive, and attempting to replicate its base in any solid material, impractical.

So if sheet wood is not suitable, then what else can we use to replicate the depth and inherent 'softness' of thatch? Laying stands of PVA-soaked wool

across a simple card sub-roof is one idea which has been recommended in the past but I tried it at Poole and found the results too inconsistent to be useful. Fortunately, creating a nicely-rounded profile in cardboard is both a feasible and a fun and relatively quick way of getting a very reasonable effect. You might care to try it, starting of course with a substantial support structure which will be familiar to any school-kit builders (Photo 535). Where the roof is straight, as above the road face, that's easy: merely add a long, reasonably-fitted piece of 1.6mm card and glue it firmly into place, ensuring the eaves are glued properly to the tops of the walls. Where a single sheet is not really practical, owing to dormers or walls of varying heights or angles, simply add much

Photo 535. Preparing the roof supports using standard, 1.6mm photo-frame mounting card, available from art shops.

Photo 536. 1.6mm card, with the corners filed off the upper surfaces, makes a tolerable base layer on to which the 'features' can be added.

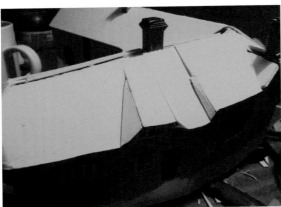

shorter pieces, beginning at the lowest level and working your way along, as per photo 536.

Where changes occur, with dormers or chimneys to work around, ensure you have a flat base either side to build up from, and then either make curved cardboard formers, bent in the fingers until they are the right shape, or build up your shapes from carefully cut segments (Photo 537). If necessary, use a file to take the edge of the card back at a chamfer of an appropriate angle so you can have a strong butt joint. You do not want anything collapsing! Continue in like fashion until you have covered the roof (Photo 538).

Having researched an appropriate pattern for the cap, carve an outline of it in cardboard and glue it just

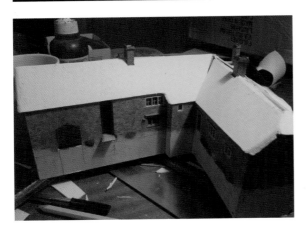

MIDDLE: *Photo 537. Dormers and the like are best accommodated with small sub-roofs. Note the gap along the roof's apex, which is deliberate.*

BOTTOM: *Photo 538. Now the basic card base is in place, but there are gaps to fill.*

below the ridge. You are only attempting to capture the lower edge, the upper being unimportant at this stage, so keep your card narrow to give you the flexibility to bend it into place if necessary. Note how there are often large 'swags' around chimneys and hips (Photo 539). At this point I will confess to a mistake – hardly my first in 30-odd years – by admitting that the card I have used here is too thin.

As you will see, I should have used 1.6mm card, as I will next time!

Don't forget to add smaller, similar sections to any odd dormers or, in fact, anywhere a cap would be vital, as here around and behind the nearest chimney (Photo 540). It will be noted that there is a narrow fillet on the nearest corner. I felt the sharp edge of the two card segments was too angular so I carved

Photo 539.   Before that, however, another layer of cardboard is added to provide the relief required for a raised cap. Shapes and flourishes tend to be regionally based, but most thatchers have their own particular style details too. If you cannot find period photos to work from, and you want to know what the local peculiarities were, ask an elderly inhabitant! Alternatively, look up 'thatch' on the appropriate local County Council website, where some record local historical practises for the county.

Photo 540.   Even thatches can have odd gables which will require their own caps and swags, as with this chimney atop a blind gable. Note, too, that the roof's thatched edge curves gently although the walls angle away from the corner in flat sections.

them away and bodged a flatter bit in. This is not a problem as it will all be hidden very shortly!

Now is the time to complete the roof 'former' by filling in any odd holes. Here you see the use of a mixture of sawdust and wood glue but these days 'decorator's caulk', or even a water-based wood-glue/filler such as 'Instant Nails', would be both quicker and easier (Photo 541). Fill, smooth and file both the top and the undersides of your card until you have those lovely rounded shapes which mirror the sensual curves of your prototype (Photo 542).

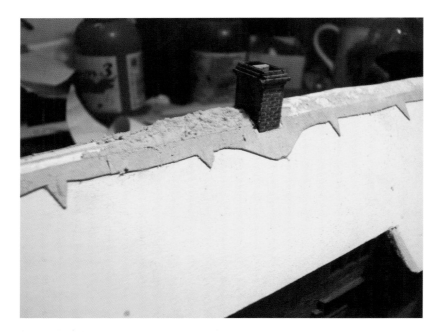

Photo 541. Filling in the gaps and providing the curved, flowing shape that thatch requires. A flat-bladed steel knife or spatula is probably best; dampen the blade for a smooth finish.

Photo 542. Leave to dry thoroughly, then finish the roof base with nicely rounded edges by filing away any unwanted ridges.

COVERINGS

Using hemp as recommended by Pendon is one possible route, and it is probably more practical than using human hair as they did at one time, but it is probably an even slower process than individual hand-tiling, and that's saying a lot! That's because every section has to be laid as a 'clump' into wood glue and allowed to dry; then it can be trimmed with tiny curved nail scissors! However, what you see on a 'proper' wheat-straw or reed thatch is merely the ends of the stalks, not any part of the length, so using any linear material might not the best answer. Certainly done well it looks exquisite – I would not argue with that for a moment – but done perhaps less well, or attempted by someone in a hurry, well; let's just say it might not be the most practical starting point for a less experienced modeller.

Dried tealeaves on the other hand, especially those from teabags, have the right colour – and if not, that is easily amended by spraying – and they also have a wonderful texture which apes thatch delightfully. Also, being part of a bush, tealeaves are a material which takes to wood glue perfectly! They certainly have a more natural, inherent 'variety' of texture and colour than any simple brown flock and are thus my preference as a standard covering for thatch.

As for application, first ensure you have to hand an ample supply of well-rinsed, dried and sifted tea-bag tealeaves. Start at one end by adding a goodly layer of slightly watered-down wood glue over perhaps a 6 inch (150mm) length and then simply throw lots of tealeaves on, stopping just short of your 'end of glue' line. Pat firmly down with the palm of the hand once or twice to ensure the leaves are in good contact with both glue and roof, then spread more glue and tealeaves along the next section and, in one continuous process, repeat until the other end of the roof is reached (Photo 543).

Leave to dry for a day or two, then patch any holes you find and, inverting the finished model, ensure you have a good further coating under any swathes of rising roof and beside any dormer windows (Photo 544). Finally, add any vegetation required such as ivy or laurel (Photo 545), and any other details such as caps to your chimneys.

At this juncture, all your hard work in creating a pattern for your thatch's cap should be rather more obvious than mine, (Photo 546), which from this angle disappears completely. But as they say, 'The man who never made a mistake never made anything', and, if it were a choice between this and a mass-produced resin cottage, I know which this modeller would prefer for his layout! (Photo 547)

Photo 543. Tip a thick layer of thatching material over the glue, pressing firmly into corners and on to edges before tipping off the loose excess for use further along the roof.

Photo 544.   Once completely dry, invert and ensure you glue a good layer over the undersides and the lower edges where the thatch rises over the dormers; then turn right side up and fill any missed patches on the main roof.

Photo 545.   Add any vegetation, such as ivy or laurel, to walls and/or roof as your last job.

Photo 546. Such speedy methods cannot produce the perfect model thatch but consider the balance of time taken versus effect achieved: this method takes but a few hours, against that of thatching a large model with hair or hemp which takes weeks, yet it still makes a pretty fair job of representing established, slightly-weathered thatch. As such, it might be less appropriate for an individual feature model but if you've a whole village to create ...

Photo 547. It is ready now to set into your landscape – where all your hard work will 'vanish' as the building blends beautifully into its surroundings. Which is just as it should be, until you deliberately peer closely for a better look!

CHAPTER EIGHT

NIGHT SCENES

THEATRE LIGHTING

I dislike resorting to opinion but it would be impossible to understand the reasoning behind my choice of subjects without expressing at least one. To me, a model railway is much like any other entertainment in that one is putting on 'a show'; providing a distraction from everyday life. Certainly construction is a large part of the fun, and operation has its own life-long fascinations, but completion should not be the aim itself, rather that after completion it

should be pass the test of, 'Now it's finished, does it work?' Does it work physically, of course, in that do the trains move properly without falling off but, more significantly, does it work visually? Does it impress as a piece of 'theatre'; and if it has a theme or story, as it should, then does that come across properly? Bluntly, does the finished work create its own 'ambience'?

As we have seen, part of that 'feel' is providing the right lighting and backdrop to create an overall impression the moment either you or a visitor

Photo 548. Tupdale's Yorkshire moors at night. With the room lights out and the door closed, the model is lit only by its own buildings' interior lighting and its sunset.

Photo 549. Modern model coach lighting is excellent but its brilliance is factory fixed, so you must adjust your own lighting if you want it to look 'balanced'.

enters 'the railway room', or at least that corner of the room wherein resides your railway. Creating such an all-enveloping environment helps to remove distractions and shows your model in, quite literally, 'the right light'. Thus a proper backscene and bright but unobtrusive lighting (which should go at least some way towards mimicking the brilliance of genuine daylight), should be a 'given' for any model railway. By way of confirmation, just look at how large and medium-sized museum models are often seen by a viewer standing in a much dimmer environment than that of the model; that is, from a room deliberately darkened to contrast strongly with the brilliance of the lit model because this makes the model seem brighter and that brilliance enhances its realism.

The opposite end of that very same environmental spectrum is taking your viewer closer and closer to the detail by dimming the whole model gradually into darkness and providing little bright spots of interest here and there: little pin-points of light to excite the curiosity. These should primarily provide a good overall impression of 'night', of course, but they should also encourage you to move in closer to

investigate the sources, to look inside structures to glimpse more intimate scenes and so, at an entirely different level of perception, to understand something else, new, about the model. The fact is, good lighting enables you to tell a better and more detailed story.

Sound and interior lighting are currently becoming available in our commercial model trains and to make best use of the latter, perhaps a few words on the theory and practice of lighting a railway and its structures might be in order so that you, too, can build dramatic night scenes to show them off in! (Photo 549)

Signals, platform and street lighting are obvious first choices but do think beyond those and look at the broader opportunities that changes of lighting give you. At the micro level you can isolate one small part of a model by creating an interior, illuminating it, and then removing all outside distractions by creating 'night time'. Drama, history, humour, period features and lifestyle: these are just a few of the things you can consider using to enrich your story by introducing by a change in lighting. On the other hand, at the macro level, for sheer visual drama nothing beats a

Photo 550. *The sunset is deliberately placed behind the viaduct to get maximum benefit from the silhouettes of trains passing in front of it as seen by a seated operator. It is also, deliberately, clearly visible from both the operating and viewing positions without the operator's head getting in the way. It's called 'planning'.*

really brilliant sunset and I am amazed it is so rarely modelled! But either way, lighting is just another way of having fun, and that's what we do it for!

LIGHTING LEVELS – THE SUNSET

The first point to consider is that ready-to-run trains with interior lighting are a done deal but while cannot readily change their intensity or colour, we can adjust our home-made lighting to best suit them. In fact, the human eye is incredibly adaptable to dim light so the overall level of illumination is, there-fore, far less important than the *balance* of one light source against another. It may be a largely subjective judgement as to whether one particular light source should be stronger or weaker than any other but it follows, therefore, that an understanding of the supposed 'real' source of that light is helpful. Are you trying to represent a candle, an oil lamp or an electric light bulb? Once we understand what effect we want, we can set our illumination levels by choos-ing the right equipment and fitting it in such a way as enables us to adjust those levels if we need to.

Photo 551. In case you think my colours are too bright, I took this real sunset over Wellington, in Shropshire, in 2008.

Take that initial photograph. The sunset is simply a long curved sheet of clear acrylic sprayed red and orange on one side and painted with clouds on the other (Photo 550). For sure, the area where I wanted illumination was generally established, the colours were sprayed and then a bulb was fitted behind and wired. The background sky-scape of blue and distant clouds came next, after which it was left until night allowed illumination only from behind.

It was now possible to decide where to paint dark colours to block out the light – the actual painting being done with the room light on, of course. The unwanted areas of back-light were sprayed black and when the 'patches' looked right when illuminated from behind, the dark areas were undercoated in light grey emulsion. It was left until daylight to over-paint the 'patches' with clouds, as you see here. And in case you think my sunset's a little bright, these are two English sunsets: the first photographed in 2008 (Photo 551) and the second from 1981, the year after Mount St Helens erupted (Photo 552). The dawn in photo 553 I photographed in 2010 from my bedroom window so no, the model sunset isn't too bright!

SIGNAL BOXES

There are very few buildings as well-glazed and open to internal inspection as a signalbox. It often has huge windows on three or more sides, so lighting one can be rather a challenge. With the sunset turned down from its full brilliance this signalbox becomes

Photo 552. This second one (from Toller Down, Dorset) is not only the best I ever saw but certainly the best of hundreds I have photographed. It dates from 1981, the year after Mt St Helens erupted.

Photo 553. Finally comes this recent dawn, seen from my bedroom window. Between them these three photos prove – as Turner noted – that it is quite impossible to match the brilliance of nature's sunlit colours using paint – but we can at least try ...

more prominent, even reflecting its light source off the roof of the passing train (Photo 554).

Of course, the days when a grain-of-wheat (GoW) bulb was the only choice are long gone and a wonderful plethora of light emitting diodes (LEDs) is now available, some in superb colours. Even so, don't dismiss the GoW out of hand entirely: those on Tupdale have been in use now for ten years and still work and in fact, of the twenty or so I originally fitted, only one was recently replaced owing to its being smashed during a move. They have one other advantage over LEDs too: they are a 'pin-point' of light, not an overall glow. Now in the general illumination of interiors this is neither here nor there but in a signal box where there is nowhere to hide the light source, and being aware that your light source might actually be visible from certain angles, a proper 'bulb' placed where it should be actually

Photo 554. As the 'modelled' sunset fades away (by your turning it down with a dimmer switch), the signalbox interior draws the visitor's attention so becoming a new focus.

Photo 555.   It is lit by a single grain-of-wheat bulb. The bare, tinned copper supply wires are run up slots in the back wall, sawn into it before fitting. The bulb was added afterwards.

Photo 556.   Two more grain-of-wheat bulbs make excellent platform oil lamps when suitably dimmed with resistors.

Photo 557.   Another advantage of 'grains of wheat' is that their incandescent light allows a mixture of colours to show up nicely, as this lever-frame proves. Modern 'warm white' LEDs now allow you to mimic the colour of real bulbs and bring out most colours equally well.

looks better than an LED (Photo 555). This obviously applies all the more so where the source can be very clearly seen, as in the 'oil' platform lamps in photo 556. Moreover, they illuminate very well, too: even reduced to 'corrected' light levels with a resistor, one GoW provided ample light to photograph this interior by (Photo 557). The levers are correctly set for a down express, by the way …

To get the power to the bulb, two single strands of bare tinned copper wire were let into two well-separated slots sawn in the inner back wall and taken right down beneath the baseboard. Here a resistor was fitted to the positive leg before connecting up to a dedicated, individually-switched, 12 volt lighting supply. Inside, the ends of the wires and the legs of

Photo 558. Where you cannot see the back of a building, just run the wires up the back so they are easily accessible if necessary.

the GoW were tinned, and then the bulb wires were merely held across the tinned copper ones and soldered in place without any mechanical joint. Ease of replacement should they blow, is the priority, and a quick touch with the iron is vital if you are not going to melt the plastic of the signal box, so struggling to free soldered loops or twisted joints is just asking for trouble: a lot of trouble!

Such devious routing is not always necessary, of course, and if the back cannot be seen, then just run

your wires down the outside as I did here (Photo 558). In either case you will eventually need to be able to remove the roof to replace the bulb since you cannot get at it any other way. That's easily done if you fit the roof with small flanges which are a tight fit inside the walls. This will not only enable the roof to become a simple push fit, but also prevent stray light escaping through any gaps.

DAY-NIGHT BALANCE

Apart from various ambient light/interior light balances, the day/night balance is worth considering too. In a normal daylight scene with no lighting, a signalbox is just another building with a stygian interior (Photo 559); light up the inside, however, and even in daylight its relevance and purpose become far more prominent (Photo 560). At night, of course, the illumination is far more dramatic (Photo 561), but you will have to model your interiors carefully as even the tiniest detail, such as these block instruments and bells, really stand out when back-lit and surrounded by darkness!

And it is not only day/night and interior/ambient lighting which has to be balanced but interior/interior lighting too. Nothing should be seen in isolation because when you stand back, if everything is not properly balanced you will still loose any sense of

Photo 559. Room lighting bright enough to simulate sunlight leaves building interiors particularly dark on a model.

Photo 560. *Switching on the interior lighting, however, allows you to see carefully modelled interior detail but without the extra illumination being too obvious.*

Photo 561. *Although the camera has failed to capture the subtlety of the colours, the drama of a well-lit interior is obvious. It's even worth turning block-bells in real brass when you can see them clearly, as the detail shows.*

realism. By way of illustration, this same signalbox looks very bright compared to the goods shed behind it (Photo 562) but so it should: the signalbox would have been well lit to enable the reading of notices and the writing of logs, while the whole huge goods shed was probably illuminated by just one or two Tilley lamps dangling from the rafters. Although bright enough to move goods around by, it would look feeble in the extreme from without, so your model lighting needs to reflect that (Photo 563). Two GoW sources, around a third and two-thirds of the way along, were thus deemed adequate and were fitted with strong resistors. Again, the roof is removable for access (Photo 564).

The pub was rather different in detail, although the approach was similar. The porch is lit by one

Photo 562. You need to understand the reality of period lighting if you want to balance the interiors of different buildings properly.

Photo 563. Unlike signal boxes, goods shed and stores interiors were often dismally lit. It was usually just about sufficient not to trip over things but you often needed a hand-lamp to read any labels!

Photo 564. This one is lit with two more grain-of-wheat's, each with its own resistor wired in series.

bulb, the bar by another (remember this model dates back to before 'warm white' and 'pale orange' LEDs were available), but the fire in the fireplace was lit by an early red LED (Photo 565). Both bulbs were very carefully placed so that while the interiors were properly illuminated, the light which 'spilled out' onto the ground outside also did so in a realistic way.

As the pub windows are just a few inches away from the edge of the model, an interior of painstaking detail was created (Photos 566 & 567), although ten years ago, my old 35mm film camera was unable to record it as well as I would have liked! Today's digital cameras are much better at close-up photography and capture a glimpse with the incredible depth-of-

Photo 565. Rural pubs rarely had illuminated signs back in the 1950s; everybody knew what and where it was so you only needed to illuminate the porch to show you were open. Even as late as the 1970s some pubs in rural Buckinghamshire didn't even bother with that, as I remember very well.

field available in daylight (Photo 568), yet are capable of capturing something through the window in the dark, too (Photo 569).

With this model it is not the roof which lifts off but the whole top floor, thus revealing the wiring to the three light sources, all on the ground floor. Each has its own resistor under the baseboard to enable the lighting balance to be properly adjusted after the building has been assembled (Photo 570). The box over the bar's lamp deliberately does not shield the light entirely from the rooms above but

a thin paper cover lets just enough light through to provide a glow upstairs, as if light from the hall was escaping through a doorway into a bedroom (see photo 565 again), which is a subtle way of suggesting life elsewhere in the building. Light is excluded from the other windows by providing full baffles (Photo 571).

LIGHTING TUBES

You will remember our leaving holes in the floor of

Photo 566. 'The Summit' pub on Tupdale has a full bar interior which was as correct for the period as could be remembered by friends old enough to have seen them. I recall considerable discussions on the likelihood or otherwise of beer mats in a rural Yorkshire moorland pub in the mid 1950s ...

Photo 567. With plates above the bar and a fireplace lit by a red LED 'The Summit' has two happy customers. The cupboard by the door hides the dartboard. The whole room measures only 40 × 50mm.

Photo 568.   Again, with the levels correct, the interior can be clearly seen in daytime, which is why it is right under visitors' noses!

Photo 569.   There's a second window in the end wall to help you see the inside from a different angle.

LEFT: **Photo 570.** *Each light has its own fused supply, then if one bulb fails, the others can continue 'the show' until you get the chance to lift the top off to replace it.*

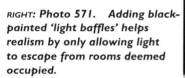

RIGHT: **Photo 571.** *Adding black-painted 'light baffles' helps realism by only allowing light to escape from rooms deemed occupied.*

our school for 'lighting tubes' (Photo 572). Where a model is situated in a location which is difficult to reach, or where making a removable roof is impractical, it is often better to fit these simple rectangular tubes of card or plastic through the floor and up into the building. With a matching hole in the scenery below you can then fit removable lighting from under the baseboard. These assemblies should have a top, to prevent the lamp being pushed up too high into the tube, and have part of one or more sides shortened by a few millimetres to let the light escape (Fig. 573).

Made square for GoW bulbs, the limited angle of light emitted by diodes means rectangular tubes allowing sideways mounting are better for these but in both cases, the idea is to move the bulb slightly up and down the tube until precisely the best level and angle of lighting is reached (Fig. 574). At that point the wires, which will need to be both flexible and insulated, can be held in place with a piece of sponge foam pushed up the base of the tube. Bulb or LED replacement from underneath is thus relatively simple and allows the building's roof to be permanently secured. It might be thought that a central location would be best as at 'a' (Fig. 575), but in most cases a corner location as in 'b' works just as well and can be used to highlight a feature or figure, as in Tupdale's waiting room (see Photo 417 in Chapter 6).

It is perhaps worth noting that you do not have to be able to see a window to be able see the light which would spill out of it at night. This concept was applied to the rear of this waiting room (Photo 576), although in this next photograph its effect on the platform face and surface opposite (Photo 577) is only visible in a large-sized photo – which is

RIGHT: *Photo 572.   Where you cannot remove the roof or upper storeys to gain access to your bulbs, you can always fit a 'lighting tube' and insert them from below, as shown here in the school.*

BELOW: *Fig. 573.   Plastic or cardboard can be used, or even rolled, glued paper – as you prefer – but if using LEDs, then make the light tubes oval or rectangular to allow you to bend the head over; most LEDs only give off light over a 30- to 60-degree angle.*

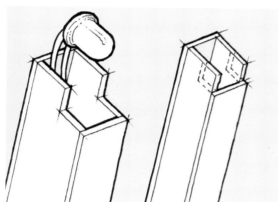

a shame because 'in the flesh' it is a subtle but very effective feature which undoubtedly adds depth and realism.

Above the station building note two other pin-points of light emanating from tiny holes in the backscene where cottage windows are painted. There are a few more tiny flecks of light in a distant corner where a town is depicted (Photo 578). In the dark they are, of course, just hints of life in an otherwise featureless landscape but they still rouse people's curiosity and get them to notice such sub-tleties later, when daylight returns.

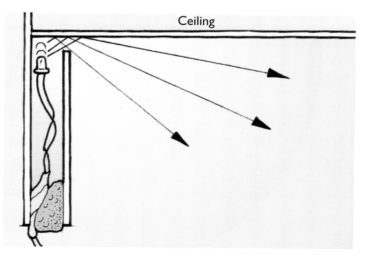

Ceiling

RIGHT: *Fig. 574.   For general interiors I suggest angling the head up slightly so that the light is reflected widely across the room by the ceiling, thus giving an even illumination. The source itself should be carefully hidden out of direct sight.*

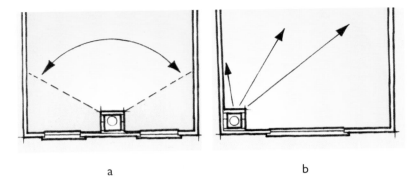

a b

Fig. 575. Note too, that a bulb fitted in the middle of the front wall (as in 'a') can find it difficult to light the nearer corners. Fitted in a corner ('b'), however, the expected 'spread' of light is reduced from 180 degrees to nearly 90 degrees, which is much nearer the limitations of an LED. Grain-of-wheat bulbs, of course, have no such problems but they do tend to burn out more quickly unless really dimmed with a resistor.

Photo 576. Use your imagination. You can illuminate rooms you can't see and have light shine out of windows you haven't made either, as here, simply by cutting suitable rectangles in back walls and fitting lamps inside …

Photo 577.   If you look closely enough, you can actually see the effect of placing a lamp behind a hole in a wall because light is spilling from the waiting room onto the face of the platform opposite. A very subtle detail but one you will find worth doing when somebody eventually spots it and goes 'wow'!

Photo 578.   In the very far corner of Tupdale I hand-painted this tiny, distant townscape. Normally invisible, you can draw attention to such details by lighting a few tiny holes here and there. These show up in the dark, excite the curiosity and so encourage closer study of the area later when the lights go up again.

RAILWAY AND STREET LIGHTING

Commercial lighting is readily available in both 2mm and 4mm scales, these platform lamps (left) and yard floodlights (Photo 579), just about passing muster in N gauge but the available range is limited. Also, only the newest releases use LEDs and these can be rather expensive. On the bright side, they all have the advantages of being simple to weather and are quickly replaced if damaged when track-cleaning. Be aware that GoW bulbs, if used in multiple, can draw a considerable current. I certainly advise measuring the total current drawn by every lighting circuit and keeping any one of them down to less than 2amps. The suggestion for larger installations is to break your lighting into sections and fit separate fuses for each (Photo 580).

Similar styles of lamps, but in much greater variety, are available in H0, many of which do well enough for 4mm scale. Even so, there was nothing even vaguely appropriate available for a rural Settle and Carlisle station so these Midland Railway type post and wall-mounting lamps are made from scratch (Photo 581). Wiring is achieved by making the post of the further one from brass tube (the return), and poking an insulated wire up the middle as the feed, while the nearer one is mounted on a 'plank' post of copper-coated paxolin strip, suitably 'gapped' up the middle.

Multiple-circuit wiring, as required for this N-gauge gantry (Photo 582), was achieved by using 'resistance wire' as used for coil-windings. These tiny single-core wires have an enamel insulation around them which is removed from the ends by heating with a well-tinned iron, after which a length of a foot or so can be soldered to the feed of each LED and

Photo 579.   When you get down to N gauge, the commercial offerings tend to be rather over-scale, but the sheer number required on a large model makes them an invaluable time-saver.

Photo 580. **Do break your lighting circuits down into separately fused sections – it's safer and makes finding faults so much quicker!**

BELOW: *Photo 581.* **Sparsely used rural stations have very few lamps so these can be hand-made to advantage, as with these two Midland-style platform lamps.**

poked down the gantry's hollow legs. Square brass tube is used for those and a rectangular section for the gantry bridge itself, again the brass construction providing a sizeable common return. The sixteen feeds so fitted into this 2mm-scale gantry to power the sixteen different LEDs are all thus wonderfully hidden! The only requirement now is to measure the resistance of the length of wire used and, where necessary, to adjust the value of each light's resistor to account for it.

The choice of resistor value for each light is up to you, of course, depending upon the voltage of your power supply, your preferences for brightness and the characteristics of the lamps or LEDs you are using. A 'multipack' of ¼ watt, carbon or wire-wound resistors containing ten of each value from 1 ohm to 100 megohms is probably your best bet, allowing you to find a favourite for any job you like, lighting or otherwise, merely buying extra multiples of the sizes you

Photo 582. *Of course, if you want a fully-working MAS gantry with five signal heads including 'feathers' and Position Light Signals to match your particular track plan, then you're probably on your own ...*

use most. As a guide, and assuming a 5v DC mains-powered or 4.8v battery lighting supply, resistances in the range of 100 to 600 ohms might suit standard LEDs, while for 12volt DC supplies start with 1k6 or so and work up or down in value as you see fit. The 'bright white' and blue examples generally require something rather higher, perhaps in the 2k5 to 6k range, while 3mm super-bright surface mount (as used in this 'limit of shunt' sign in photo 583, for 'position light signals' post-mounted below MAS, and in pairs for the 'feathers' on the gantry), might be as much as 47k. The new very tiny surface mounts now available, like the 1.6mm × 0.6mm example in photo 584, will require something even stronger however, perhaps in the 60–80k range, depending largely upon the colour they emit.

The 2mm-scale ground signals made using these miniscule LEDs (Photo 585), are a real struggle to wire. The result though, when you've added hoods, name panel and some grey paint to the back, are these phenomenally-tiny working ground signals less than 2 scale feet across, shown 'on' in photo 586 and 'off' in photo 587. But now I am straying into the area of electrics and wiring, which is a whole different book all of its own.

Fine detail like this right under people's noses is always important however, especially as N-gauge models tend to be rather flat owing to the small scale. If you can get people's eyes right down to track level then their whole perception of reality really kicks in simply because ground level is where you see the real world from and in the smaller scales, a lower

Photo 583. '*Surface-mount' LEDs now allow you to make tiny illuminated signs, such as this 3.6 × 2mm, 1:148th scale 'limit of shunt' signal. The face was simply painted black, and the 1.5mm high lettering scratched away.*

viewpoint really helps the perception of realism. Put another way, what you are looking at suddenly becomes entirely familiar from down at the human perspective and thus it seems far more realistic.

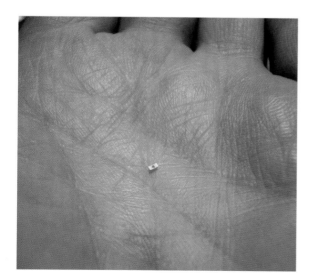

Photo 584.   *The smallest lights I have used to date are these 1.6 × 0.6mm surface-mount LEDs sourced in Germany.*

IN CONCLUSION

So, in the fervent hope that you will take at least some inspiration from the foregoing, I take my leave by encouraging you to embrace an intelligent, thoughtful approach to realism based partly on using your time where it is of the greatest benefit to the overall project, but also by not forgetting the other side of that very same coin: that it is the 'getting rid of sore thumbs' – those odd, small, unrealistic bits which destroy that vital 'suspension of disbelief' – which is the aim of the best modellers. This sounds complicated but really it just means standing back and having a good, long, hard look; and if something doesn't look 'right' then change it – you'll be all the happier for it when you do! (Photo 588)

Remember that 'quality' can be as complex as creating a highly detailed and very specific building just to establish 'place', or as simple as a flick with a brush, damp with a smear of the right paint in the right place, to highlight something which is less obvious than it should be. The trick is merely to learn which is the most appropriate in each instance and that is best done by observing reality, closely.

Photo 585.   Three of these minuscule LEDs are super-glued to a black plasticard 'face' with the three negatives in the middle. You get one chance only to solder a short length of tinned copper wire to all three at the same time ...

Photo 586.   The 2mm-scale ground signals thus produced are a real struggle to wire but what a result! 'On'.

Photo 587.   The same signal 'Off'. There are more than a dozen of these on this layout.

Putting every possible detail into a model not only takes ten times as long but, in the end, makes everything bland because as a whole, giving everything equal prominence offers no clues to the observer as to how to understand what he is presented with. Therefore, you are almost forced to make choices and the key in making them is to realize that what you leave out is as important as what you put in. With any model you are telling a story and you can either tell yours through a wandering, un-plotted narrative without any real form or function, or you can think through your history, your location, your narrative and, by including only the relevant and discarding the irrelevant, tell a story rich with drama, interest and lucidity. It is both what you put in, and what you leave out, which enables you to create a physical representation of your cerebral knowledge, your *understanding* of your subject matter, and so give a purpose to the reality you are creating. And as with every story: the better you tell it, the more enjoyable it becomes.

Photo 588. Tupdale's Up Advanced Starter is seen against a sight panel of white-painted stonework. The new, tiny surface-mount LEDs allow you to light both signal lamps and even ground signals with relative ease, and to add illuminated tail lamps if you want to. But these are really just all extras at the end of the day, and can be a distraction from creating that overall realism which can only be achieved by standing back and looking at the overall effect to find and resolve 'sore thumb' problems. The devil is truly in the detail, in fact. And talking of 'at the end of the day', did I mention my 'working sunset' experiment? Remind me to tell you all about it sometime ...

GLOSSARY OF BUILDING TERMS

Architecture   Structures designed by architects or masons, according to rules, and drawn up on carefully prepared plans.

Ashlar Stonework   'Won' stone fastidiously sawn into precisely finished blocks in which the joints are almost invisible. Expensive to produce.

Barge-board   A timber board or assembly attached to a gable end for both protection and decoration; sometimes pierced, often shaped.

Batten   A strip of wood of small size, used horizontally to attach individual rows of tiles or slates to roofs or walls.

Blade   One of two huge curved timbers forming a cruck.

Bond   The pattern of bricks in a wall.

Brace   Any timber fitted diagonally as triangulation to increase rigidity.

Brought to course   A 'lift' of random masonry brought to regular horizontal lines – each often being one day's work for one man.

Cames   Pre-formed lead strip, grooved both sides to accept small pieces of glass and used to make 'leaded lights'.

Capstones   Single stone blocks, often decorated, covering joints at the top of walls, especially gables.

Casement   A window which is hinged along one edge and so opens.

Catslide   A form of continuous roof extension which reaches nearer the ground than the rest of the roof.

Cladding   Any material which is used as a finish to a wall but which is not structural.

Closer   A brick of less than standard length or width used to alter the bond to that of a straight line at reveals or corners.

Collar   A horizontal timber used above wall height to tie together a pair of rafters.

Coursed   Laid in rows more or less horizontally.

Crenellations   Serrated upper edges of, typically, castle and church walls. Also known as battlements.

Cruck   A particular form of half-timbered cottage gable construction.

Damp-proof Course   A (normally) horizontal layer of impervious material placed in a wall to prevent rising damp.

Dentils/dentilations   Bricks set slightly proud of a wall's surface for decorative effect.

Dormer   A vertical wall, usually fitted with a window, projecting from a sloping roof and having its own roof.

Dripstone   A projecting stone or moulding used to direct rain away from the wall, door or window below.

Eaves   That part which forms the underside of a roof between its edge or gutter and the wall.

Fascia Board   Horizontal plank, originally painted timber, set vertically on edge, nailed to the ends of the rafters and on to which guttering is fixed. Positioned parallel to and just inside the roof edge.

Footing   An invisible support under a masonry structure, often concrete.

Gable   The triangular top of a wall extending to the apex of a roof.

Gauge   That part of a tile or slate which is visible and can thus be measured, equating to the distance between its battens.

Header   A brick laid in a wall so that only its end shows.

Herringbone   A pattern, usually of bricks, laid in alternating diagonal rows forming a zig-zag pattern.

Hip   The external joint formed when two sloping roofs intersect.

Inglenook   The partially wall-enclosed area around a fireplace or chimney.

Jamb   The timber vertical edge of a door or window at a wall.

Jetty   The cantilevered projection of an upper storey over a lower in a timber-framed house.

Joist   One of many horizontal timbers supporting a floor.

Lacing Course   Horizontal band of stone or bricks in a rendered or flint wall.

Lath   A thin strip of wood sprung into slots as a base for plaster.

Ledge   The horizontal timbers of a 'ledge and brace' door.

Ledge and Brace Door   An early type of door formed of vertical planks nailed to (usually three) horizontal timbers to which the hinges were secured, the latter braced by (usually two) diagonal timbers, resting on and rising from the hinge side towards the closing face.

Liggers   Hazel or willow rods used to secure thatch at caps and eaves.

Light   A vertical or near-vertical area of glazing, including glazing bars, but undivided by walls, mullions or transoms. A 'light' may be, or may contain, a 'casement' but not vice versa.

Lintel   A horizontal, structural beam over a door or window.

Mortar   A wet material used to bed and secure masonry to build a wall and for its pointing after construction.

Mullion   A vertical structural component sub-dividing a window. (*See also* 'transom'.)

Outshut   An extension of a building under a sloping roof.

Pitch   Angle of slope on a roof.

Plinth   A visible support under a masonry structure, usually proud of the wall's surface.

Pointing   The use of mortar to create a neat, waterproof exterior finish between pieces of masonry in walls.

Purlin   A longitudinal horizontal roof timber part-way up and supporting common rafters, sometimes exposed at the gable end. (*See also* 'wall-plate' and 'ridge'.)

Quoin   Distinctive brickwork or dressed stones at a reveal or corner of a wall.

Rafter   One of several sloping timbers running from wall-plate to apex of a roof, usually paired and usually supporting battens.

Rag Slates Large, random-width, diminishing length slates normally from 40in down to 26in long.

Rails The horizontal structural timbers of a framed door. (See 'ledge'.)

Random Not laid in courses.

Random Slates Traditional roof of slates varying in length and width and laid in diminishing courses.

Rendering A cement or lime-mortar covering over a wall.

Reveal The side masonry of a deep opening in a wall for a door or a window.

Ridge The apex of a roof.

Ridge beam A timber running along the apex of a roof.

Rubble Unsquared and undressed stone, usually 'found' rather than 'won' or 'worked'.

'Rusticated' Stonework Squared stonework in which the rear, sides and edges of the face are smoothed neatly but the middle of the face is left undressed and usually deeply rounded.

Sash A glazed wooden window or light which slides in guides, often counter-balanced by weights on ropes.

Shuttering Timber planks or boards used to line trenches to retain mud or wet concrete.

Shutters Timber constructions used to protect glazed lights and doors.

Sill Lower edge of a window opening in a wall: made of timber or masonry and normally projecting from the wall to throw water off.

Soffit The underside of a lintel, beam or arch.

Spars One of many names in thatching for the pegs which secure liggers and 'sways', their embedded cousins.

Squared Stonework Stone 'won' from quarries and sawn or worked into rectangular shapes.

Squinch A masonry arch formed across an interior angle between two adjoining walls to support weight above it – originally designed to support a round domed roof over a square room.

Stiles The vertical structural timbers of a panelled door.

Stretcher A brick or stone laid so that its longest face is visible.

Strut A supporting timber, usually vertical, often used in roofs.

Tie-beam The main horizontal timber of a truss tying together the feet of common rafters.

Torching The name for rendering the underside of tiles or slates.

Transom A horizontal structural member subdividing a window. (See *also* 'mullion'.)

Truss A triangular or triangulated framework spanning a structure or walls.

Valley The usually lead-lined gap between two sloping roof surfaces either at their foot or at the junction when two roofs meet at an internal angle.

Vernacular Architecture Structures not designed by architects or masons but merely by individuals or builders following or adapting local traditional methods. Often sketched freehand if committed to paper at all!

Wall-plate Horizontal timber fixed along the top of a wall to which rafters can be nailed.

Yoke A short horizontal timber joining two rafters near their tops.

ECCLESIASTICAL INSPIRATIONS

Not being a architect, it is with a certain trepidation that I present this collation of images of real churches, some of which provided the inspiration for the model featured in Chapter 4. I say that because, unlike most architecture, every church in the UK is unique and they nearly all have an architect's imprint, if not in all of their features, then at least some. That architect generally came from an established major, and almost exclusively city-based, practice. However, many of the more successful lived in the country where local contacts and Victorian munificence means that while your local town church might be generally credited to a recognized architect, it could actually have been designed, under supervision, by some unknown apprentice; while on the other hand, the unremarked church of some tiny hamlet could have been designed by such as Sir Gilbert Scott of Houses of Parliament fame – you'll never know until you look it up!

Now, with regard to vernacular architecture, it matters not whether you are on the side of Pevsner or Betjeman, (discuss!), but they certainly agreed upon the value of pompish Victorian architecture and explain it's attractions well in their writings – thus compensating for today's commonly held opinion that it was far too flowery and fussy. In fact, of course, it was not one style but many: from the squat neo-Norman of the 1840s to the (often very) High Gothic of the late period, one or more of which a multitude of zealous church 'restorers' visited upon 80 per cent of our admittedly crumbling English and Scottish churches during Victoria's reign. But whether or not these 'restorations' appeal to you visually, their representation in model form is a vital component of almost any church on a model railway since so many were, to a greater or lesser extent, transformed in such fashion during the railway age. Most, of course, are still with us which, had they just been left to crumble, might now be a very different story a century and more later.

Whitcombe, Dorset's, sixteenth-century church tower: banded, buttressed and castellated but without further decoration.

Early 'Victorian Revival' architecture in Dorset. East Stour's neo-Norman tower of 1841: decorated panels and a white wash suggesting Caen stone.

St. Mary's, Hale, Staffs (by Sir Gilbert Scott): built new in 1856 replacing a wooden one destroyed by fire. Note the higher levels of detailing, illustrated overleaf.

Elongated mythical creature gargoyle at Hales.

Winged lion gargoyle on another corner of the same tower.

Henstridge, Somerset; Church tower dating from 1900 with plinth, string courses, battlemented parapet with fanciful corner pinnacles and angled corner buttresses.

LEFT: Stalbridge, Dorset, St. Mary's Church tower, as rebuilt completely in 1866 – an early example of 'Late Perpendicular'.

RIGHT: Henstridge's unusual ship weathervane, originally by the RNAS 'HMS Dipper' in 1946, here as recently replaced in the same style by current apprentices.

St Swithun's, Cheswardine, Staffs, 'restored' 1887–9 under Loughborough Pearson shows the heights of monied Victorian Gothic, complete with chunky 'gargoyles'.

Nineteenth-century demons: 'grotesques' at St Swithun's.

Another grotesque further along, placed over a rain spout thus, being separate, not a gargoyle.

Wide gable-wall copings surmounted by crosses, Stalbridge; fifteenth century but 'restored' 1878 by T. H. Wyatt (and re-roofed 1928).

Stalbridge: fifteenth-century wall, masonry tower detail of 1866, extended nave wall of 1878.

Cheswardine again: flush-sided coping-styled buttress steps and ...

RIGHT: ... gravestones removed to boundary wall.

BELOW LEFT: Quality ironwork, Henstridge.

BELOW RIGHT: Poignant cherub, Stalbridge.

Fine wooden porch or 'narthex', Cheswardine.

Lych gate, date unknown, Henstridge.

Curious Cavalier and Roundhead detailing at Hale, reflecting a local civil war battle.

Twelfth-century nave window, Whitcombe.

LEFT: Fifteenth-century chancel-extension window, further along the same wall.

RIGHT: Authentic nineteenth-century high gothic windows with mullions and tracery, Stalbridge.

HEADERS UP!
A Simple Introduction to Brickwork

When representing brickwork, most modellers have traditionally used brick papers or, more recently, embossed card or plastic as a basis for their brick surfaces. Early railway modellers incised their patterns into plain card and then hand-coloured their bricks. Still today, the more demanding modeller will do the same to achieve specific effects. Here are a few pointers as to when embossed surfaces are useful and why, and when the hand carving, or incising, of mortar lines into card remains a useful tool in the modeller's armoury …

Regular Flemish-bond brickwork from near Derby: it is neat enough for an embossed base but the colours are far more varied and far too specifically distributed for any printed brick paper. It may be a fluke, but note especially how much paler the colours are where water runs, below the upper sills, and where traffic sprays the walls, although presumably the bottom foot or so is mud-splashed and thus stained somewhat darker.

A wall, from a barn in Staffordshire, showing typical local brick colouration: it is built in English Garden Bond, in which each row of headers is surmounted by three rows of stretchers. The wrought ironwork spreads the pressure of a tie-rod – fitted to counteract bowing walls.

RIGHT: This wall, from a barn near the one shown in the previous photograph, is in Common Bond, which is much the same except the number of rows of stretchers above each row of headers can vary considerably; here only from four to three, but six or more can occasionally be found.

A wonderful example of a vernacular variation, from a barn in the next village, showing a type of Common Bond but here with no more than two headers together, to tie the inner face of bricks to the outer. We might call it 'Uncommon Bond, variant 2H'.

This wall, which is a gable end of the first Staffordshire barn, seems to have no pattern to its structure at all. One might have assumed it had collapsed and been rebuilt by an amateur, except that the other end was just as bad, if not worse!

LEFT: An example, found in Shropshire, also with no apparent pattern, and yet considerable pains have been taken to add brick dentils (teeth along the crown). Most peculiar!

RIGHT: When replacing lath-and-plaster with noggins, each row of bricks is generally begun from opposite ends, with a partial brick cut precisely to fill any remaining gap. Note also the use of headers below, indicating a double-skin wall, but none above, suggesting these are only a single skin thick.

In Dorset, a considerable effort has been made with these recent noggins to make attractive angled patterns, known as 'raking bonds'.

North to the Welsh Marches for these lovely warm-coloured bricks which have been laid without a string, merely following the slope of the ancient timbers they are infilling. Rather cleverly, I suspect those thin horizontal timbers have been planed down and inserted half-way up each panel to most precisely make up any height adjustment needed, since only full-height bricks have been used above and below each one.

BELOW LEFT: This example, from south Shropshire, shows how the weight of upper storey walls and roof can be shared between timber beams and brick relieving arches, which latter take most of the weight. Indeed, the timbers are probably little more than joists, supporting just the arch infill and the floor of the hay loft above.

Some brick buildings have a curved corner, commonly made of consecutive rows of headers. This example in Staffordshire (less than a mile from the barns shown previously, despite the entirely different colouring), also shows how the bricks are progressively cantilevered out to a normal corner so as to support a standard roof structure.

BELOW RIGHT: A pigeon loft or dove-cot once provided a valuable food source for 'the gentry' and is suggestive of an 'estate' farm. This particular example would be a challenge to reproduce well as a model, though. Fortunately, wooden ones are more common!

ROOFS
A Brief History of Keeping the Rain Out

At the dawn of railways, thatch was the standard cheap roofing material. The most substantial properties tended to use solid stone for roofing, where it was available, and hand-formed clay tiles where it wasn't. Stone slabs got smaller over time, moving from locally sourced large slabs, through gradually smaller stone-slate, to pure slate. This was first commercially cut in north Wales around 1820, distributed initially by sea and then, much more widely, by the railways. Later still, machine-made tiles appeared and were generally quicker to fit – important as labour costs increased – and nowadays are so widely used that real stone, thatch and reclaimed period tiles are considered 'luxury end' roofing materials.

Although railway modelling has continued happily despite the passing of the steam age, roof coverings devised since then are both well-known and easy to find if you want to model them, so they are not covered here. Perhaps another time …

THATCH

When we think of a thatched cottage, most of us have an idea of what one looks like but, as with everything else man-made, there is a surprising number of variations for so simple an idea as bundling up some form of soft, natural material and pegging it down to form a roof. Where once wheat straw was commonly used, the short varieties bred these days for combine harvesting are useless for thatching and with reed and long-straw thatching tending to remain in specific areas where it was once traditional, both wheat-straw and long-straw thatchers now often grow their own, older-type varieties just for thatching. Also note that today, as ever, there are many different cultivars of thatching straw, each with implications of cost, longevity, style and colour for the finished work. Indeed, some caps or ridges (different names for the same thing) are made of different straw to the rest of

The simplest of all thatches to model: flat, plain cap, with ends hidden by elevated masonry gables. (The grainy effect is not pixellation but a covering of chicken wire, used today to protect the straw from vermin and birds wanting nesting materials.)

Here the thatch overshoots the gable end forming broad shoulders separated by a protruding chimney. Unusually, it has been trimmed short around a slated gable.

This lateral gable has its verges joined by a flush, rounded cap, which is formed into a point at the top.

More commonly, thatched gables have a half-hipped rounded ridge end, as on this barn.

Full hips are quite common too: note also the narrow slated strip between these two adjacent (and very grey), long-straw thatches.

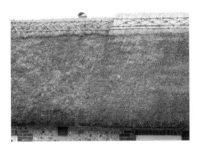

Two contiguous combed wheat thatches of similar age at a property boundary: note the subtlely different treatments, probably indicating work by different thatchers.

North-facing thatch among trees can accumulate a lot of green lichens. Note the exaggeratedly pointed end to the cap.

The very slight edge to this cap ('shallow blocking'), is a notable feature of this decidedly brown thatch. It would seem there's a prototype for my model after all!

the roof while, because most caps are replaced more often than the main roof, even using the same straw type can lead it to exhibit much less weathering and therefore to noticeably different colourings. As for precise details, you would have to ask an expert: I am merely an observer of the finished works.

With each thatch taking a skilled man several weeks to complete, even with a helper, there were once hundreds – perhaps thousands – of working thatchers around the country, each one producing work which would have been individually recognizable to another local thatcher. Sadly, with a useful life of between but twenty to fifty years, few, if any, of the top coats we see in pre-war period photos

are likely to have survived this long. However, good thatchers today have nurtured those early skills and, travelling much further afield for jobs than they used to, are thus distributing their styles and practices more widely than was once the case, although English Heritage and most councils try very hard to retain local thatching characteristics. Even so, a single village (if of sufficient size and amply thatched), can sometimes offer the curious a lot of variations to study. Here I first present some of the variety I found around just two Dorset villages, Piddletrenthide and Broadmayne, and then I offer examples from elsewhere for comparison, leaving the reader to study the particular local period traditions in their own area of interest.

A much paler, almost fawn-coloured cap sits here above a browny-grey thatch.

Notable features here are: the 'cross rods' or 'pattern pieces' (the diagonals between the horizontal liggers) are much more numerous and closer together than hitherto; the cap end is formed into a 'ridge peak' (like a fo'c's'le on a ship); the windows are denoted by vestigial raised arcs ('eyebrows'); and we see a thatcher's signature – two long-tailed straw birds facing each other.

This old thatch has been around for a while and lost about half of its cross rods. See how the lower edge (eave), takes no account of the window; then note also the subtle yealm edges every nine inches or so down the face of the roof, highlighted in places by the moss, suggestive of a long-straw roof.

Here, not only do we have deeper eyebrows over the windows but they are formed using slightly raised sections, almost dormers but not quite. Note too, the sparse cap decoration of a single point (far) and a single club or trefoil (near). The grey colour indicates a wheat thatch (reed thatches turn a deep golden-brown with age), while the fur-like finish shows this to be a combed wheat thatch, in which the stalks are 'shut' neatly together using a biddle or beater so that only their ends show.

LEFT: Now the eyebrows are deeper still, this time with horizontal central sections, while this cap is decorated with three equal and evenly-spaced points.

This time the thatcher's really gone to town: there's not a horizontal edge anywhere along that deep 'block cap', it being continuously decorated with alternate points and scallops, while the chimney is highlighted by a dramatic quintrefoil drop, swag or sway; and a trefoil at the verge. These birds would appear to be carved in wood and painted!

Where a landlord owns a row of cottages he is likely to have had them all re-thatched at the same time. If so, the cheapest way of accommodating an increase of building depth is to sweep the thatch upwards (and if necessary, backwards as well), so as not to have to form complex edges. The light grey of the cap suggests it is both newer and of a different straw type to the variegated deep browns of what looks to be a mature marsh or 'Norfolk reed' roof.

Here an outhouse, part of a larger barn, has been roofed by a continuous thatch sweeping downwards; but the main roof has failed and is covered with what looks like sailcloth.

ABOVE: These true dormers – defined by the windows standing (at least partly) higher than the main wall – have individually raised roof sections reaching some three-quarters of the way up the roof. Note the vestigial 'cheeks', and those slight horizontal lines in the thatch, revealing the layered yealms of a long-straw thatch – very common in Dorset.

LEFT: This delightful little dormer is made up of straight lines with notably sharp edges, but observe that the 'cheeks' here extend only halfway down the dormer sides, fading then into the roof-line proper.

Another option is to fill in between the windows and so form a single broad dormer.

This end view shows how the roof generally, and the dormers in particular, have that 'poured on and set' look which characterizes a good thatch.

Chimneys, of course, protrude through roofs and, where the two meet, a seal is required. This used to be done with 'pugging' which was, I am told, a lime-mortar and sand mix.

Here's another example, first seen from the one side, and then ...

... from the other. Two sides of the same chimney can be notably, or subtlely, different.

A chimney nicely centred on its gable will generally exhibit a balanced thatch, however, and is here sealed with a modern, plasticized cement.

Here we see both cement and a bitumen strip.

Where a chimney is surrounded by thatch, a short 'apron' can usually be found below it.

Thatching around a chimney; on a gable, with a lower-roofed extension beyond; can require a very particular solution ...

A round-topped thatch on a porch makes an attractive feature.

So does a pointed one.

In Devon, unlike in Dorset, thatches tend to droop downwards at the verge – known as a 'rolled gable' – as seen here on some alms houses at Moretonhampstead. I presume this helps keep out the driving rain for which the area is famed.

Another option is to project the thatch further out from the gable, as here at Dunsford, also in Devon.

Here at Wedmore on the Somerset levels, this thatch flows, like wavelets, over its house.

These dormer's thatches are highly complex in form but match beautifully! Note that the chimney joints are protected with lead flashing in this instance.

A detail of the sharply pointed end to this ridge, along with another fine signature bird.

A pair of semi-detached cottages in the Cotswolds, the far one with a plain cap, the other with a boxed cap using pointed detailing and swags around the chimneys. Note too the 'catslide roof' at the rear where the main roof is continued, unbroken, over an outshut.

This gable and dormer in Little Stretton, Shropshire, end in a vertically cut face which I have not noticed elsewhere. The gable's thatch is also very wide and supported by extended timberwork.

From the same village, a scalloped block ridge (which is perhaps not as evenly formed as it might be), while another extended gable suggests that this is a local variation. Here, however, it is supported by massive extended purlins and substantial barge boards.

An old, much worn thatch which has suffered from 'robbing' by birds. Note: the exposed spars, used to secure the thatch to the base coat; and how far the ridge has sunk away from the pugging round the chimney. The main body of old 'base' thatch beneath, which can often be original, would appear to be in some danger!

Invisible beneath thatch, but clearly visible today on houses no longer thatched, are various patterns of protruding masonry intended to help weather-proof the joint between chimneys and thatch. This old stack with its protruding brick row immediately above a tiled roof is typical and is usually evidence that the property was once thatched.

Looks can be deceptive, however. These bricks only protrude perhaps a quarter of their width and are purely decorative – this building was new in 1872, was never thatched, and these are its original slates! Conflictingly, an older cottage across the lane was once thatched but now has plain chimneys because it was burnt down twice and, although the walls are original, the chimneys were replaced when the owner fitted a new tiled roof!

These, however, are genuine indicators of a once-thatched roof and show how the inner, or roof, side of chimneys was commonly dealt with, whereas the outside was often plain.

Similar rain protection to that achieved with bricks was earlier effected with stone-slates.

Another trap for the unwary! These stones are above the remains of the thatch pugging and are both thicker and level, rather than downward sloping, and so probably once supported wooden scaffolding, a practice which can still today be found in Switzerland.

Here is more convincing evidence that a roof was once thatched: these stone-slates, carefully built into the tower, turned water away from the wall into the body of the thatch, where it could run harmlessly down the straw and out at the end of the yealms.

LEFT: *Further evidence, this time of pugging, which remains extant long after the thatch has been replaced. Those fine stone slabs conveniently lead us nicely into the next section ...*

Further information can sometimes be found published by local government, such as;–
www.devon.gov.uk/thatching.pdf
www.wiltshire.gov.uk/thatching.pdf

SLABS, TILES, SHEETING AND SLATES

This fabulous old barn in the far south of Somerset must be at least 300 years old, if not more, and the accretion of delightful yellow, green and brown mosses which its old stone flags have acquired over the years provides a wonderful example of weathering.

This close-up shows the original stone slabs, complete with double row at the eaves.

Recently, the need to replace rotted timbers meant the old tiles came off and, in due time, were replaced. Restoration of the full original roof (to remove a skylight and later dormer), plus damage replacement, meant adding newly quarried flags: the difference in colour is obvious, but give it another hundred years ... The difference between direct sunlight and shade on the wall's apparent colour is also remarkable.

Cotswold stone flags tend to be smaller and are, perhaps, a bit more grey. Note the 'guardian angel' on the porch.

Although the original barn dates from 1380, it was not converted into the Arlington Row cottages until the 1600s when this dormer was added. One can only assume that nothing as prosaic as lead was permitted, as the valley is formed with carefully angled flags.

A new stone roof using very thin slabs which are either reconstituted or machine sawn.

And so to slate, which eventually garners its own lichens: but is it the lime washing out, or the lead, which inhibits its growth below the chimney?

Some walls are so posh that they have their own roof. Here's one in slate ...

... and another in tiles!

Having covered interlocking tiles in the text, I turn here to regional differences in hand-thrown plain tiles – starting with this delightfully ramshackle old shed in Dorset.

This close-up shows how each tile is hand-cut to a slightly different size (no moulds here!), and even the bonnet hip tiles look haphazard in the extreme!

These plain clay tiles from Somerset are much more regular – and what a brilliant red some of them are!

Also available in green! I presume these 'ornamental spade' shaped tiles were left over from some other job to find themselves used up on a simple barn. You'd need some alchemy to understand why they're green but seeing is believing!

These 'Staffordshire Blues', as they're called – and yes, these are in Staffordshire – are interesting not only for their colour but for the special 'tile-and-a-half width' tiles at the gable end. Observe, too, how the ridge tiles sport flanges to overlap the next.

More Staffs blues, just down the road, show varying flatness and illustrate 'arris hips': hip tiles designed to suit specific roof angles and which thus lie flush with the plain ones.

I had not seen these edge tiles before – they're on the same roof – but they are obviously designed in two widths, to be alternately fitted so as to match the plain tile's stagger.

Corrugated iron dates from the Industrial Revolution and comes in different-sized panels. Used for many purposes, from barns to chapels, it was also a common, cheap repair for leaking old thatch at one time, being merely laid over the top.

It also came in curved sheets, but whatever the original finish, both types tend to end up the colour of old rust …

Asbestos was another cheap form of corrugated roofing material common on farm buildings, until it was proved to be carcinogenic. The cost of specialist removal tends to mean much of it survives – more or less – until it falls down!

To Cornwall now – Polperro – for this rendered roof, so treated to stop the gales sweeping under the tiles and blowing them off. Presumably slate (Cornwall has long quarried its own local slates), these roofs are common in the far south west.

I have yet to attempt modelling Cornish port roofs, but they certainly have character …

WELSH SLATE

Roofing slate, being a natural product, comes in several minor colour variations and is available in large sizes for large buildings ('kings and queens', up to 36in long), and in over twenty-five different sizes for housing from 26 × 16in to 10 × 5in. These are generally available in the following qualities: 'best quality'; in 4mm, 6mm, 8mm and 10mm nominal thicknesses, and 'rustic quality', which presumably varies somewhat. Other types, sizes and qualities are no doubt available.

SOME WELSH SLATE NAMES

(NB; the veracity of some sizes quoted – and of 'Ladies' in particular – is suspect since different sources do not always agree. I suspect some quarries may have argued over the true names of different sizes, which would explain the variations, or it could be just that memory has failed with the years so that in retrospect, the wrong names have been associated with particular sizes.)

Singles	Historical name for 10 × 5in slate.
Doubles	Historical name for 12 × 6in slate.
Small Header	Historical name for 13 × 10in slate.
Headers/Small Ladies	Historical name for 14 × 8in slate.
Narrow Ladies	Historical name for 14 × 7in slate.
Ladies	Historical name for 16 × 8in slate.
Broad Ladies	Historical name for 16 × 9in slate.
Wide Ladies	Historical name for 16 × 10in slate.
Viscountess	Historical name for 18 × 9in slate
Wide Viscountess/Small Countess	Historical name for 18 × 10in slate.
Countess	Historical name for 20 × 10in slate.
Broad Countess	Historical name for 20 × 12in slate.
Wide Countess/Marchioness	Historical name for 22 × 11in slate.
Wide Marchioness/Small Duchess	Historical name for 22 × 12in slate.
Duchess	Historical name for 24 × 12in slate.
Princesses	Historical name for 24 × 14in slate.
Empress	Historical name for 26 × 16in slate.

INDEX